ADOBE PHOTOSHOP™ 5

Advanced Digital Images

PRENTICE HALL
Upper Saddle River, NJ 07458

Library of Congress Cataloging-in-Publication Data

Adobe Photoshop 5: advanced digital images/Against The Clock.
      p.   cm. -- (Against the clock series)
ISBN 0-13-021324-1
1.Computer graphics. 2. Adobe Photoshop. I. Against The Clock (Firm)
II. Series.
T385.A35828 1999
006.6' 869 -- dc21

                         99-12147
                         CIP

Acquisitions Editor: *Elizabeth Sugg*
Developmental Editor: *Judy Casillo*
Supervising Manager: *Mary Carnis*
Production Editor: *Denise Brown*
Director of Manufacturing & Production: *Bruce Johnson*
Manufacturing Buyer: *Ed O'Dougherty*
Editorial Assistant: *Brian Hyland*

Formatting/page make-up: *Against The Clock, Inc.*
Printer/Binder: *Banta*
Cover Design: *Joe Sengotta*
Icon Design: *James Braun*
Marketing Manager: *Shannon Simonsen*
Creative Director: *Marianne Frasco*
Sales Director: *Ryan DeGrote*
Director of Marketing: *Debbie Yarnell*

©1999 by Prentice Hall, Inc.
Upper Saddle River, New Jersey 07458

Printed in the United States of America

10 9 8 7 6 5 4 3 2

ISBN 0-13-021324-1

Prentice Hall International (UK) Limited, London
Prentice Hall of Australia Pty. Limited, Sydney
Prentice Hall Canada Inc., Toronto
Prentice Hall Hispanoamericana, S.A., Mexico
Prentice Hall of India Private Limited, New Delhi
Prentice Hall of Japan, Inc., Tokyo
Pearson Education Asia Pte. Ltd., Singapore
Editora Prentice Hall do Brasil, Ltda., Rio de Janeiro

Table of Contents

PURPOSE

The Against The Clock series has been developed specifically for those involved in the field of graphic arts.

Welcome to the world of electronic design and prepress. Many of our readers are already involved in the industry — in advertising and design companies, in prepress and imaging firms, and in the world of commercial printing and reproduction. Others are just now preparing themselves for a career somewhere in the profession.

This series of courses will provide you with the skills necessary to work in this fast-paced, exciting, and rapidly expanding business. Many people feel that they can simply purchase a computer, the appropriate software, a laser printer, and a ream of paper, and begin designing and producing high-quality printed materials. While this might suffice for a barbecue announcement or a flyer advertising a local hair salon, the real world of four-color printing and professional communications requires a far more serious commitment.

THE SERIES

The applications presented in the Against The Clock series stand out as the programs of choice in professional graphic arts environments.

We've used a modular design for the Against The Clock series, allowing you to mix and match the drawing, imaging, and page layout applications that exactly suit your specific needs.

Titles available in the Against The Clock series include:

Macintosh: Basic Operations
Windows: Basic Operations
Adobe Illustrator: An Introduction to Digital Illustration
Adobe Illustrator: Advanced Digital Illustration
Freehand: An Introduction to Digital Illustration
Freehand: Advanced Digital Illustration
Adobe PageMaker: An Introduction to Electronic Mechanicals
Adobe PageMaker: Advanced Electronic Mechanicals
QuarkXPress: An Introduction to Electronic Mechanicals
QuarkXPress: Advanced Electronic Mechanicals
Adobe Photoshop: An Introduction to Digital Images
Adobe Photoshop: Advanced Digital Images
File Preparation: The Responsible Electronic Page
Preflight: An Introduction to File Analysis and Repair
TrapWise: Digital Trapping
PressWise: Digital Imposition

We've designed our courses to be "cross-platform." While many sites use Macintosh computers, there is an increasing number of graphic arts service providers using Intel-based systems running Windows (or Windows NT). The books in this series are applicable to either of these systems.

All of the applications that we cover in the Against The Clock series are similar in operation and appearance whether you're working on a Macintosh or a Windows system. When a particular function does differ from machine to machine, we present both.

ICONS AND VISUALS

Pencil icon indicates a comment from an experienced operator. Whenever you see the pencil icon, you'll find corresponding sidebar text that augments or builds upon the subject being discussed at the time.

Bomb icon indicates a potential problem or difficulty. For instance, a certain technique might lead to pages that prove difficult to output. In other cases, there might be something that a program cannot easily accomplish, so we might present a workaround.

Pointing Finger indicates a hands-on activity — whether a short exercise or a complete project. This will be the icon you'll see the most throughout the course.

Key icon is used to point out that there is a keyboard equivalent to a menu or dialog-box option. Key commands are often faster than using the mouse to select a menu option. Experienced operators often mix the use of keyboard equivalents and menu/dialog box selections to arrive at their optimum speed.

If you are a Windows user, be sure to refer to the corresponding text or images whenever you see this **Windows** icon. Although there isn't a great deal of difference between using these applications on a Macintosh and using them on a Windows-based PC, there are certain instances where there's enough of a difference for us to comment.

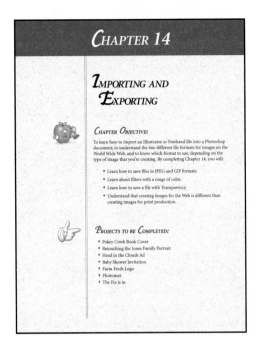

CHAPTER OPENINGS *provide the reader with specific objectives.*

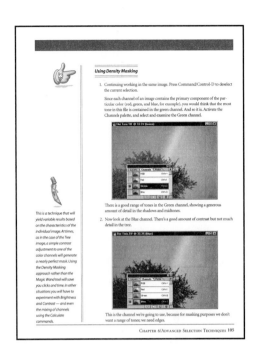

SIDEBARS and HANDS-ON ACTIVITIES *supplement concepts presented in the material.*

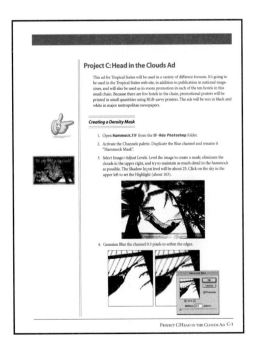

SUPPLEMENTAL PROJECTS *offer practice opportunities in addition to the exercises.*

PROJECT ASSIGNMENTS *will result in finished artwork — with an emphasis on proper file construction methods.*

The Against The Clock course materials have been constructed with two primary building blocks: exercises and projects. Projects always result in a finished piece of work — digital imagery built from the ground up, utilizing photographic-quality images, vector artwork from Adobe Illustrator, and type elements from the library supplied on your student CD-ROM.

This course, *Adobe Photoshop 5.0: Introduction to Digital Images*, makes use of several projects that you will work on during your learning sessions. You will find the projects that you will complete by the end of the course displayed on the inside front and back cover of the book. Here's a brief overview of each.

PROJECT A: POKEY CREEK BOOK COVER

The *Pokey Creek Book Cover* requires you to use many of the skills you've developed during the course, including setting highlight and shadow points. This is an RGB image, as are all projects, and color correction is an integral part of completing the work. You will create images for the cover, spine and back cover, and combine them to create the entire image. Type is an important component of the job as well, and will be handled using Photoshop's Type tools.

PROJECT B: RETOUCHING THE JONES FAMILY PORTRAIT

The *Joneses* photograph doesn't look bad — at first glance. Retouching it includes modifying the positions of feet and legs to improve the overall look of the photo. It also includes colorizing an element using the Hue and Saturation palette. Finishing touches on this project include removing unsightly blemishes and adjusting the overall look of the photograph to give it a professional touch.

PROJECT C: HEAD IN THE CLOUDS AD

Many of the effects you see in advertisements in everyday commercial work are actually composed using Photoshop. You will have the opportunity to create such a visual when you complete the *Head in the Clouds Ad*. Using type, layers, compositing, and other skills you've learned in the course, you will complete an advertising visual that's ready for a magazine.

PROJECT D: BABY SHOWER INVITATION

In this project you will work with Selection tools and paths, and will bring selections from one photo to another. You'll have an opportunity to work with Layer Transform tools, and to alter the color of images using the Curves image adjustment. You'll also work with Layer Masks to create a "realistic" effect for each of the 14 layers you create. In addition, you'll work with merging layers to conserve RAM, and with Photoshop's Type and Layer Effects tools.

PROJECT E: FARM FRESH LOGO

In keeping with modern design considerations, a logo needs a fresh and ever-evolving look. The *Farm Fresh Logo* begins with a simple graphic, imported from Adobe Illustrator, and adds depth and contour to the design elements, virtually jumping off the background. You have the opportunity to work with the Paste Inside feature, and to simulate droplets of water that look real enough to roll off the fruit they cover.

PROJECT F: PHOTOMAT

The *Photomat* project also originates with a graphic imported from Illustrator. You work with a variety of effects, starting with simple noise and drop shadow, then adding airbrushed highlight and shadow to individual "photo frames." Frames are constructed in a variety of ways, from using Photoshop's Paste Inside function to using the painting and airbrush tools, to creating custom textures with filters. In addition, you'll apply artistic filters to the content of the frames, to achieve variety in the entire presentation.

PROJECT G: THE FIX IS IN

This is your "final exam" — a damaged black-and-white photo that not only needs to be repaired, it also needs to be colorized. You'll use the Pen tool to create selections, and use the selection in a number of ways. You'll manufacture missing elements and create detail where there is none, using the Rubber Stamp tool. Colorizing the image will be done primarily with Adjustment Layers using Hue and Saturation. Along the way, you'll discover a number of tricks to put in your personal bag.

FOR THE STUDENT

On the CD-ROM, you will find a complete set of Against The Clock (ATC) fonts, as well as a collection of data files used to construct the various exercises and projects.

The ATC fonts are solely for use while you are working with the Against The Clock materials. These fonts will be used throughout both the exercises and projects and are provided in both Macintosh and Windows format.

A variety of student files have been included. These files, necessary to complete both the exercises and projects, are also provided in both Macintosh and Windows formats.

FOR THE INSTRUCTOR

The Instructor Kit consists of an Instructor's manual and an Instructor's CD-ROM. It includes various testing and presentation materials in addition to the files that come standard with the student books.

- **Overhead Presentation Materials** are provided and follow along with the course. These presentations are prepared using Microsoft PowerPoint and are provided in both "native" PowerPoint format as well as Acrobat Portable Document Format (PDF).

- **Extra Projects** are provided along with the data files required for completion. These projects may be used to extend the course, or may be used to test the student.

- **A Test Bank of Questions** is included within the instructor kit. These questions may be modified, reorganized, and administered throughout the delivery of the course.

- Halfway through the course is a **Review** of material covered to that point, with a **Final Review** at the end.

ACKNOWLEDGMENTS

I would like to give thanks to the writers, illustrators, editors, and others who have worked long and hard to complete the Against The Clock series. Foremost among them are Rob McAllister, Susan Hunert, Bob Simonds, Ray VillaRosa, Michael Barnett, and Jim Wheaton, whom I thank for their long nights, early mornings, and seemingly endless patience.

Thanks to the dedicated teaching professionals whose comments and expertise contributed to the success of this book, including Ed Mineck and Patricia Russotti of Rochester Institute of Technology, Doris Anton of Wichita Area Technical College, Ron Bertolina of The Graphic Arts Technical Foundation, and Dr. Mitchell Henke of Bemidji State University.

A big thanks to Judy Casillo, Developmental Editor, and Denise Brown, Production Editor, for their guidance, patience, and attention to detail.

A special thanks to my husband for his unswerving support and for living in a publishing studio.

Ellenn Behoriam, December 1998

Against The Clock (ATC) was founded in 1990 as a part of Lanman Systems Group, one of the nation's leading systems integration and training firms. The company specialized in developing custom training materials for such clients as *L.L. Bean, The New England Journal of Medicine, Smithsonian,* the *National Education Association, Air & Space Magazine, Publishers Clearing House,* The *National Wildlife Society, Home Shopping Network,* and many others. The integration firm was among the most highly respected in the graphic arts industry.

To a great degree, the success of Systems Group can be attributed to the thousands of pages of course materials developed at the company's demanding client sites. Throughout the rapid growth of Systems Group, founder and General Manager Ellenn Behoriam developed the expertise necessary to manage technical experts, content providers, writers, editors, illustrators, designers, layout artists, proofreaders, and the rest of the chain of professionals required to develop structured and highly effective training materials.

Following the sale of the Lanman Companies to World Color, one of the nation's largest commercial printers, Ellenn embarked on a project to develop a library of training materials engineered specifically for the professional graphic artist. A large part of this effort is finding and working with talented professional artists, writers, and educators from around the country.

The result is the ATC training library.

Ellenn lives in Tampa, Florida with her husband Gary, and her dogs Boda and Chase.

ABOUT THE AUTHORS

Every one of the Against The Clock course books was developed by a group of people working as part of a design and production team. In all cases, however, there was a primary author who assumed the bulk of the responsibility for developing the exercises, writing the copy, and organizing the illustrations and other visuals. In the case of *Photoshop: Advanced Digital Images,* that author is Rob McAllister.

Rob McAllister has been speaking and writing about creating effective pages since before desktop publishing was invented. In the process of teaching others, he has written various "how to" guides and training manuals. Rob is a contributing editor for Hayden Books' FreeHand Graphics Studio Skills, and is the author of a series of eight books for Delmar Publishers on a variety of desktop publishing topics.

Rob is a technical editor for Electronic Publishing and contributing editor for Printing News in addition to Project Manager for Against The Clock.

Ed Mineck is an associate professor in Digital Imaging & Publishing Technology at the Rochester Institute of Technology. He is also a trainer for professionals and a regular presenter at national and international conferences. Ed creates and delivers state of the art skill building curricula that enables future independent learning on a wide range of imaging topics. He has been training and presenting on Photoshop since the first version of the application.

Gary Paul Howland, PhD, is a well-known and respected systems integrator, consultant, and trainer to the graphic arts industry, was one of the earliest adopters of desktop prepress, and has been designing and creating course materials, educational programs, and support systems for over twelve years. His expertise includes Macintosh and Windows platforms. Gary lives in Nokomis, Florida.

Bob Cusano has seen the graphic arts evolve from the days of hot metal through creating art and pages on personal computers to migrating those pages to the internet. He lives in Hamden Connecticut, and is lead instructor for Desktop Publishing for the Graphic Arts courses at Gateway Community Technical College in North Haven, Connecticut.

Lisa Bochatey has been involved with graphics and computers for over twenty years. She spends her time training and consulting for Newspapers, publishers, designers, and general business clients in the midwest. Lisa has Masters degrees in both Print Technology and Management, as well as in Instructional Design from Rochester Institute of Technology.

Bill Morse has been involved in computer graphics since the late 1970s, pioneering a computer-driven special-effects camera system that produced high-resolution transparencies which predated the era of Photoshop — photocompositing with rendered art, glows, textures, motion graphics, and natural media simulation. He was dragged, kicking and screaming, into the Digital Age, and now does his artwork primarily in Adobe Illustrator, Adobe Photoshop, and MetaCreations Painter.

John Parsons has been involved in commercial printing since 1975. John held the position of Training Operations Manager for Imation Publishing Software, where he developed the Certified Imation Consultant training program. He is currently president of Parsons Consulting, Inc., a prepress training and workflow consulting business in Bainbridge Island, Washington.

Win Woloff teaches Adobe Photoshop, at Hillsboro Community College and The International Academy of Merchandising and Design in Tampa, Florida. He has been a commercial Photographer for over 25 years and holds the degree of Master of Photography and Photographic Craftsman from the Professional Photographers of America. Win has lectured throughout New England and Canada on a variety of photographic topics. Win currently heads the digital department at Eagle Photographics and Digital Imaging.

Debbie Rose Myers Debbie Rose Myers is an energetic instructor at the Art Institute of Fort Lauderdale. She is a state certified art instructor who has provided in-service training with Photoshop and Illustrator for educators throughout the United States. Debbie has won inclusion in two national jurried museum shows as well as Best in Show at her recent M.F.A. graduate art show. Her work can be viewed as part of the permanent collection at the Lowe Art Museum, in Coral Gables, Florida.

GETTING STARTED

Platform

The Against The Clock series is specifically designed to apply to both Macintosh and Windows systems — the courses will work for you no matter what environment you find yourself in. There are some slight differences in the two, but when you're working in an actual application, these differences are limited to certain types of functions and actions.

Naming Conventions

In the old days of MS-DOS systems, file names on the PC were limited to something referred to as "8.3," which meant that you were limited in the number of characters you could use to an eight-character name (the "8") and a three-character suffix (the "3"). Text files, for example, might be called *myfile.txt*, while a document file from a word processor might be called *myfile.doc* (for document). On today's Windows-based systems, these limitations have been somewhat overcome. Although you can use longer file names, suffixes still exist. Whether or not you see them is another story.

When your system is first configured, the Views are normally set to a default that hides these extensions. This means that you might have a dozen different files named *myfile*, all of which may have been generated by different applications and be completely different types of files.

On a Windows system, you can change this view by clicking on *My Computer* (the icon is on your desktop) with the right button, and choosing View>Options. From this dialog box you may choose whether or not to display these older, MS-DOS file extensions. In some cases, it's easier to know what you're looking at if they're visible. This is a personal choice.

To ensure that the supplied student files are fully compatible with both operating systems, we've named all the files using the three-character suffix — even those on the Macintosh.

Key Commands

Key commands are fairly consistent between the Macintosh and the Windows versions of Adobe Photoshop. The major difference lies in the names of special function keys. The Macintosh has a key marked with an Apple and an icon that looks like a clover leaf. This is called the Command key. The Command key is a *modifier* key; that is, it doesn't do anything by itself, but changes the function of a key pressed while it's being held down. A good example is holding Command while pressing the "S" key: this Saves your work. The same thing applies to the "P" key; hold down Command and press it to Print your work.

On Windows-based systems, the Control key is almost always the equivalent of the Command key on the Macintosh. (This is sometimes confusing to new users, since the Macintosh also has a Control key, although, on the Macintosh, it's hardly ever used in popular applications.)

Another special function key on the Macintosh is the Option key. It's also a modifier key, and you'll need to hold it down along with whatever other key is required for a specific function. The equivalent modifier key on a Windows system is called the Alt key (for alternative). Besides these two nomenclature issues, there isn't really a lot of difference between using a Windows system and a Macintosh system (particularly when you're within a particular application).

The CD-ROM and Initial Setup Considerations

Before you begin using your Against The Clock course book, you will have to set up your system so that you have access to the various files and tools that you'll need to complete your lessons.

Student Files

This course comes with a complete collection of student files. These files are an integral part of the learning experience, as they're used throughout the course to help you construct increasingly complex elements. Having these building blocks available to you throughout your practice and study sessions will ensure that you will be able to experience the exercises and complete the project assignments smoothly and with a minimum of time spent looking for the various required components.

In building the Student Files folders, we've created sets of data for both Macintosh and Windows users. Locate the appropriate version of the "**SF-Adv Photoshop**" folder for your platform of choice and simply drag the icon onto your hard disk drive. If you have limited disk space, you may want to copy only the files for one or two lessons at a time.

Creating a Project Folder

We strongly recommend that you work from your hard disk. However, in some cases you might not have enough room on your system for all of the files that we've supplied. If this is the case, you can work directly from the CD-ROM.

Throughout the exercises and projects, you'll be required to save your work. Since the CD-ROM is "read-only," you cannot write information to it. Create a project folder on your hard disk and use it to store your work-in-progress. Create this folder while you're looking at your desktop so that it will be at the highest level of your system, where it will be easy to find. Name this folder "Work in Progress".

Fonts

Whatever platform you're working on — Macintosh or Windows — you will have to install the ATC font library to ensure that your lessons and exercises will work as described in the course book. These fonts are provided on the student CD-ROM. Separate versions for Windows and Macintosh are provided.

Instructions for installing fonts are provided in the documentation that came with your computer. If you're using a font utility such as Suitcase or Font Juggler, then be certain to refer to the instructions that came with the font management application for installing your ATC fonts onto your system.

Preferences

We recommend that you throw away your Preferences file before you begin the lessons in this course. The "Adobe Photoshop 5 Prefs" (Macintosh) and the "Adobe Photoshop 5 Prefs.psp" (Windows) files may be found inside your Adobe Photoshop 5.0>Adobe Photoshop Settings folder (Macintosh) or the Photoshop 5.0>Photoshop Settings folder.

Prerequisites

This book assumes that you have a basic understanding of how to use your system. Whether you're working on a Macintosh or a Windows workstation, the skill sets are basically the same.

You should know how to use your mouse to point and click, and how to drag items around the screen. You should know how to resize a window, and how to arrange windows on your desktop to maximize the space you have available. You should know how to access pull-down menus and how check boxes and radio buttons work. Lastly, you should know how to create, open, and save files.

If you're familiar with these fundamental skills, then you know all that's necessary to utilize the Against The Clock courseware library.

Notes:

*1*NTRODUCTION

The concepts and organization of this book make certain assumptions about your knowledge and experience. You should be familiar with Photoshop's tool set, and with the concepts of channels, layers, and the variety of selection techniques available to you.

If you have concerns that you don't have an adequate grasp of these fundamentals, let your instructor know before class starts.

Photoshop is an extremely robust program, with exciting features that go well beyond photo manipulation. There are dozens of books about Photoshop, and each one can teach you something new and useful about the program.

While Photoshop is capable of producing a wide variety of effects, each successive version of the program has made creating them easier. What this means for the creative professional is that time can be spent designing a dynamic piece, either for print or for the Web, rather than executing tedious details. For the design professional, it means increased productivity.

It has been our goal, in creating exercises and projects, to first of all help you see that you can create "cool stuff" quickly and easily, using Photoshop's built-in features; then to make it even more interesting by employing additional effects. While becoming expert in Photoshop is hard work, it should also be fun and fulfilling.

As you progress through this course, we encourage you to pay attention not only to the details — how to do the tasks associated with the exercises and projects — but also to the principles behind them. While there are some projects and exercises that demand absolute attention to each detail, many give you more latitude. In many parts of this course, we encourage you to experiment with similar effects, rather than limit you to ideas that the authors find interesting. We hope you will do so, and expand your creative vision.

Additionally, we encourage you to look at the "big picture" — what you're actually creating — and make decisions based on that reality, rather than establishing a blanket rule for production.

The goals of this course are to:

- Build on your existing knowledge.

- Expand your "toolbox" of creative techniques.

- Temper creative technique with production reality.

- Explore advanced uses of Adobe Photoshop.

While this course is strongly slanted toward design and design-related techniques and functions, it also explores many practical realities. The course touches on color correction, but does not immerse itself in the details that are needed for high-end color adjustment. If this is your need, consider attending additional courses following the successful completion of this material.

CHAPTER 1

COLOR MODES

CHAPTER OBJECTIVE:

To learn about the various color modes, or *color models*, supported by Photoshop; to gain an understanding of where and when specific file types are best utilized. After completing Chapter 1, you will:

- Know how to access the Mode setting for an image.

- Understand the definition of each of the eight different color models supported by Photoshop.

- Be comfortable with the concept of color gamuts, or the range of colors that be can achieved from each of the available color models.

- Know how to change an image from one mode to another.

- Know how to convert images from RGB to CMYK color — an important skill in the workplace.

- Have built an understanding of color correction, and how differ- ent color models affect this critical process.

Color Modes

Photoshop uses several different color modes (also called color models) when working with images. Each mode represents a different way of storing color information in memory, a disk, a web site, or printing to film or paper. They all have their uses and advantages in certain situations.

Each color mode represents itself differently in the Channels palette. This allows alteration to individual channels of color (brightness, contrast, etc.), without changing the attributes of the entire image. Spot colors, or colors that are chosen from a palette, can also be analyzed for the CMYK quantities used.

Look under the Image>Mode menu to see your options. Note that each color model has a number of different bit depth options for importing, viewing, and printing that will be explained.

Remember that the resolution of an image is effectively changed if it is scaled in a page layout program such as QuarkXPress or PageMaker.

If a bitmap image is going to be printed on an imagesetter with a 1200 dpi resolution, its own final resolution should be as close to 1200 ppi as possible. This can be accomplished by placing a 1200-ppi scan in a document at 100%, or by placing a 300-ppi image at 25%.

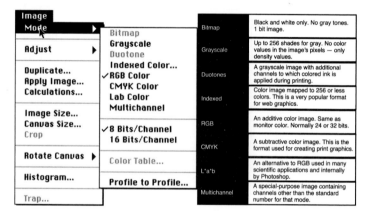

Bitmap Images

Also known as 1-bit images, bitmap images are black-and-white pictures. Each pixel can be only black or white — no grays, no colors. This format is used mainly for high-resolution line art and in multimedia projects. Many page layout programs can colorize and overprint bitmap images without affecting the other graphics behind them.

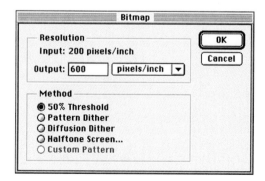

Bitmap images can be created as new documents, or they can be made by creating Grayscale or Multichannel images. With Photoshop, you have several options when converting to Bitmap mode:

1. 50% Threshold — Every pixel darker than 50 percent gray will turn to black, and every pixel lighter than 50 percent gray will turn white.

2. Pattern Dither — A pattern of white and black dots are mixed up to form the image.

3. Diffusion Dither — The dot pattern will form a mezzotint image, similar to looking at an image through a window screen. This method is usually preferred over the Pattern Dither.

4. Halftone Screen — Creates a pattern that looks like a halftone picture.

When using the Halftone Screen option, the shape of the pixel, or dot, can be designated.

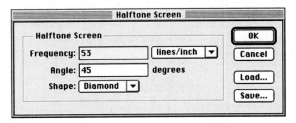

When preparing bitmaps for printing, the image resolution should match the printer resolution, if possible. Otherwise, the imagesetter has to "guess" whether to make a pixel black or white, which results in "stairsteps" or "jaggies."

Grayscale

Grayscale images in Adobe Photoshop use up to 256 shades of gray, including black and white. Each pixel uses 8 bits of memory to store a number ranging from 0 (black) to 255 (white), resulting in about a 0.4% difference between each shade of gray. While a 0.4% difference is impossible to see with the human eye, many films and density calibration equipment can recognize this minute difference. Some page layout programs can colorize grayscale images, but they cannot usually overprint them transparently; the image will "knock out" or prevent the printing of items that are beneath it. Grayscale images are the basis for many special effects in Photoshop.

Duotone

Duotones are grayscale images that are printed using two colors of ink. Usually the black plate is used to emphasize highlight and shadow areas, and the color emphasizes the midtones. They can only be created from images in Grayscale mode.

Photoshop's Duotone mode actually includes monotones, duotones, tritones, and quadtones, which use 1, 2, 3, and 4 inks, respectively. Pixels are colorized with a

When preparing Grayscale, RGB, or CMYK images for print, the final image resolution (ppi) should be 1.5 to 2 times the halftone screen frequency (lpi). If the printed size is greater than the original, multiply the resolution (ppi) by the enlargement factor.

Select a resolution and line screen according to the amount of detail in an image. For images with little detail, lower resolutions may be used. Images with a great deal of detail require higher resolution.

A monotone image is an image that uses just one non-black ink to reproduce the picture.

percentage of each ink depending on their original grayscale value. The curve/ink combination modifies the output without affecting the original grayscale image. Because the curve data is PostScript information, duotones can only be printed as EPS files; the actual grayscale pixel color information is stored in 8 bits. While any color may be assigned to the inks, be aware that on screen colors won't match printed output in most cases.

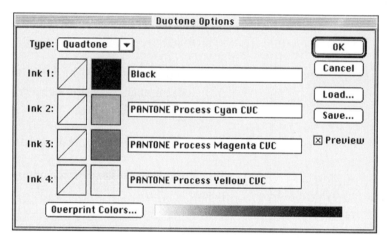

Later in this chapter, you will learn how to make a duotone image.

Indexed Color

An indexed color image is yet another 8-bit-per-pixel format. Like an 8-bit grayscale image, each pixel is represented by a value from 0 to 255. Instead of a shade of gray, though, the value refers to a position on a color lookup table. Each position on the table contains a specific color, with 0 as black, and 255 as white. Indexing is often used as a method of reducing the range of colors stored in an image to only those actually used: storing four or five colors instead of 256 or 16 million. When a particular color is not found, the Index color option will find the color closest to it in the Index palette.

*LUT — Lookup Table
CLUT — Color Lookup Table*

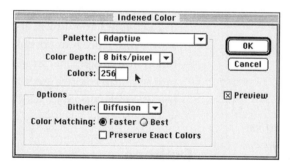

Wallpaper image — an image that will be used as either a design for your desktop or as a background for a web page.

Indexed color images may contain fewer than 256 colors. These colors are designated in powers of 2 (2, 4, 8, 16, 32, 64, or 128 colors).

Filters are not available for use with indexed images.

Converting an image to an Indexed color using an Adaptive palette and no dithering can create a better posterized image than the Posterization command.

The Index Color mode has several palettes for you to use, depending on what you plan to use the image for:

- Exact — If the image already uses less than 256 colors, then this option will appear as the default. Used mainly for high-contrast or screen shot images.

- System — The System option is really two options. Images can be worked on either in a Macintosh or Windows-based format. Best used when producing a wallpaper or custom icon image.

- Web — When producing an image that will be used on an internet web page as a GIF, you can use this palette to make use of the Web palette's 216-color LUT.

- Uniform — Mainly an unused option. This palette uses a uniform sampling of all the colors in the image.

- Adaptive — Allows the use of different bit depths to reproduce different degrees of color quality. Photoshop will sample the image, and design a palette to use the color spectrum most common in the image.

- Custom — A Custom palette can be constructed, or one can be obtained from another source.

These considerations are critical if you intend to use a vector-based illustration program to design graphics for the World Wide Web. Although you can use Photoshop to convert such files for the Web, understanding Indexed color will allow you to specify colors that will appear correct on a variety of monitors regardless of the program in which they were created.

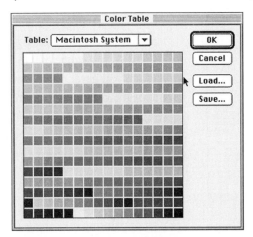

Many page layout programs won't separate Indexed color images, which must originate as RGB; make certain that you convert them to CMYK before sending them to an imagesetter if you intend to use your graphic in a print project. In addition, once an image is converted to Indexed color, much of the continuous tone detail will be lost. When possible, convert to CMYK from the original RGB image.

RGB

RGB is the color model used by scanners, monitors, and film recorders; it is based on light, and is referred to as an Additive Color mode; each shade is created by adding three components of light together — red, green, and blue. The RGB color gamut (or range of colors available from a particular mode) covers a large part of the visible spectrum. RGB can be a 24- or 48-bit color mode; each pixel is represented by three values from 0 to 255, one value each for red, green, and blue. The more light that is added (the higher the values), the brighter (closer to white) the color becomes. When you add the maximum amounts of red, green, and blue light, white is produced. Lower values result in darker colors.

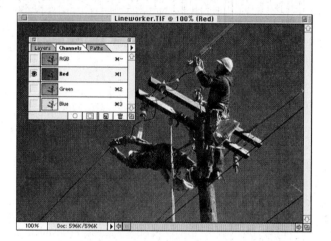

CMYK

What RGB is to computer screens, CMYK is to printing presses. CMYK is a subtractive color model. When light hits a printed page, some of the light is absorbed, or subtracted, by the pigments on the page; the remaining light is reflected back and perceived as a color. Each of the CMY primaries (cyan, magenta, and yellow) is specified in a range of 0 to 100%, as is the black which is added to the color model. When you have 0% ink coverage, the paper remains untouched, and the image appears white. One hundred percent each of cyan, magenta, and yellow makes a dark, muddy brown. Black is added to provide density in shadows and details that would be impossible to achieve using combinations of cyan, magenta, and yellow alone. The CMYK mode can use either 32 or 64 bits of data per pixel.

The color gamut of the CMYK mode is much smaller than that of the RGB mode because the printing process depends on inks absorbing light, not on light itself. Each set of printing inks created by a different manufacturer will produce a different CMYK color gamut. CMYK images are used extensively in printing, but not in multimedia.

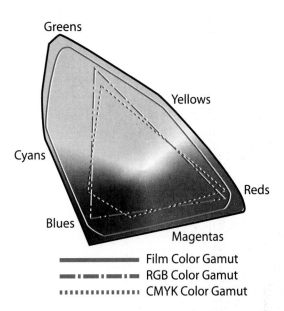

Graphical representation of the RGB and CMYK color gamuts inside the range occupied by color film and the overall CIE L*a*b colorspace.

L*a*b*

Covering the entire range of the visible spectrum, the L*a*b* model is used by Photoshop internally to convert images from one mode to another, as well as for a number of other operations. Another 24-bit system, L*a*b* color stores 8 bits of information for luminance or lightness (L), and 8 bits each for two color axes: (a) from green to red and (b) from blue to yellow. L*a*b color can be useful for special effects, and allows us to convert an RGB or CMYK image to L*a*b and back again with no loss of color information. L*a*b images may be printed to a PostScript Level 2 or Level 3 printer.

The L*a*b* color mode is a format that is device-independent, meaning that it will be represented consistently across different types of computers or color management systems.

Converting Between Modes

1. It's simple to convert images from one mode to another using the Image>Mode menu in Photoshop. Open the image **Lineworker.TIF** from your **SF-Adv Photoshop** folder. This is an RGB image. Examine it by selecting the Image>Mode menu. You'll see a check mark next to RGB Color. Notice that the selections for Duotone and Bitmap aren't available to you.

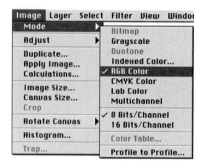

When matching image colors to a process color book, make certain that the inks match the inks with which you will be printing. One designer we know was working on a difficult color correction job — the images had been lit from overhead with fluorescents, with incandescent sidelighting. After painstakingly correcting the image, matching it carefully to the swatches in a process color book, she went to film. When she examined a proof, the colors were completely wrong. It turned out she'd matched the images to a Toyo ink book rather than a SWOP ink book. She had to start over from scratch.

2. Create a copy of the image by choosing Duplicate from the Image menu. Name the copy "Lineworker CMYK.TIF" and save it in your **Work in Progress** folder.

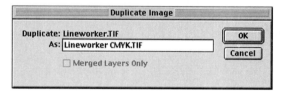

3. Select CMYK Color from the Image>Mode menu. This will convert the image from RGB to CMYK. You will probably see a shift in the color on the screen. Notice, too, that the title bar of the Image window will display the new color mode next to the Image title.

4. Click on the Image>Mode menu; Bitmap, Duotone, Indexed Color and are now unavailable.

5. Make a copy of **Lineworker CMYK.TIF** by choosing Duplicate from the Image menu. Name the copy "Lineworker Grayscale.TIF".

6. Select Grayscale from the Mode menu. Click OK when the warning dialog box asks if you want to discard all color information. This will convert the image from CMYK to grayscale. Click on the Mode menu, and you'll see that all of the options in the Mode menu are available for a grayscale image.

7. Keep **Lineworker CMYK.TIF** and **Lineworker.TIF** open for the next exercise. Save **Lineworker Grayscale.TIF** in your **Work in Progress** folder. Close the image

Dot gain is the tendency of halftone dots to spread, or become larger on the printed page, resulting in a darker image. As a general rule, finer halfton screens and more porous papers result in higher amounts of dot gain. Photoshop allows you to adjust for dot gain (in the CMYK Setup dialog box, within the Color Setting controls) when converting images to CMYK.

There are many common colors not reproducible in CMYK. Examples are neon colors, metallics, fire engine red, and vivid colors in a sunset.

Converting Between RGB & CMYK

Digital designers have been able to use desktop scanners to put images into their layouts for a decade now. Recent advances in the quality of desktop scanners and a growing availability of digital stock photography have made the quality of desktop color separations (conversion from RGB to CMYK) much better. As the amount of printed material being repurposed for multimedia grows, more work is now being converted from CMYK to RGB, as well. It *sounds* easy enough; you know how to use the Mode menu, right?

When Should You Convert?

The biggest factor in determining when to convert from one color mode to another is: "Where is the color most critical?" A poster-sized CMYK image that's 100MB in size will be only 75MB as an RGB image, but manipulating the color of the RGB image and then converting to CMYK will almost certainly create flattened tone. Conversely, creating images for multimedia productions that will only be used in "quick-and-dirty" printed promotional pieces may not require a high level of quality.

A CMYK image has a smaller gamut than an RGB image, but allows for smaller variations in color of the shades it does produce. Simply put, images that are converted to and modified in CMYK are going to be different from the same images modified in RGB. The differences between CMYK and RGB begin to stack up as more color changes are made to an image. Consequently, you should never convert back to RGB after converting an image to CMYK. To demonstrate, we'll compare CMYK and RGB versions of the same image using the Difference blending mode.

Examining Color Variation with the Difference Command

1. Activate the image **Lineworker CMYK.TIF**, which you converted in the last exercise.

2. Convert the image to RGB in the Mode menu. Press Command-A (Macintosh) or Control-A (Windows) to select the entire image, then Command- or Control-C to copy the image to the clipboard.

3. Activate the image **Lineworker.TIF**. This is the original RGB version of the image. Press Command-V (Macintosh) or Control-V (Windows) to paste the converted image into the original file.

4. On the Layers palette, change the blending mode of Layer 1 from Normal to Difference. Now visible are the pixels whose CMYK color had no equivalents in the RGB palette.

5. Close both images without saving.

The Hue, Saturation, and Lightness (also called Brightness or Value) color model seems to make more sense to users with traditional art backgrounds.

With over 16 million colors in Photoshop's RGB color gamut, you'd think that there wouldn't be any problem matching every possible CMYK color. But the CMYK mode actually has more colors (over 4 billion), and because the CMYK color gamut covers a smaller part of the visual spectrum than the RGB gamut, the steps between CMYK colors are smaller than they are in RGB.

Why Convert Before Color Correction?

Scans from even the most expensive drum scanner aren't always perfect. In most cases, desktop scans are going to need adjustments in color before they're ready for film or screen. Even small color corrections can affect images in ways that aren't at first visible, but which compound with every step.

When you correct color in an image, you are usually *removing* information from a file. When you convert from RGB to CMYK, more information loss results. Even if you have already corrected a file, a converted image often needs more correction to compensate for the "flatness" caused by the conversion. Eventually, so much information is lost that the image will show "posterization" or distinct banding between colors.

As a general rule, perform gross corrections in RGB, then, for images to be printed, convert to CMYK and fine-tune the image.

Summary

The ability for Photoshop to work with, and save, in different color modes, allows the designer to use one program to create, alter, and export images in a multitude of formats. Whether the image will be used in print production, transmitted presentation, or with a web site, Photoshop can accomplish these tasks. By knowing how colors react, and the limitations of converting one color mode to another, the designer can maintain the highest quality of color in an image.

ADVANCED IMAGE ADJUSTMENT

CHAPTER OBJECTIVE:

To learn about the concept of Levels and Curves, and how they affect the overall control of the tonal range of your images; how to modify these tools to achieve the best possible results. By completing Chapter 2, you will:

- Know what Levels are, and how they affect the appearance of your images.

- Understand how to read a Histogram, which provides a visual representation of how an image's tones are balanced.

- Learn the difference between shadows, midtones, and highlights, and how these values affect the appearance of your image.

- Learn about different types of images, and how to adjust Levels in an image to improve its appearance.

- Learn how to use Levels for other effects, such as cleaning up an image with rough edges.

- Understand the Curves dialog box, and how the graphic it presents relates to various tonal ranges within an image.

- Understand the relationship between Curves and Levels, and when each technique is most effective.

Advanced Image Adjustment

While there is a debate among Photoshop users regarding which color correction tool (Levels or Curves) is better, a few facts should be noted. Both commands adjust the white and black points on the different channels. The Levels Command uses a Histogram as a reference tool. Many users find using a Histogram easier and quicker than the more elaborate controls available in the Curves command. If an image only requires an overall adjustment to the brightness, contrast, and gamma settings of a channel, then the Levels Command will suit the purpose.

However, if a greater degree of control is desired, especially in particular areas of grayscale representation of channels, then the Curves Command is the proper tool to use. Adjustments and anchor points can be set to particular levels of grayscale representations of channels using the Curves command. This will give the user a greater control of the entire color correction process.

The specific controls available with both the Levels and Curves commands are explained in this chapter, and it presents examples showing where each control works best.

Levels

Levels allows you to adjust the brightness, contrast, and gamma (or contrast in the midtones) of an image. Often an image that seems to be lacking in detail is simply a low-contrast image; a quick adjustment of the image brightness levels can drastically improve such an image. You can adjust the contrast of either the entire image, or an individual color channel, such as red, green, or blue in an RGB image.

The Levels dialog box is accessible from the Image>Adjust>Levels submenu or Command/Control-L submenu.

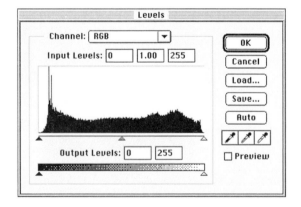

The most dominant feature of the Levels dialog box is the Histogram, the graph in the center of the box. The Histogram represents the distribution of lighter (or white) and darker (or black) pixels for each channel, or the entire image.

Some "blurry" images are not really out of focus — they just have a low contrast problem.

Mapping — the method to represent the distribution of light and dark pixels over an entire image.

There are two sets of sliders to control Input Levels and Output Levels. Both sets have a black slider for adjusting the shadows in an image, and a white slider to adjust highlights. In addition, the Input Levels slider has a gray triangle in the center of the slider bar for adjusting gamma, or midtones.

Input and output levels may be changed by moving the slider, entering actual values in the boxes above the slider sets, or by using the Eyedroppers to select the brightest and darkest points in the image.

The basic theory behind the Levels sliders is simple. To increase the overall contrast in an image, move the Input sliders toward the center of the slider bar. To decrease contrast, adjust the Output sliders. To adjust the contrast in the midtones of an image, move the Gamma slider left or right. The use of the Levels as it relates to color correction to individual channels, as well as numerical controls will be discussed in the next chapter. For now, an understanding of the use of the slider is in order.

Identifying the Problem

With a little experience you'll often be able to recognize the adjustments necessary to improve an image. Learning to read the Histogram can be very useful for identifying a potential problem. Keep in mind that the examples listed are very general rules regarding images; sometimes an image is simply by nature a low- or high-contrast image, and shouldn't be adjusted at all.

A well-balanced image generally displays a well-balanced Histogram. There will usually be peaks or valleys somewhere in the graph, but over all, the distribution of pixels covers the entire brightness range; the Histogram is a gradual curve with the majority of the pixels represented by midtones.

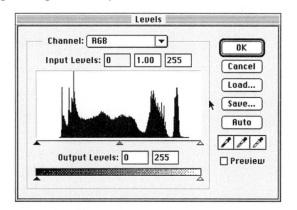

A low-contrast image tends to have all the pixels piled into a smaller range of the graph, usually in a very sharpened curve shape. This is likely the most common problem you'll find when adjusting the brightness and contrast of images.

Use the histogram to quickly determine whether an image is well-balanced, very light, overly dark, high contrast, or flat.

Use the Histogram to quickly determine whether an image is well-balanced, very ligt, overy dark, high contrast, or flat

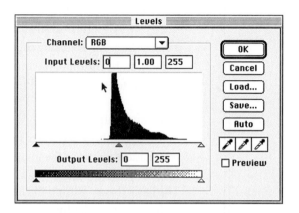

This Histogram shows clearly that there is a lack of very dark shadows; there are no pixels on the left hand side of the graph. In addition, this image lacks highlights — evident by the absence of information on the right hand side of the graph. Image detail is often defined by highlights and shadows; an image lacking these may appear fuzzy.

The Histogram for a high-contrast image may have a spike or two, particularly at the left (in the shadow areas) or far right (in the highlights), but overall, the center area (or midtones) is rather flat.

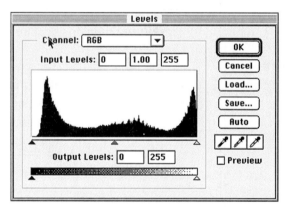

Don't forget that the paper stock you print on will also affect color and contrast.

While this is a rather uncommon profile for an image scanned from an adequate photograph on a properly calibrated scanner, other input devices may not have the contrast controls that photographic film and cameras have. It's a good thing they're not too common: this type of image can be very difficult to correct. Why? In order to reduce the contrast (by adjusting the Output Levels sliders inward) we have to remove highlights and shadows in the image, and as stated previously, these are usually the components that define detail in the image. Striking a balance between detail and contrast can be tough. While it is often easier to simply rescan or choose a different image, today's Photoshop user has to be prepared to optimize these images.

Other Image Types

There are many other types of Histograms. For example, you may find a Histogram where all of the pixels are piled up on the left, indicating a dark, and usually low-contrast, image. Some images are very light, which yields a Histogram with all of the pixels on the right side of the graph. Be cautious when adjusting these types of images; depending on the subject, an image can be very light or very dark and still be well balanced.

It is quite common to find an image that combines two or more of the basic types. For example, an image could be adequately balanced throughout the highlight areas, and still have a contrast problem in the shadows. A Histogram for this type of image would look like this:

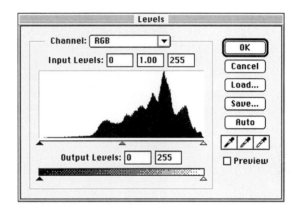

Adjusting Image Levels

1. Open the image **Fishing.TIF** from your **SF-Adv Photoshop** folder.

2. Examine the image. Notice how faded and washed out the image is, and the lack of detail.

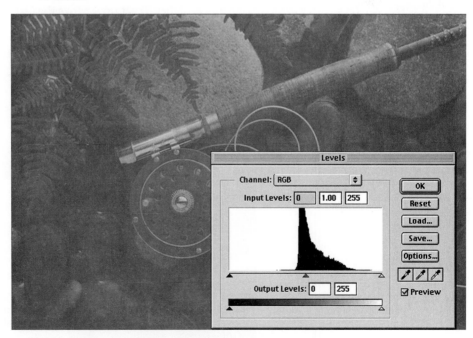

3. Press Command/Control-L to activate the Levels dialog box.

4. Move the black Input slider to the right so it touches the edge of the beginning of the curve. Move the white slider to the left so that it touches the end of the curve.

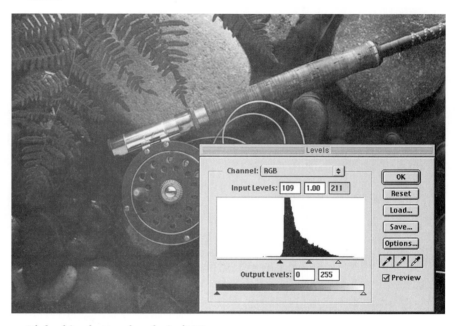

It's looking better already, isn't it?

5. The gray Gamma slider in the center of the image is used to adjust the contrast in the midtones. By moving the Gamma slider you are adjusting the ratio of dark midtones to light midtones. If you move the Gamma slider to the right, the distance between the black slider and the Gamma slider is larger than the distance between the Gamma slider and the white slider, so the ratio of darker shades is higher. Try it now. Move the Gamma slider to the right until the middle box above the slider bar reads 0.70.

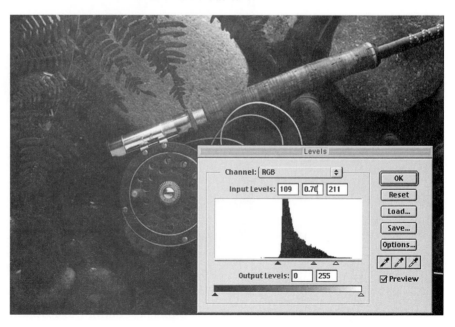

To properly adjust an image using the Levels slider and Histogram, you need to manage the relationship between highlight, shadow, and midtone (gamma).

The middle tones of the image are much darker, but the highlights are not greatly affected.

6. Now move the Gamma slider to the left to make the distance between the Gamma slider and the white slider larger; a setting of about 1.20 should do the trick. Notice the increase in the detail of the image. Click OK.

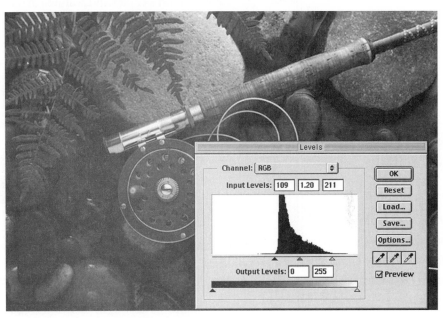

7. Save the image as "Fishing Leveled.TIF" to your **Work in Progress** folder.

Other Uses for Levels

Sometimes the "artwork" you'll receive will be less than perfect. Sometimes the original art was lost, or a hard disk crashed without a backup, and the only existing copy of a logo is a very nasty enlarged Xerox copy or fax document. This type of image tends to have ragged edges, or "jaggies" which greatly reduce the usability of the artwork.

While you might try to rebuild the artwork by hand, you can often recover a large portion of the work using Levels and a few simple techniques.

Cleaning Up Simple Bitmaps

1. Open the file **Bad Logo.TIF** from your **SF-Adv Photoshop** folder. This is an example of a document printed at a small size on a low resolution printer, enlarged on a copier and scanned at 600 ppi, then converted to grayscale and reduced. Not exactly camera-ready art, is it? Press D to return the foreground and background to their default colors.

When cleaning up a black-and-white logo with sharp edges, the Polygon Lasso tool and Path functions are invaluable.

2. First, clean up any obvious "dirt," the unwanted spots picked up by the scanner. Just circle them with the Lasso or Square Marquee tools, and press the Delete key. Use the Lasso tool to select any large "bubbles" or blobs on the edge of the image, and delete these also.

3. Activate the Layers palette. Duplicate the Background layer by dragging the layer name over the Create New Layer icon at the bottom center of the palette. Rename the layer "Art".

4. Click on the Art layer and select Filter>Blur>Gaussian Blur. Adjust the blur value so that most of the jaggies disappear. The image will appear quite fuzzy. For our example, we used a value of 7.

This document was scanned as a bitmap. The size and resolution were intentionally much larger than we needed (the logo will be reproduced at 1″ high) to give us more information to work with. We used Image>Mode> Grayscale with Size Ratio set at 1 to reduce the file size.

5. Set the Blending mode for the Art layer to Difference. You will see a hazy white outline, along with a jagged white outline on a black background.

6. Select Image>Adjust>Levels. Pull the black slider to the right and the white slider to the left until most, but not all, of the white disappears. The sliders will be very close together. The white that is remaining is the Anti-Aliased edge of our new artwork. Click OK.

7. Change the mode for the Art layer to Normal. If the artwork was mostly curves and began at a high enough resolution, this may be all you need to make it a viable graphic.

8. Select Image>Image Size. Make certain that the Resample Image check box is checked, allow the method to default to Bicubic, set the Print size height to 1.25″ (to allow for the background) and the resolution to 200 ppi.

9. Sometimes a little more cleanup is required. You can blur a little more, and level again, or use the Lasso tool to clean up the few corners (which should be sharp) and smooth the round edges.

10. Close the image without saving.

Curves

The Curves dialog box is used for brightness and contrast adjustments, changing image gamma, and performing color correction, just as the Levels command does; the difference is in the degree of control available.

Levels allow you to adjust the highlights, shadows, and gamma of an image. Curves, on the other hand, allow you to adjust any gray level in the image; at the same time, you can "lock in" up to 15 values along the grayscale curve.

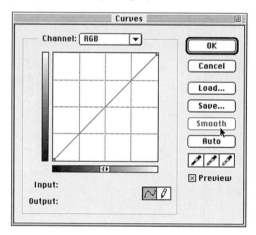

To change the view of the Curves dialog box from percentage view (the grid is divided into tenths) to quarter-tone view, use Option/Alt-mouse click.

When working on an RGB image, the Curves dialog box works from the darkest grays to the lightest, from left to right (notice the gradient band at the bottom of the dialog box). The diagonal line in the middle of the box is the "curve."

In RGB, raising the curve at any point along the graph lightens the brightness levels which correspond with the gray level shown at that point on the gradient bar. In other words, if you raise the curve beginning at dead center of the diagonal line, you are adjusting the 50% grays within the image. Lowering the curve would darken the image in that range of brightness levels.

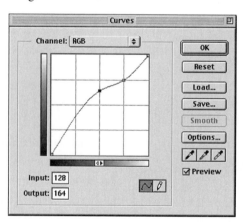

When performing color correction on a CMYK image, the gradient bar is reversed — the lighter grays are on the left and the darker grays are on the right. In this case, raising the curve darkens the brightness levels and lowering the curves lightens the brightness levels.

Notice that even though we only wanted to raise the 50% area, the line is remapped into a curve. This prevents abrupt drop-offs in color, allowing gradual transitions between lighter and darker shades of gray.

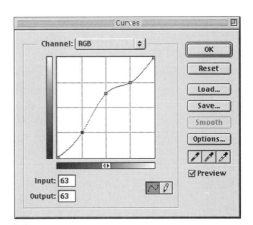

See the point in the middle of the line? Clicking anywhere along the curve adds a point which "locks in" that level of brightness. For example, if we needed to lighten the shadow areas and midtones without affecting our highlight areas, we could lock the highlights and adjust only the problem areas in the image. Adding more than one point is often required to "protect" a part of the curve.

Comparing Curves and Levels

1. Open the image **Old Man.TIF** from your **SF-Adv Photoshop** folder.

While the linear Levels adjustment is adequate to managing the highlight, shadow, and gamma values in an image, it is often necessary to adjust the grays in specific areas. The Curves adjustment is ideal for this.

2. This image is very dark. First, we'll try to adjust it using Levels. Press Command/Control-L to activate the Levels dialog box.

   Bring the black slider to the beginning of the Histogram bump; move the white slider to the left until his shirt brightens and the colors become clear.

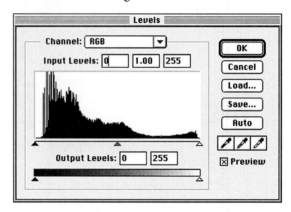

3. Examine the image. Note the lack of detail in the highlights on the left side of his face and hat.

4. Move the white slider back to the right until the highlight details return. Now try to brighten the shirt with the Gamma slider. Move the Gamma slider to the left to increase the ratio of white in the image.

   To bring out the tones in the shirt, the gamma has to be adjusted so far into the white range that the image appears flat. We're losing the medium-dark shadows in the midtones.

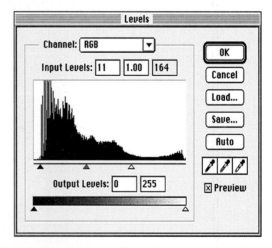

5. Click Cancel, and select Image>Adjust>Curves or press Command/Control-M to activate the Curves dialog box. First of all, we know that it is necessary to preserve the highlights within the image. Click on the curve to add a locking point in the upper right quadrant of the Curves dialog box.

6. We need to lighten the rest of the image overall. Click dead center in the grid and drag a point a little more than halfway up to the next horizontal line. Notice

that the Input and Output numbers at the bottom of the dialog box change as you move the cursor. These represent the "before" and "after" of the curve's adjustment, and are shown in a scale of 0, or black, to 255, or white.

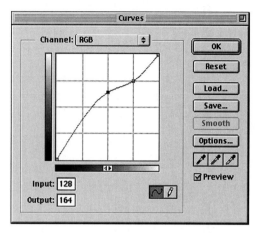

Adding locking points to keep highlight and shadow detail is known as protecting the image.

7. Notice that the image is getting flat again, the same as it did when we adjusted the gamma in the Levels palette. We need to preserve some of the darker midtones and lighter shadows of the image; they need to be lightened, but not as much as the lighter midtones.

   Add another locking point near the lower left quadrant to restore the shadows. (If you accidentally add a point you don't want, simply drag it to any existing point, or to either end of the curve.)

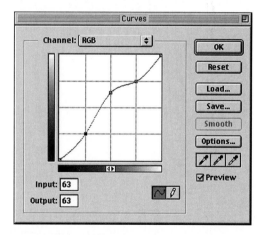

8. Click the Preview check box off and on to compare the image before and after curve adjustment. Fine-tune the brightness and contrast until it looks just right to you by moving the points up and down or side to side.

   Click OK to apply the changes to the image.

9. Open the Curves dialog box again and spend some time adjusting curves up and down to get a feel for how they work.

10. Close the file without saving.

Arbitrary Curve Maps

So far, the curves that we have worked with have been very simple. The Curves command is capable of much more, however; "Arbitrary" curve maps are special maps drawn with a pencil directly on the grid. They're extremely useful for special effects.

Creating an Arbitrary Curve

1. Create a New 5″ × 5″ RGB document at 200 ppi. Set the background to white.

2. Press D to reset to default colors. Activate the Linear Gradient tool (Command/Control-G). Set Gradient to Foreground to Background. Draw a gradient from top to bottom while pressing the Shift key.

3. Press Command/Control-M to activate the Curves dialog box. At the bottom of the box are two buttons: one illustrates a curve, the other a pencil. Click on the Pencil button.

4. Use the pencil to draw a squiggly line on the grid; any line will do. Watch the different areas in the Gradient Fill change to banding shades of gray.

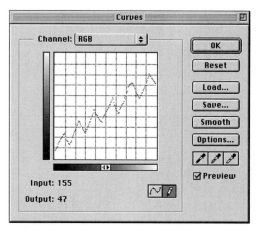

What you are actually doing is remapping one shade of gray to another. For example, the far left of the curve represents the black pixels in the image. By clicking the mouse at this part of the curve at the top of the grid, you will turn all of the black pixels in the image white.

5. The changes are probably pretty abrupt. Press the Smooth button to make the tonal shifts more gradual.

6. Hold down the Option key (Macintosh) or Alt key (Windows) to change the Cancel button into a Reset button, and click Reset. This resets the dialog box, changing the curve back into a straight line.

7. Select the Pencil button. Click once in the lower left corner of the grid, then press the Shift key. Go straight up to the top of the grid, then slightly to the right, and click again. The Shift key constrains the pencil to a straight line.

   Continue clicking top and bottom until you have a zigzag pattern. The gradient should now look a little like a pile of fabric.

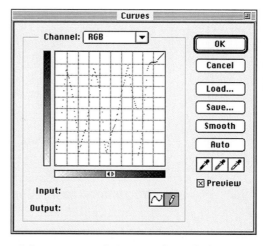

8. Click the Smooth button several times, and watch the curve become more gradual. Eventually it will become a straight diagonal line again.

9. Reset the dialog box again. Select the Pencil button. Draw a series of tiny dashes at the top and bottom of the grid. Repeat until the image is entirely made up of thin, rough black-and-white stripes.

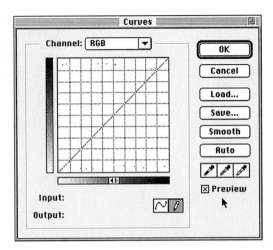

10. Click the Smooth button once, then press the Curves button (to the left of the Pencil button). The arbitrary map is now converted into a normal curve that can be adjusted point by point.

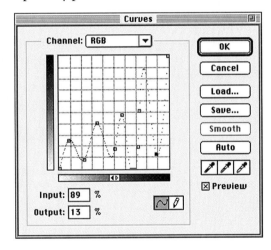

11. Close the file without saving.

Creating Inline/Outline Type Using Curves

1. Create a New grayscale document. Make it 5″ × 1.5″ at 200 ppi, with a white background.

2. Choose File>Place and select the file **Sale.EPS** from the **SF-Adu Photoshop** folder. Press the Return key to place the image.

3. Select Filter>Blur>Gaussian Blur. Enter a value of 7 and click OK.

4. In the Channels palette, duplicate the Black channel. The new channel will default to Black Copy, because there is only one channel in a grayscale document.

5. While in the Black Copy channel, press Command/Control-M to activate the Curves dialog box. Click the Pencil button to activate the arbitrary curve function.

6. Using the Pencil, draw little lines at the top and bottom of the grid, as shown below.

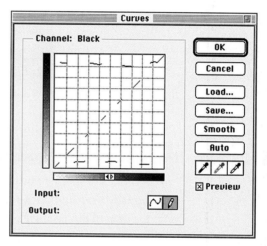

7. Click the Smooth button, then click the Curves button next to the Pencil. Adjust the points up and down. Moving a point down adds a white stripe. Moving a point up adds a black stripe. Make certain that the far right point is in the upper right corner, and the far left point is in the lower left corner. These points determine the background color and the color in the center of the text. Click OK.

The inline/outline effect works great with duotone images.

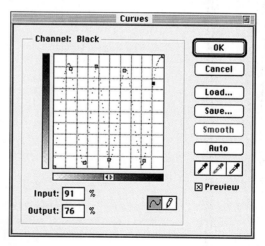

8. Activate the Black channel. Choose Select>Load Selection and choose Black Copy. Make certain that the Invert box is checked, so that the type is loaded as a selection rather than the background. Click OK, then activate the Reflected Gradient tool. Set Gradient Foreground to Transparent. Change Opacity to 50%. Click the Reverse box.

When creating several pieces of inline/outline type for a project, Save your Curves Settings in the Curves dialog box. That way, all the pieces of type will remain consistent.

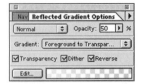

9. Set the foreground color to white. While pressing the Shift key to constrain the gradient to a straight line, make a gradient from the center of the text to the top edge.

10. Deselect to admire your work, then Close the file without saving.

Understanding Duotones

A duotone is a special type of colorized image made from a grayscale photograph. Essentially, information is added to the image which replaces or augments the black in the image with another color. The color may be a PMS or process color.

Duotones are used to enhance a two-color printed piece for artistic effect, or to colorize selected areas of a black-and-white image. Duotones used to be painstakingly created on a camera, but Photoshop gives you the ability to easily create not only duotones, but tritones (black and two spot colors) and quadtones (black and three spot colors) as well.

Creating a Duotone

1. Open the image **Chargit.TIF** from your **SF-Adv Photoshop** folder. This is a grayscale image.

2. Select Image>Mode>Duotone to activate the Duotone Options dialog box. If Type is not set to Duotone, change it now.

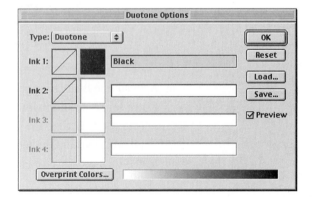

3. Click the box with the diagonal line next to Ink 1. The curve and grid are similar to those in the Curves palette, but they work a little differently. Click in the 50% box, and type 40. This will cause every pixel in the image which is at 50% black to display only 40% black. The rest of the curve is redrawn to smooth the transition between gray shades.

4. Click the 80% box, and change the value to 90%. While duotone curves can be adjusted point by point similar to regular curves, it is often easier to make the initial selection by typing in values, then adjusting if necessary later. Click OK.

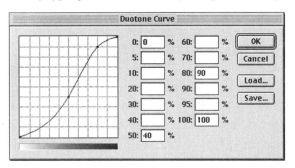

Remember that duotones can be made with process colors as well as spot colors.

5. Click the second box to the right of Ink 2 in the Duotone Options dialog box to activate the Color Picker. Select the Pantone Coated Book. Type 144 (there's no box to type into) to select Pantone 144CV and click OK. Alternately, you could scroll in the color bar until you find the color you're looking for. If you know the color, type it in and save some time.

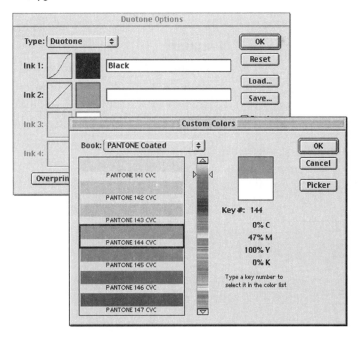

All the information for a duotone is stored in a single grayscale channel. The color is added according to the formula for the curve you specify. To view (but not to edit) the plates that will print when you output a duotone, convert the image to Multichannel mode.

6. Click the Duotone Curve box next to Ink 2. Change 10% to 5% and 100% to 80%. Notice how this brings all the values between 10% and 80% on the graph to well below their normal levels. To pump a little more color into the image, select the 30% box and change it to 30%, which will lock it in at that value. Click OK.

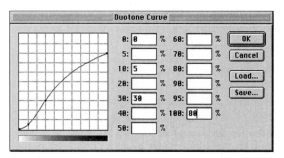

Duotones are a great way to spice up drab images used in process printing, too. Just convert the image to grayscale, build the duotone, and convert to CMYK.

7. Examine the gradient bar at the bottom of the dialog box. Notice the orange-brown shades in the midtone section. The pixels that correspond to these shades in the image will be recolorized. Click OK.

8. To print a duotone properly at a service bureau, it must be saved as an EPS file before being placed into a page layout program.

   Choose File>Save As, and select Photoshop EPS as the file type. Change the file name to "Duotone.EPS" and save to your **Work in Progress** folder. Select Binary Encoding to keep the file smaller, and an 8-bit preview for accurate on screen viewing in your page layout program. Click OK.

Summary

Through the Levels and Curves tools, tonal correction that would normally take hours for the photographer or printing vendor is reduced to minutes. Understanding when to use the proper tool will maximize the Photoshop user's time for more creative tasks, such as building duotones.

CHAPTER 3

PRACTICAL COLOR CORRECTION

CHAPTER OBJECTIVE:

To learn the basic concepts required to correct an image's color tones; to learn the tools provided by Photoshop for color correction, and to understand where to begin. Color correction is a complex science and art rolled into one. After completing Chapter 3, you will:

- Have a better understanding of the differences between RGB and CMYK images, and know why an image can look great on screen yet not reproduce with the color quality you expected.

- Learn about Photoshop's color correction tools, beginning with the Color Balance dialog box.

- Become comfortable with using the Levels command in both RGB and CMYK images to balance specific color ranges.

- Expand your knowledge of the Curves dialog box, as you see how curves can control the balance of one color against another.

- Know how to use Hue and Saturation to change colors within specific ranges.

- Understand Neutrality, and see how balancing the neutral tones in an image is the key to professional, high-quality color correction.

PROJECTS TO BE COMPLETED:

- **Pokey Creek Book Cover**
- Retouching the Jones Family Portrait
- Head in the Clouds Ad
- Baby Shower Invitation
- Farm Fresh Logo
- Photomat
- The Fix is in

Practical Color Correction

While the theory of color correction is not needed to understand the tools within Photoshop, in the real world of image manipulation and production, practical color correction is imperative. Production and printing houses have found some of the most time efficient ways to color correct Photoshop files for output.

Every Photoshop user has found his or her own techniques to minimize the time they spend on color correction. With all of the creative tools available within Photoshop, technical tasks, such as color correction, should be streamlined; the Photoshop user can then devote more time to the artistic side of creating high-quality images.

Most Photoshop users do their color corrections in the RGB color mode because:

- The spectrum of colors is greater in the RGB color mode than CMYK.

- A monitor represents and transmits colors in the RGB color mode.

- Quality color conversion software is available through Photoshop and many interpolation and RIP applications.

- Files in an RGB color mode are naturally smaller (only three channels), thereby easier to work with.

This first exercise is to find the best manner to identify the printable highlight and shadow point of an image. Since images can be acquired through many sources, and the quality of the image can vary, having a method to establish these points is imperative to color correction. The Histogram, Levels, Color Sampler, and the Info palette can make finding the highlight and shadow points easy and painless.

Finding the White and Black Point by use of the Histogram

1. Open the file **Bishop's Harbor.TIF** from the **SF-Adv Photoshop** folder.

2. Choose Image>Histogram to open the Histogram window. A representation of the overall pixel distribution of the image in a composite (luminosity) and the individual color channels can be shown.

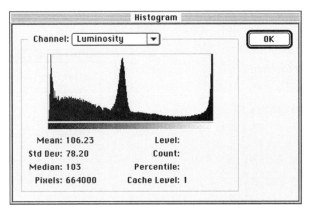

Depending on the resolution of your monitor, the Histogram may show substantially different numbers.

3. Use the Histogram to view the overall distribution of the pixels from the shadow to the highlight area. High concentrations of pixels are in the darkest and lightest area of the image, with another concentration just to the darker side of the midpoint of the Histogram. This shows that even though there are a great amount of detail pixels in the highlight, shadow, and midpoint areas of the image, not too many pixels are in the other areas.

To further review the Histogram dialog box, let's review the Mean, Standard Deviation, and Median values. The Mean is an average point of the brightness values in the image. A Mean of 128 usually identifies a well-balanced image. Images with a Mean of 170 to 255 are light; images with a Mean lower than 85 are dark. The Standard Deviation (Std Dev) represents how widely the values vary. The Median shows the middle value in the range of color values. As shown above the image is slightly on the dark side (Mean of 106.23). Close the Histogram window.

4. To determine the proper highlight and shadow points in the image, use the Color Sampler tool and the Info palette. Open the Info palette by choosing Window>Show Info, then select the Color Sampler.

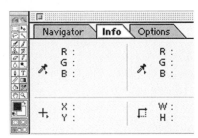

5. With the Info tab selected, click the black Triangle drop-down menu and select Palette Options. Select two separate readouts. For this exercise, use Actual Color, or the current color of the image for the First Color Readout, and RGB Color

The Histogram provides a great deal of information about the image. Reading the Mean will tell you if an image is light (over 170), dark (under 85), or normal. It tells you at a glance the distribution of pixels in the image.

The Color Sampler tool is a flyout option from the Eyedropper tool on the Tool palette.

for the Second Color Readout. While two different Color modes can be selected, the First Color Readout selection should be the Color mode of the image as acquired, and the Second Color Readout selection should be the final Color mode to which the image will be output, so that comparisons can be evaluated. Click OK.

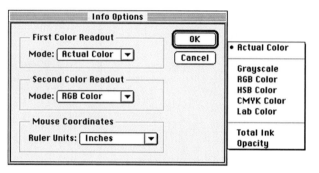

6. Place the Color Sampler tool over a portion of the image that appears to be a light (highlight) area of the image that has some detail and Shift-click. A number "1" will appear and the setting for the area will appear in the Info Palette window. Try three other locations on the image. The Color Sampler will record up to four areas on a single image. To remove a point, Shift-click on the point, and drag it off the image.

7. Do the same with the shadow area of the image.

8. There isn't a great deal of difference in the shadow area either. Whichever area is selected for the highlight and shadow area will be appropriate.

9. Close the file without saving.

Understanding Neutrality

The purpose of basic color correction is to create truly neutral grays in an image and thereby remove any unwanted color casts.

It is a common misconception that neutral gray is made up of equal parts of cyan, magenta, and yellow inks. As you learned earlier, printing pigments are impure; in other words, the magenta ink isn't an absolutely pure magenta. In addition, different sets of printing inks are different — the yellow in Toyo inks, a set of inks quite common in Japan, contains more magenta than SWOP (Specifications for Web Offset Publications) yellow, which is an industry standard in the U.S. Finally, due to the way the human eye perceives color, a gray needs to contain a little more cyan than other colors to be perceived as "neutral."

A prime value of creating a neutral gray is that when a neutral state has been achieved, color caste is removed, and the image may be color corrected much more easily.

Creating Neutral Grays

1. Create a New document, 300 × 300 pixels (no other settings matter) in CMYK mode.

2. Press D to reset the foreground and background to their default colors.

3. Click on the foreground color swatch to bring up the Color Picker. Locate the values for CMYK in the lower right corner of the dialog box. Enter 100 each for C, M, and Y, and set black (K) to 0. Click OK.

4. Depending on your monitor calibration, the foreground color probably looks fairly black on screen. We're about to demonstrate how much of a fallacy this is. Select the Linear Gradient tool. Draw a gradient from top to bottom with the gradient on the Options palette set to Foreground to Background.

5. As you can see, the gradient isn't neutral at all. It should appear as a warm brownish gray. If your Info palette is not already on screen, select Window>Show Info. Set the palette options to show CMYK and RGB color. Drag the cursor over the image while watching the numbers change on the palette. Contrary to what the screen seems to be telling you, every shade of gray in the image contains equal amounts of cyan, magenta and yellow.

6. Select Image>Adjust>Curves. Select Cyan from the Channels pull-down menu.

7. Click and drag the middle of the curve upward to increase the percentage of cyan throughout the image. As you drag, you'll see the image become more and more neutral.

8. Notice the Input and Output readings at the bottom of the box. The Input level is the ink percentage before correction, reading from 0 to 100, left to right. The Output level represents the ink percentage after correction. Raising the curve increases this number; lowering reduces it.

9. Adjust the curve until Input reads 50% (the middle of the graph horizontally) and Output reads about 65%.

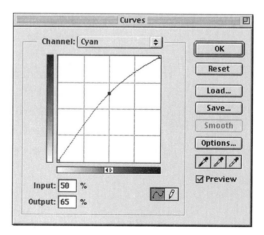

10. Position the cursor over the image again, and look at the numbers on the Info palette. The first number listed after a color is the ink percentage before correction and the second number is what the new percentage will be if you click OK. The magenta and yellow are unchanged, but the cyan is boosted. Notice that there is a larger percentage increase of cyan in the middle of the image (the midtones) than there is in the highlight and shadow areas.

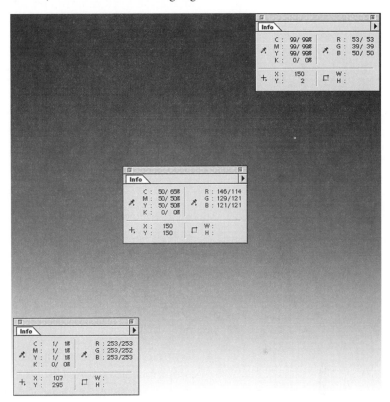

11. Check and uncheck the Preview check box a few times to compare the image before and after correction.

12. Click Cancel and Close the file without saving.

Adjusting an Image

1. Open the file **Poolside2.TIF** from the **SF-Adv Photoshop** folder.

2. Open the Info palette. Open the Palette dialog box. To see the color points in the RGB and CMYK color modes, set the First Color Readout mode to RGB Colors and the Second Color Readout mode to CMYK Colors. Click OK.

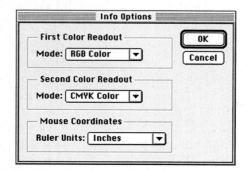

3. Select the Color Samplers tool in the Tool Bar, or press Shift>I, and in the Color Sampler Options palette, select 3 by 3 Average.

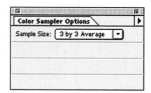

4. To correct colors in the RGB color mode, and have it relate directly to CMYK, complementary colors is the vehicle to use. As described in Chapter 2, the complementary color for red is cyan, green is magenta, and blue is yellow.

5. Examine the image carefully. Notice the yellow cast in the skin tones, and the greenish cast in the sky. It may not be apparent on an uncalibrated monitor, but if you place the Eyedropper tool over these areas you will find a high proportion of yellow. If you place the Eyedropper tool over the sand in the foreground, you'll find that it is nowhere near neutral. Red is running 215-230 (Cyan: 15-25%); and Blue is running as high as 185 (Yellow up to 40%).

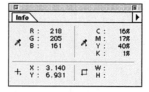

6. Check a few locations in the image, and check the values of both Yellow and Blue values. The relationship should be approximately the same.

7. Choose a point of neutral color in the foreground sand that shows a value between 215-230 Blue values and between 15% and 25% Yellow values in the Info palette. (We used *x* 2.760, *y* 6.950 as our point of reference.)

8. Select Image>Adjust>Curves. Since we want to remove yellow, activate the Blue channel in the Curves pull-down menu. Make certain that the Preview check box is activated.

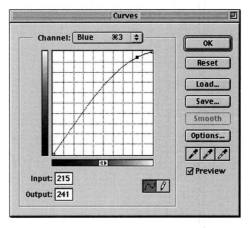

9. Move that point in the curve to equal the Red value (around 240) — or simply click on the curve line and type the Blue value in the Input box and the Red value of that point in the Output box. Notice that the image starts to lose its yellow cast. If we picked the right point, we'll notice that the Red, Green and Blue values are pretty equal. If not, we'll have to adjust the Red and Green channels, as well, because the white will start to wash out.

10. When the neutral area is about 240 for all three colors, you'll find that the skin tones have become more natural and the sky and water have lost most of the greenish cast.

11. Save as "Poolside Corrected.PSD" in your **Work in Progress** folder, and leave it open for the next exercise.

Once the color cast has been adjusted, you're ready to refine your image adjustment. Here is where Photoshop experts stand out from the pack, and you're about to learn the "trick" that makes them expert.

Refining Image Adjustment

1. Open the Curves palette. Set the highlight so there will be a printable dot. Double-click the Highlight Eyedropper to open the Color Picker and set C=5, M=3, Y=3, K=0. Click OK.

2. Set the shadow so it won't go completely black. Double-click the Shadow Eyedropper and set C=95, M=82, Y=82, K=80. Click OK.

3. Set the midtone. Double-click the Midtone Eyedropper and set C=62, M=50, Y=50, K=80. Click OK.

   Even though you're working with an RGB image, you want to use these CMYK curve values, so you'll have good translation to the printing process.

4. Find the highlight in the image and click on it with the Highlight Eyedropper.

5. Find the shadow in the image and click on it with the Shadow Eyedropper. Usually, as is the case here, this will adjust the image appropriately, and you will be able to skip to Step 10. The following three steps may be indicated by certain jobs.

6. Adjust the brightness by dragging up or down at the 50% point of the RGB curve, if needed.

7. Increase contrast by adding up to 10% to the Input in shadow areas and subtracting up to 10% in highlight areas.

8. Flatten an image by subtracting up to 10% to the Output in shadow areas and adding up to 10% in highlight areas.

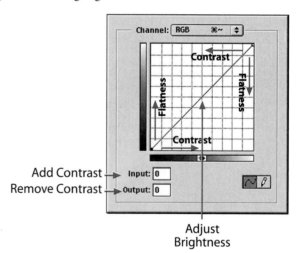

9. As a last step, convert from RGB to CMYK. Close the file without saving.

Here's where the relationship between the Histogram and the Curves dialog occur. After determining the kind of image you're working with from the Histogram, you can apply steps 7, 8, or 9 with confidence. If you couldn't tell what kind of image you had, you would only be guessing how to handle it.

Color Correction with HSV

In this exercise, we're going to change the time of day from around noon to sunset — or at least make a good start of it. We're going to do this by changing the color of the sky and water.

1. Open **Poolside Corrected.PSD** from your **Work in Progress** folder.

2. Using the Magic Wand tool, select an area of sky, then choose Select>Similar.

3. Switch to the Lasso tool, and holding down the Option/Alt key, deselect everything below the point where the trees meet the sky.

4. From Image>Adjust>Hue, Saturation, change the Hue to +170 and the Saturation to +65. Leave the lightness alone. Click OK.

5. Now select the ocean water and change its Hue to +170. Leave the saturation and lightness at zero.

6. Select the pool — it's a little trickier. We're going to lighten the hue to +160, and desaturate to –20, with the lightness set at –5.

7. To give the scene the overall "setting sun" look, choose Image>Adjust>Variations, and click twice on "More Red."

8. To finish the impression, we would lenthen the shadows — but that is outside the scope of this exercise.

9. Close the file without saving.

Things to Remember About Correcting Images

Like many other things in Photoshop, image correction takes time to learn before it can be done easily and accurately. Here are some things to remember while gaining experience in color correction:

- Approach all image correction with a plan of attack. Examine the image carefully before correcting, and formulate a logical work path for correction.

- Leveling may be done in either CMYK or RGB mode.

- Leveling *removes* information from the file. Never level more than once. Make certain that you save an uncorrected copy to revert to if necessary.

- Do most color corrections in the color mode in which the image has been scanned. Correct in RGB, then make final tweaks after converting to CMYK for images intended for traditional offset printing, or after converted to Indexed if the image is to be used as a GIF.

- Never convert back to RGB after converting an image to CMYK or Indexed, unless absolutely necessary.

- Realize that some filters and blending modes don't work as expected, or don't work at all, in CMYK mode. Examples are the Lighting Effects filter, which only works in RGB mode, and the Hard Light Blending mode, which is dependent upon a 50% RGB gray to define transparent areas.

- If you have to use an image in both forms; i.e., for both a web page and a printed piece, do most of your corrections in RGB, then convert a copy to CMYK and fine-tune the color adjustments.

- Make certain that you don't overcorrect images. A sure sign of overcorrection is *posterization,* an image that is divided into distinct areas of color rather than blending smoothly from one to the next. Another way to tell is to examine the Histogram for each channel in the Levels dialog box. The more space there is between the bars in the graph, the less color information exists in the file.

- Not all images need color correction, though most need a levels adjustment.

- It can often take several steps and different commands to correct a single image. For example, you may want to level the image, correct color with Curves, then use Selective Color or Hue/Saturation to correct areas of shifted color. Occasionally, you'll need to select an area, such as a sky, with selection tools before correction; that way, you can adjust the blue in the sky without adjusting the blue in water or other blue objects in the image.

- Never trust the monitor when dealing with CMYK color. The only sure way to predict color in output is to use the information on the Info palette and a process color book, which shows swatches of colors printed with various proportions of cyan, magenta, yellow, and black.

- Finally, realize that color correction is a *science,* dealing with values that are verifiable. However, with the acquisition of experience, you'll find that you know almost instinctively what adjustments are necessary to produce a beautiful, well-balanced color image.

Complete Project A: Pokey Creek Book Cover

CHAPTER 4

TRANSFORMING IMAGES

CHAPTER OBJECTIVE:

To learn about Photoshop transformations; to understand the specific commands in Photoshop for transforming graphics; to learn how to use guides and grids in your artwork. After completing Chapter 4, you will:

- Know the three ways to use Transform commands, and understand how the transformation applies to layers.

- Understand how grids and guides allow you to make precision alignment of images.

- Learn how to scale with Free Transform while maintaining aspect ratio.

- Understand how to transform 2-dimensional artwork into a 3-dimensional object with the 3D Transform filter.

PROJECTS TO BE COMPLETED:

- Pokey Creek Book Cover
- Retouching the Jones Family Portrait
- Head in the Clouds Ad
- Baby Shower Invitation
- Farm Fresh Logo
- Photomat
- The Fix is in

Transforming Images

It is good practice to determine the required transformation(s), such as scaling, rotating, and skewing in the page layout program, and apply those numbers as Photoshop transformations. You may be able to link directly from the layout application, opening the high-resolution image into Photoshop.

It's often necessary to rotate, skew, scale, or otherwise transform an image. While most desktop publishing applications have commands to achieve these effects, printing an image transformed in a layout application can slow output, or stop it entirely, since the output device must calculate and execute the transformations of the high-resolution image.

Transformations that are executed in a page layout are applied only to the low-resolution preview image you see on your monitor. The actual commands are stored in the layout as OPI comments, along with the information on the external location of the high-resolution version of the image.

Transform Commands

Photoshop contains specific commands for transforming graphics. A selected path or even selected points on a path can be transformed. In these cases, the menus change to read Transform Path (or Points).

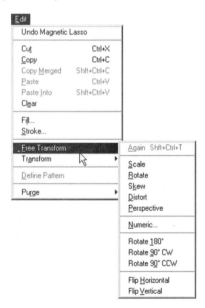

- The Scale command allows you to resize a layer, a series of linked layers, or a selection, either proportionally or nonproportionally.

- The Rotate command rotates image data in either direction, in 0.1-degree increments.

Rotating an image to other than 90, 180, or 270 degrees will result in image degradation, especially in situations with marginally adequate resolution. Given the choice, rescanning an image mounted to the correct rotation angle will always give higher quality results.

- The Skew command allows you to lock two or three corners of the image while distorting the remaining points.

- The Distort command allows you to warp an image in any direction, giving you the ability to place image data on a 3-point perspective plane.

- The Perspective command twists the image into a one-point perspective.

There are three different ways to use Transform commands. You can access one command at a time; access all commands at the same time using Free Transform; or enter specific values for transformation using Numeric Transform. Whichever method you choose, it's a good idea to perform all transformations on the image, apply the transformation only once. Otherwise, the image may degrade because Photoshop has to recalculate pixel values for each transformation.

The Transform commands work on any layer except the Background layer when there is no active selection, on the Background layer when a selection is active, or on a selected portion of a normal layer. If the active layer is linked with one or more layers, the transformation applies to all linked layers.

To convert the Background to a standard layer, simply double-click on it.

Using the Transform Commands

1. Open **Archery Target.TIF** from the **SF-Adv Photoshop** folder.

2. Double-click the Background layer, then click OK to let the layer name default to "Layer 0".

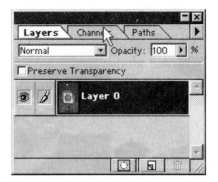

3. Select Edit>Transform>Scale. Hold down the Shift key and drag a handle from any corner. The image is scaled proportionally, maintaining height and width aspect ratio. If you drag a handle from the center of the top, bottom, or sides, the image will be nonproportionally scaled.

4. Release the Shift key and drag a corner handle. The image is resized again, only this time, the height and width aren't proportional.

5. To return the image to its proper aspect ratio, select Edit>Transform> Numeric and check the Constrain Proportions check box; click OK. To apply the transform press Enter.

6. From the File menu, choose Revert. Double-click on the Background layer to convert it to Layer 0. Select Edit>Transform>Rotate. Hold the cursor over any handle and drag to rotate the layer. The rotation will display immediately. Double-click on the image, or press the Enter key to apply the transformation.

Unless you have increased the Canvas Size dimensions, the corners of the rotated image will be cropped.

7. Select Image>Rotate Canvas>Arbitrary and enter 45 degrees clockwise to automatically increase the canvas size when you rotate (any degree of rotation will work).

When transforming images, try to perform all the transformations before applying. It will reduce the resulting image degradation. And if you decide that you do not want a transformation, do not use a transformation to reverse the effect. Instead, use the History palette to go back to a stage before the transformation; or revert to the last saved version of the image.

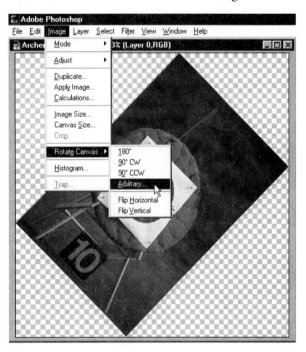

8. Revert the image again, changing the Background layer to Layer 0, and scale it down to about 50% of its original size (Edit>Transform>Scale). Now rotate the image about 45 degrees. It has enough canvas room to avoid cropping the corners.

Hold down both Option and Shift keys to scale the image from the center.

9. With the Move tool, drag the image to the upper left corner of the canvas. Select Edit>Transform>Skew. Drag the right center handle down. When dragging any side handle, the two corner points opposite the handle are locked into position.

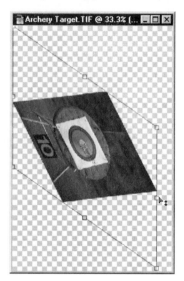

10. Now drag a corner point; the remaining three corner points are locked into position.

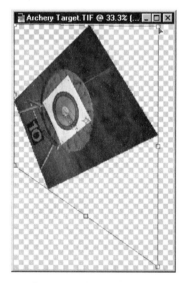

11. Revert to the "Make Layer" state in the History palette.

12. Resize to 50% again. Select Edit>Transform>Perspective. Drag the upper right corner handle to the left. The image is pulled into a one-point perspective. If you drag another handle after the first drag, you're essentially applying a Distort or Skew transformation.

13. Select Edit>Transform>Distort. Pull any handle in any direction. Distort allows you to move any point without constraining the other points around the image.

14. Press Escape and leave the file open for the next exercise.

Using Free Transform

1. With the transformed **Archery Target.TIF** image still open, select Edit>Free Transform.

   Scaling with Free Transform is achieved the same way as when using the Scale command. Simply drag a handle; hold down the Shift key to maintain aspect ratio.

2. Rotate the layer by positioning the cursor just outside any handle until it turns into a curved two-sided arrow. If you press the Shift key while dragging, the rotation is constrained to 15-degree increments.

3. Press the Command/Control key and drag any handle; this is the equivalent of the Distort command; the other handles will remain fixed.

4. Press Command/Control-Shift and drag a handle. The image is skewed just as if you were using the Skew command.

5. Finally, press Command-Option-Shift/Control-Alt-Shift (Windows) and drag a corner handle; the image is pulled into a one-point perspective.

6. To undo the last adjustment select Edit>Undo, or Command/Control-Z.

7. Press Enter or double-click on the image to finish the transformation.

8. Keep the image open for the next exercise.

Using Numeric Transform

1. Select File>Revert to return the image to its original saved form; double-click the Background layer to turn the Background into a Regular layer.

2. Choose Edit>Transform>Numeric; the Numeric Transform dialog box appears.

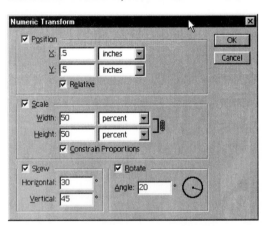

3. Using this dialog box you may perform any transform except Distort and Perspective. The check boxes next to each command designate which transformations will take place. Make certain that all check boxes are checked.

4. To move the layer within the image, enter values in the X and Y boxes in the Position box. The Relative check box, when checked, moves the layer the specified distance from its current position; if unchecked, it moves to absolute points on the ruler. Enter 0.5″ in both boxes, and leave the Relative check box checked.

5. Scale allows you to scale the image to specific dimensions or a percentage. Enter 50% in both boxes. If the Constrain Proportions check box is checked, when you enter a number into one box it is automatically duplicated in the second box.

Unless there's a reason to play with an image to achieve the effect (because you'll "know it when you see it") it's usually best to use the Numeric Transform palette. It's most accurate, and all transformations can be performed quickly.

6. Enter "30" in the Horizontal Skew box and "45" in the Vertical Skew box to skew the image.

7. Enter "20" in the Angle box to rotate the image. Click OK and the transformations are performed. These are very complex calculations; it may take a minute for your screen to reflect the changes.

8. Close the file without saving.

Guides and Grid

As useful as the guides and grid feature are, they are not a substitute for the Info palette, where you will get the most accurate and complete information about an image's position.

The ability to freely drag a portion of an image into another shape is a useful feature. Often, however, a little more precision is required, particularly when using the Distort command. Photoshop allows you to specify a grid and drag out non-printing guides to assist in aligning objects. They're really helpful in precisely positioning items on a page.

Using the Preferences>Guides and Grid dialog box, you may specify the spacing between grid lines, the distance between subdivisions within the grid lines, and the colors of the grid and guides.

The grid is turned on and off in the View menu. The View>Snap to Grid menu option automatically aligns objects to grid points as you move them if the grid is visible, and the moved object comes within a few pixels of a grid line.

Guides are created by clicking and dragging from either ruler. The rulers must be visible in order to create guides; once guides are created the rulers can be turned off. Guides may be moved with the Move tool unless the View>Lock Guides option is checked. When dragging or moving guides, pressing the Shift key while moving causes the guide to snap to whatever ruler tick marks are visible on screen. If the Shift key is not pressed, and the Snap to Grid option is turned on, the guide will snap to the grid if it is near a grid line when released. You can make objects snap to the guides with the View>Snap to Guides option. To hide guides, select View>Hide Guides.

If you have a standard set of guides that you use repeatedly, record their setup as an Action. If you will need to switch between sets of guides, the first step in the Action should be Clear Guides.

Actions are discussed in Chapter 15: Working Smarter.

Using Guides and Grids

1. Create a New RGB document, 5″ square at 100 ppi. Set Contents to White.

2. If rulers aren't visible on the screen, press Command/Control-R. The Ruler Units are set from the Info palette. Activate the Info palette and click the plus sign in the lower left corner of the palette, or select Palette Options from the flyout menu, to ensure that the units are set to Inches.

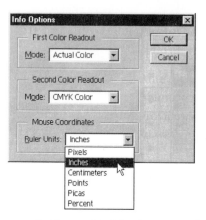

3. Select File>Preferences>Guides and Grid. Change Gridline Every to 1 inches and Subdivisions to 8. This will create a grid in 1/8″ increments.

4. The grid and guide colors may be changed by clicking on their respective swatches. For now, leave these at their defaults. You can also specify the type of line used denoting grids or guides. Selecting Lines style displays solid lines and the Dashed Lines style displays a lighter, dashed line style. These options are available for both grids and guides. The third style choice, Dots, places a dot at each subdivision of every grid line. This choice is less distracting than the others. Change the Grid Style to Dots. Click OK.

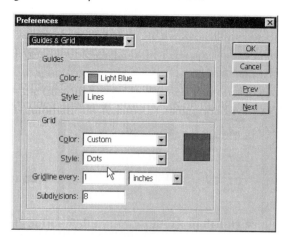

5. If the grid is not visible, select View>Show Grid and make certain that the Snap to Grid option is checked.

If you don't need the "snap to" function of the grid and guides, turn it off. There's nothing more aggravating than an element trying to snap to a point that you don't want it to snap to.

6. Click and drag the horizontal ruler down into the image area. Release it near a grid line to draw a guide.

7. Click and drag the vertical ruler across the image area; release it on a ruler tick mark.

8. Check that View>Snap to Guides is on. Create a rectangle using the Rectangular Marquee tool; notice how the marquee tends to "stick" to the guides and grid.

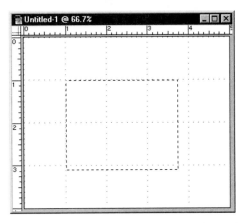

9. Move the selection border; again, it sticks to the guides and grid.

10. Turn off Snap to Grid and Snap to Guides. Now move the selection border again. Though the grid lines and guide lines are still visible, the selection moves freely throughout the image. If you hold down the Command/Control key, the selection border will stick to the guides, but not the grid.

11. Activate the Move tool. Click on a guide and drag it to a new position.

12. Close the file without saving.

Creating a Cube

1. Open the image **Beach Boy.TIF** from the **SF-Adv Photoshop** folder.

2. If the grid is visible, select View>Hide Grid. If rulers aren't visible, press Command-R (Macintosh) or Control-R (Windows). If not already set, change the ruler units to inches by clicking the plus sign in the lower left corner of the Info palette and select Inches.

3. Double-click the Background layer and rename it "Top". Duplicate the layer twice; name one layer "Left" and the other "Right".

4. Select Image>Canvas Size. Resize the image to 2″ × 2″, keeping the Anchor located in the center.

5. Double-click the Zoom tool to size the image to 100%.

6. Make certain that Snap to Guides is on. Hold down the Shift key and drag horizontal guides to the following positions: 1/4″, 1/2″, 3/4″, 1-3/16″, and 1-1/2″.

7. Again, hold down the Shift key and drag vertical guides to the following positions: 3/8″, 1″, 1-5/8″.

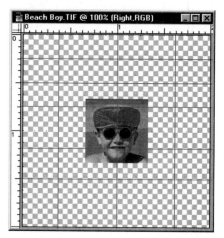

8. Turn off all layers except Left. With the Left layer active, select Edit>Transform>Distort. Drag the upper left corner of the image to the intersection of the first vertical guide and the second horizontal guide. Drag the upper right corner of the image to the intersection of the middle vertical guide and the middle horizontal guide. Drag the lower left corner to the intersection of the first vertical guide and the fourth horizontal guide. Drag the lower right corner to the intersection of the middle vertical guide and the last horizontal guide. Press Return or Enter.

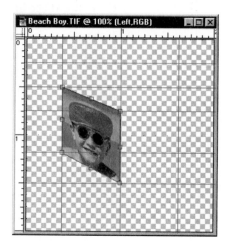

9. Turn off the Left layer, turn on the Right layer, and activate it. Select Edit>Transform>Distort. Drag the upper right corner of the image to the intersection of the last vertical guide and the second horizontal guide. Drag the upper left corner of the image to the intersection of the middle vertical guide and the middle horizontal guide. Drag the lower right corner to the intersection of the last vertical guide and the fourth horizontal guide. Drag the lower left corner to the intersection of the middle vertical guide and the last horizontal guide. Press Return or Enter.

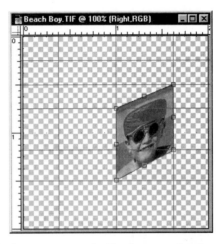

10. Turn off the Right layer, turn on the Top layer, and activate it. Select Edit>Transform>Distort. Drag the upper left corner of the image to the intersection of the middle vertical guide and the first horizontal guide. Drag the upper right corner of the image to the intersection of the last vertical guide and the second horizontal guide. Drag the lower left corner to the intersection of the first vertical guide and the second horizontal guide. Drag the lower right corner to the intersection of the middle vertical guide and the middle horizontal guide. Press the Return or Enter key.

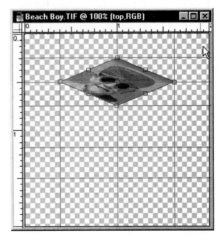

11. Turn on all layers, then Close the file without saving.

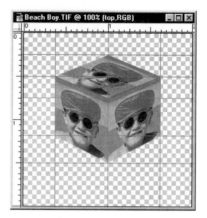

3D Transform Filter

Transforming 2-dimensional artwork into a representation of a 3-dimensional object is made somewhat easier by the 3D Transform filter. Through the use of primitive cube, cylinder, and sphere wireframe shapes, a flat array of pixels can be manipulated in space to apply the artwork to the selected shape.

We have just completed a manual approach to creating a 3D cube; but manually rendering a cylindrical or spherical shape would be much more challenging. It must be noted that other, specialized software is available that applies more powerful and sophisticated shape rendering. For occasional use, the tools in Photoshop are adequate for many purposes.

Render a Cylindrical Shape

1. Open the file **Martin Salt.TIF** in your **SF-Adv Photoshop** folder. This is a rather simple salt container label. The purpose of the exercise is to use the 3D Transform to wrap the label around a cylindrical container.

2. Select the Filter>Render>3D Transform menu item. Select the cylinder tool and draw the shape on top of the label artwork in the 3D Transform window. If you don't get it exactly on the position shown, use the Solid Arrow tool to reposition the wireframe; and use the Direct Selection (hollow arrow) tool to drag the anchors into position.

   If you reshape the wireframe into an impossible-to-render position, it will turn red. Correct the position and continue.

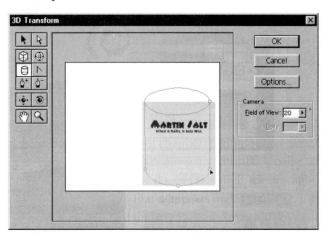

3. To rotate the salt box, use the Trackball tool from the 3D Transform palette and drag the rendered cylinder into a position that appears to be pouring salt. Use the Camera Field of View and Dolly adjustments on the right side of the window to keep the cylinder in view. You may also move the cylinder with the Pan Camera tool.

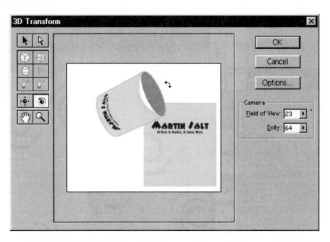

4. When you are satisfied with the position of the salt box, click OK.

5. To isolate the rendered salt box, use the Pen tool to draw a path around it; and Make Selection from the path.

The cylinder can be rotated in virtually every direction and it may take some practice to manipulate the cylinder in the desired direction. Keep clicking and dragging from different points of the cylinder and in different directions to get a feel for the movement technique.

You may choose to use the Magnetic Lasso tool, but you probably need the Pen tool practice.

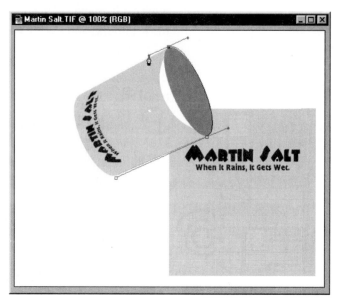

6. Press M to invoke the Marquee tool; and then Control-click (Macintosh) or Right-click (Windows) for the contextual menu. Select Layer Via Copy to isolate the cylindrical salt box to its own layer. Or use the shortcut Command/Control-J.

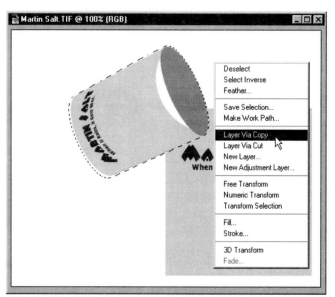

7. Fill the original label layer with a solid background color of your choice — perhaps a pale blue.

8. Add a layer below the Salt Container layer. Change the foreground color to white. Then Airbrush, with Option set to Dissolve, to paint salt granules pouring out of the container. A very soft brush works best.

9. For an additional effect, with the Salt layer active, choose Filter>Noise>Add Noise. Select Gaussian and Monochromatic; move the Amount slider around until you're satisfied with the result. Click OK.

10. Save the file as "Martin's Salt.PSD" to your **Work in Progress** folder.

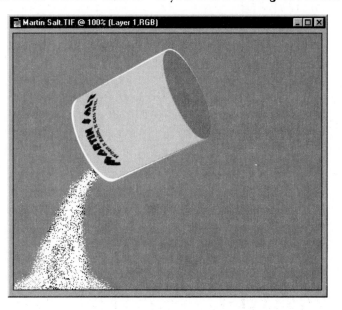

Notes:

CHAPTER 5

ADVANCED CHANNEL OPERATIONS

CHAPTER OBJECTIVE:

To build an understanding of how all images use channels to record color information and selections; to understand how density masks are used to create professional compositing, filter effects, and fades for shadows and reflections. After completing Chapter 5, you will:

- Know how to create depth in your images.

- Understand how to create special Alpha channels, and how to combine them to create special effects or complex masks.

- Become familiar with the Calculations dialog box, and understand how to use calculations to create special effects.

- Understand how Apply Image blends the image and channel of an image into the active file image.

- Understand the Channel Mixer, and learn how to mix channels of an image.

PROJECTS TO BE COMPLETED:

- Pokey Creek Book Cover
- Retouching the Jones Family Portrait
- Head in the Clouds Ad
- Baby Shower Invitation
- Farm Fresh Logo
- Photomat
- The Fix is in

Advanced Channel Operations

All images use channels to record color information. How much red, green, and blue should appear in each pixel to create the illusion of a red Jeep in a green meadow? Designers and production specialists manipulate the grayscale of each channel to adjust color. They also use channels as a tool to create shadows, smoothly composited images, and effects such as embossed type and 3-D highlights and shadows.

Channels serve two simple purposes. First, they act as a grayscale print of each primary color. When overlaid on screen (RGB), white areas in the Red channel, for instance, display red, black areas display no red. (CMYK is reversed.) An amount of 25% (202) shows as 75% gray, while 60% (102) shows as 40% gray.

The second purpose for channels is to record selections. The selection might be a complex tracing of shapes to isolate them from the rest of the image. This selection/ channel could have a hard edge or may include a feather value so that changes blend with unchanged areas. The advantage of channels is that they record what is selected (white), what isn't selected or is masked (black), and what is partially selected (the gray areas) in direct proportion to the gray value.

Channels and Density

The ability to record density or grayscale values provides great power and flexibility in the hands of users to control how much (light) or how little (dark) an applied effect will have on different parts of the image. A channel containing a gradient from light to dark will have the effect of gradually protecting or hiding pixels in the image that appear where the Gradient channel darkens. Density masks are used to create professional compositing, filter effects, and fades for cast shadows and reflections. A good way to learn this concept is through an exercise that uses a Gradient mask.

Using Gradient Masks

1. Type D to reset the Foreground and Background color defaults. Open **Pokey.TIF** in the **SF-Adv Photoshop** folder. Crop the image at 3.125″ as shown to eliminate the lower portion, including the man fishing.

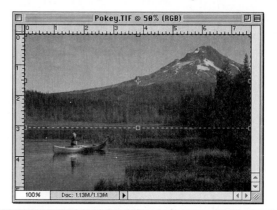

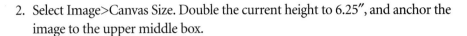

Using gradient masks in image compositing is vital. Gradient masks allow smooth blends at the edges of both images, soften or fade one into another, or simulate the reflection of one object onto the surface of another.

2. Select Image>Canvas Size. Double the current height to 6.25″, and anchor the image to the upper middle box.

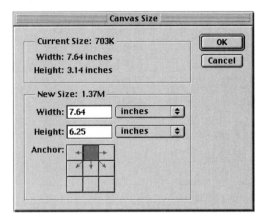

3. Using the Magic Wand tool, select the white area at the bottom of the image. Click the Save Selection as Channel icon to convert the current selection into a new Alpha channel. Double-click to rename it "Gradient."

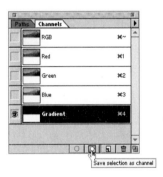

Try this:

Load the Gradient channel as a selection. Apply a small amount of the Twirl filter to the image — just enough to slightly distort the lower reflected surface. Then, apply the ZigZag filter with the Pond Ripples option. Very realistic.

4. Working in the Gradient channel, double-click the Linear Gradient tool and set it to Foreground to Background. Make certain that white is the foreground color and black is the background color and that the tool opacity is set to 100%. Press the Shift key and drag the gradient from the bottom to the top of the white region of the mask.

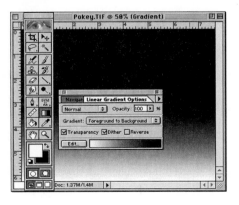

5. Return to the RGB channel. Choose Select>Inverse to select the top scene. Press Command/Control-C, then Command/Control-V to paste a copy of it into a new layer. Choose Edit>Transform>Flip Vertical and position it at the bottom.

Don't try to use Gaussian Blur through a gradient density mask; weird artifacts will result!

6. Load the Gradient selection mask (Command/Control-click on the Gradient channel). Press Delete, which will delete pixels not protected (white area) by the mask. The result is a smooth fade out in the direction that the mask lightens. These pixels are less protected from being deleted.

7. Close the file without saving.

Creating Depth Where None Exists

Light defines how we see in the world. The surface of an object absorbs, reflects, and redirects light according to its shape, giving the object dimension. High points reflect a lot of light — sometimes eliminating detail. These areas are called specular highlights. Normally, lit areas, called highlights, give the illusion of raising items off the surface. Indentations and low areas cast shadows.

Highlights, shadows, and midtones comprise the tonal range in an image. So-called "specular highlights" are outside normal tone calculations — they are ignored when determining the brightest point in the image. An example of this might be the sparkle of a diamond.

The direction, hardness, and color of created highlights and shadows also affect how the 3-D illusion appears. For an image to appear raised from the surface, shadows are generally placed at the bottom and right sides of the shape or selection. To give the illusion of being depressed into the surface highlights are used in this position. The edge thickness and fuzziness determines how far the object appears to be from the surface. Thicker and fuzzier shadows make the shape very depressed or embossed, while harder, narrow edges give only the slightest hint of dimension. To be most realistic consider the colors of both the object and the surface. In real life, shadows and highlights have a tint of the predominant color(s) in them. They aren't just gray.

This exercise demonstrates how to visually raise a two-dimensional object from a surface. To do this, we're going to learn how to create two types of special Alpha channels. One will simulate highlights, and the other will create the shadows.

Creating Highlight and Shadow Masks

1. Open **Rough Stone.TIF** from the **SF-Adv Photoshop** folder. It's a basic stucco background, perfect for three-dimensional type and artwork.

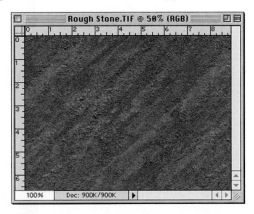

"Load" a channel means to load this channel as a selection. "Activate" a channel means to highlight that channel name in the Channels palette.

2. Make certain that the Layers and Channels palettes are showing. Choose File>Place. Select **Tropical Interiors.EPS** from the **SF-Adv Photoshop** folder. Click "Place" to place it directly onto a new layer. Resize the image, holding down the Shift key to maintain aspect ratio and position it as shown. When you're satisfied that it roughly matches this visual, press the Return or Enter key.

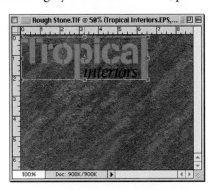

If your machine has enough RAM and Adobe Illustrator, you can copy paths from Illustrator and paste them directly into a new layer.

If you choose to continue to work with the image as paths, click "Paste as Paths" in the dialog box that appears when you paste into Photoshop.

When something is truly embossed, it's raised from the surface but maintains a sharply defined, flat surface with soft shadows on the slope. This exercise creates that effect with a more sophisticated result than the Photoshop Emboss filter.

3. Command/Control-click on the new layer created to get a selection of it. In the Channels palette, click the Save Selection as Channel. This turns a selection of the placed graphic into a channel. Double-click its name in the Channels palette; name it "Type Inside".

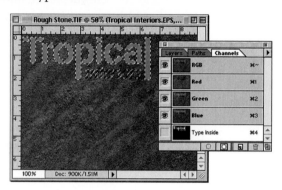

4. Copy the channel by dragging it to the New Channel icon. Double-click on this channel to rename it "Type Outside".

5. With the selection still active, choose Select>Modify>Expand. Enter 3 pixels and click OK. This will expand the selection by 3 pixels all the way around.

6. Press D followed by X to change the foreground color to black, then hit the Delete key to clear the extra regions of the mask. This expanded outline of the type will contain the shadows and highlights that we're going to create.

7. Duplicate the Type Outside mask by dragging it to the New Channel icon, and name it "Blur Mask". At this point, you should have 3 additional channels.

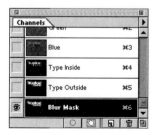

8. With the Blur Mask channel active, press Command/Control-D to deselect. Choose Filter>Blur>Gaussian Blur. Use a radius of 2.5 pixels to soften the edges of the mask.

9. Duplicate the Blur Mask channel; name it "Highlights". Choose Filter>Stylize>Emboss. Enter the figures shown below, and click OK when done.

10. Duplicate the Highlights channel. Rename the new channel "Shadows".

11. Activate the Highlights channel by clicking on it once. Press Command/Control-L to activate the Levels dialog box. Select the black point Eyedropper tool.

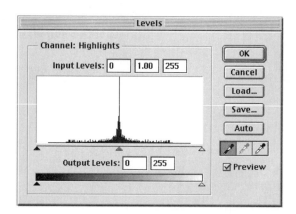

12. With the black point Eyedropper tool, click anywhere on the gray image area. This will set 50% gray as the darkest tone in the image, resulting in all of those areas turning black. The upper left edges of the type objects retain their tonal values, thus creating the highlight mask. Click OK.

You can Invert the tonal map of an image by simply pressing Command/Control-I. This eliminates the mouse clicks needed to activate the menu selection.

13. Activate the Shadows channel. Select Image>Adjust>Invert or press Command/Control-I to create a negative or tonally opposite mask. What was light is now dark and vice versa.

14. Press Command/Control-L to repeat the Level adjustment executed in Steps 12 and 13 (set the black point by clicking on a gray area of the image). Since the image was inverted before selecting the black point, the highlights have been reversed — we now have a shadow mask. Click OK.

15. Make sure that the Background layer is active. If it's not, the next steps won't work. This also activates the RGB composite.

16. Now we'll use these channels as selections to highlight and shadow the pixels in the actual color image. In the Channels palette, Command/Control-click the Highlights mask to load it as a selection. Press Command/Control-L to open the Levels dialog box. Lighten the shadow tones in the Highlight selection area by sliding the white (right) Input Levels slider to the left as shown. Click OK.

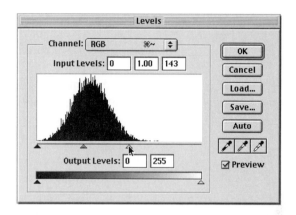

17. Load the Shadows mask channel. Again, in Levels, slide the black (left) Input Levels slider to the right. This will darken the selection to create the shadows. Click OK. Deselect.

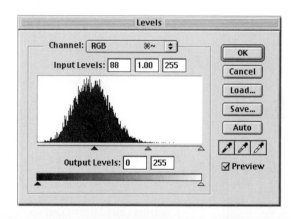

Make certain that the Background layer and the Layers palette are active, or else the tonal adjustments you're making to create the highlights and shadows will be executed on the transparent portion of the Type layer — it won't work.

18. Save the file as "3D Text.PSD" in your **Work in Progress** folder before closing; we'll be using it in the next exercise.

Almost all these channel effects can be more easily accomplished using Layer Effects. So why bother learning to do them the hard way?

In the real world, you're liable to have to work on an image created before Layer Effects were available, and unless you understand how it was built, you'll have no clue about how to fix it.

Channels are also useful for color correcting portions of an image. For example, if you need to pull green out of all parts of an image except the grass, you can create a channel which excludes the grass and then apply curves to the image.

Practicing Complex Techniques

This same basic technique with minor modifications can create a range of different effects. Once the concept of creating highlight and shadow masks is familiar, practice the technique until it can be repeated without thinking. We're serious about this. Complex yet commonly required techniques such as this one should be as natural as writing your name so they can be applied automatically when creative genius strikes.

Sometimes, it helps to list complex techniques in order of execution:

a. Load or create the background.
b. Place or create the artwork.
c. Create and save the "inside" mask.
d. Duplicate and expand.
e. Blur and Emboss.
f. Duplicate twice — name one channel "Highlights" and the other "Shadows."
g. Set the "black point" of Highlights to 50% gray with the Levels command.
h. Invert the "tone map" of Shadows, set the black point to 50% gray.
i. In the composite image, load/lighten highlights, then load/darken shadows.

Many variations are possible with this technique. For example, on a high-res file, the embossed channel can be made "tighter" (with smaller, more defined edges). The technique can also be used to sharpen edges by loading the inside mask into the blur channel and filling it with 50% gray. You can also use the channels to add noise, etc.

Using Channel Calculations

The Image>Calculations command allows Alpha channels to be combined in unusual ways to create special effects or complex masks. Channel calculations are similar to the blending modes used with layers and painting tools. The difference is that they work on channels rather than layers, and the calculation results are saved as a new channel, an active selection, or into a new document.

Channel calculations can seem pretty confusing at first. The best bet is to experiment with different channel operations, then, when a pleasing effect happens, write it down! Depending on the document, the Calculations dialog box can generate thousands and thousands of different possibilities. One small setting change will generate an entirely different effect. Keep a record of the changes to duplicate the effect any time.

The Calculations dialog box is divided into four sections:

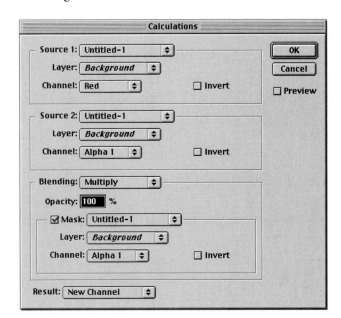

- Source 1 and Source 2 specify which channels will be included in the calculations. Source channels may be from any open document (specified in the Source pull-down list), provided the channels are the same height and width in pixels. Color channels (i.e., Red), an Alpha channel (created or saved from a selection), or an existing selection can be used. When using a color channel, specify which layer the channel should be extracted from or if it should come from all layers Merged. Invert the channel before calculating if that works.

- The Blending section determines how the Source 1 image/channel will be combined into the effect; choose a Blending mode and Opacity value. In addition, a Mask can be applied to confine the contribution of Source 1 using a channel as a density mask. The mask may also be inverted.

- The Results section specifies where the results of the calculation should be saved. Choose to save in the current document as a new channel, in another document having the same dimensions, or as an active selection that can be used or additionally altered.

Type Effects Using Calculations

1. Open the document **3D Text.PSD** created in the last exercise. Once open, duplicate the Type Inside channel so we can blur and offset it.

2. Choose Filter>Blur>Gaussian Blur, and blur the channel 2.5 pixels.

3. Press D to change the background color to black. Activate the Move tool and use the arrow keys to move the mask 3 pixels to the right and 3 pixels down. Rename the channel "Offset Mask".

4. Choose Image>Calculations. Make certain that Preview is checked.

5. Set Source 1 Channel to Offset Mask. Make certain that the layers are Merged and the Invert box is checked. Set Source 2 Channel to Type Inside. Again, make certain that the layers are Merged, but this time leave Invert unchecked. In the Blending section, change the blending mode to Add. In the other fields that appear, change Scale to 2. Do not check the Mask box. In the Results section choose New Channel. The dialog box and image should look like this:

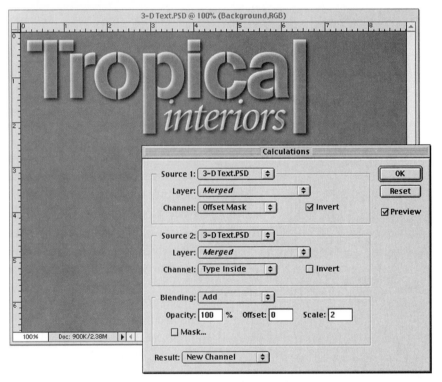

6. Click OK. A new channel "Alpha 1" has been created.

7. Choose Image>Calculations again. Source 1 should be 3-D Text.PSD, Layer: Merged, Channel: Alpha 1. Make certain that Invert is not checked. Source 2 should be 3-D Text.PSD, Layer: Merged, Channel: Offset Mask. Make certain that Invert is not checked. Change Blending to Difference. The dialog box and image should look like the following:

When using the Calculations command, what's really happening when you choose "add," "subtract," "multiply," etc., believe it or not, is that the numeric values of the pixels are actually added, subtracted, multiplied, etc. This explains why the Multiply mode results in a darker image. Multiplying two numbers together always results in a higher number than the original; in the case of calculations, higher numbers create darker colors.

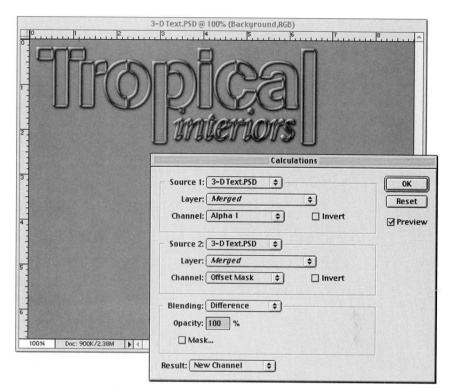

8. Click OK. A new channel, Alpha 2, appears.

9. With Alpha 2 active, Select All and Copy it to the clipboard.

10. Activate the Background layer and turn off (or Hide) the Tropical Interiors Logo.EPS layer. Select Edit>Paste to paste to a new layer.

11. Change the blending mode for the layer to Hard Light.

12. Close the window without saving.

Apply Image

Apply Image is a little different from Calculations. It blends the image and channel of this or another image into the currently active file image. It can blend from the source file any combination of a layer and channel or merged layers and composite channel. While it provides the same blend features as Calculations, Apply Image offers the ability to apply the effect to composite channels; Calculations does not. If desired, the result can utilize a mask from either of the documents from any layer or channel. The source image and the slave mask can be inverted as well. The result is often psyche-delic, but with certain blend modes it produces a haunting ghost or embossed effect of the image's texture using light and shadow.

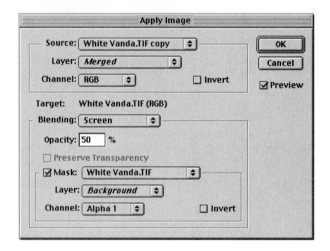

Channel Mixer

This dialog box provides yet another method to adjust and play with colors in an image based on the existing color information. In the Channel Mixer, choose which primary color to work with and add to the image. Sliders for each color channel are the means to do this. For example, if Red is chosen in the pop-up menu, red is added or subtracted (cyanadded) to the image, regardless of which slider is changed. Dragging the Green slider would add or subtract magenta using the Green channel as a density mask. It would be like telling the monitor to shoot more or less red phos-phors through the Green channel or printing magenta ink through the cyan negative (if you're in CMYK mode, the choices and sliders are C, M, Y, K). Dragging sliders to the right (positive) adds color up to twice (200%) the current amount, to the left (negative) subtracts color and adds its complement.

The Contrast slider heightens or subdues the effect created by other adjustments. Checking Monochrome converts the image to appear grayscale (all color channels will end up the same). This works well for creating density masks which isolate backgrounds or contrasted objects in the image.

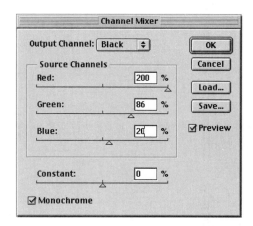

The following exercise using both of these features provides opportunities experimentation.

Mixing channels of an image

1. Open **White Uanda.TIF** from the **SF-Adu Photoshop** folder. Choose Image>Duplicate to create a temporary copy of the file that we can play with. Open the Channels palette so it can be viewed while Channel Mixer is open.

2. Choose Image>Adjust>Channel Mixer. Check Preview, and using the description above, along with some creativity, play with the controls a bit. Use Red as the Output channel and watch the lower leaf on the left. Changing the Green slider makes it very red, but changing the Blue slider doesn't as much. That's because its area contains green throughout, but blue only in a small patch. Watch the Channel icons in the palette to monitor how adjustments affect the image. Constant adds or subtracts red all over. Match the following settings to continue with the exercise.

When using Monochrome in the Channel Mixer, notice that all color channels end up the same in the document. The image is still in RGB but appears grayscale. When using Channel Mixer for this purpose, work on a duplicate file and drag one of the color channels back to the original document to use it as a channel mask.

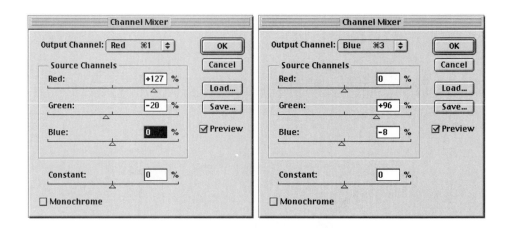

3. Click OK. Return to the original file and make another duplicate. With Copy 2 active, choose Image>Adjust>Channel Mixer again. This time we'll use it to create a mask of the flowers. Check "Monochrome" and use the following settings:

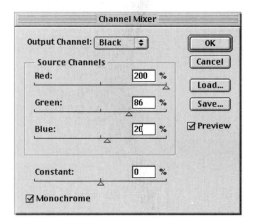

4. Click OK. With the Magic Wand tool, click in a white area inside the flower shape. Choose Select>Inverse (or Command/Control-Shift-I).

5. Press D for default colors and Press Option/Alt-Delete (Fill with black). This creates a mask through which only the flowers show through or can be selected. Drag the blue channel from Copy 2 into the window of the original document

so we can use it. It will be saved in the Channels palette of the original as Alpha 1. Close the window of Copy 2 (black-and-white image) without saving it.

6. Two document windows should be open: the original unchanged image and the copy whose color we changed. Activate that copy. Open the Layers palette and drag the Background layer to the New Layer icon to copy it. With that layer active, and with no selection, choose Filter>Stylize>Find Edges. Set this layer to Soft Light mode.

7. Activate the original image file with the RGB Composite channel active and choose Image>Apply Image. While having preview checked, start with the settings displayed, then experiment with the blending modes and try inverting the source file to see its effect. The settings used indicate that a composite (RGB) of the duplicate, using both layers (Merged) as they are in that document will be applied to this original image using 50% Opacity of the copy in Screen Mode. Using the Alpha 1 mask means that only the flower section of the duplicate image will be applied.

Apply Image only works when both documents are in the same color mode and have the same pixel dimensions.

If using Apply Image on a layer of the active or target document that has transparent areas, click on "Preserve Transparency" to prevent the image being blended from appearing in those areas.

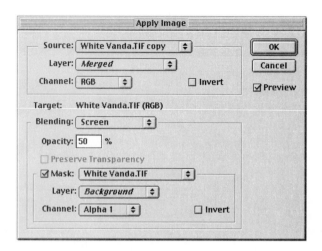

The final image looks like this, only in color.

8. Close the file without saving.

Managing Channels

Channels are great, but when working with large images they can consume a lot of RAM and bloat file sizes. These two related strategies can help. In the last exercise we dragged a channel from one image to use in another. That means that we can borrow a channel from another document if images are the same pixel dimensions.

Channel Libraries

Documents can contain just channels as a scrapbook or library. Simply create another document of the same pixel dimensions and drag channels into it; it doesn't need an image. Save it as a TIFF if using RGB or CMYK mode; save it as a Photoshop DCS 2.0 if using Multichannel mode or outputting the file.

To use the library without dragging channels from it, open the library file and the image file. From the image file, when a channel is needed, choose Select>Load Selection. In the Document pop-up menu, choose the file name of the library file and select which channel to load. To save selections directly to the library, choose Select>Save Selection and choose the library file name in the Document pop-up menu. Channel libraries are most efficient if they are converted to Multichannel mode (Image>Mode>Multichannel).

If a document contains many channels that you want to make a library out of, Save a Copy of the file. Then delete the RGB or CMYK color channels (to reduce file size) and save it as a TIFF.

Before converting Duotones to Multichannel, make certain that all adjustments are satisfactory. Multichannel images can't be converted back to Duotone mode to alter the ink coverage.

Multichannel Mode

While Multichannel images cannot be printed in color (they have no composite because none of the channels are assigned to RGB or CMYK), they are useful for several purposes. Since they contain only channels they're perfect for a Channel library. Remember that channels must be the same pixel dimension as the target image.

This mode can also be used to swap Cyan and Magenta channels as a special effect. Just convert the image to Multichannel, reorder the channels in the palette, then convert it back to CMYK mode. Another use for Multichannel is to help improve duotones. Once adjustments are complete in Duotone mode, convert to Multichannel. The advantage is that each color channel can be adjusted tonally using curves or levels. Save Multichannel files as Photoshop DCS 2.0 or Photoshop native format.

Transparency as a Channel

Conservation of channels is often important when file size grows. Saving every selection may not be necessary, especially when elements are on separate layers. The transparency of a layer acts as an automatic selection; just Command/Control-click on the layer name to get a hard-edged selection of what's on that layer. A layer can even be used in the Select>Load Selection command dialog box.

Layers can also act as their own channel mask. For any layer, click on "preserve transparency" to create a channel around the elements on that layer. Areas that are currently transparent become masked so that painting, pasting, filter and other channel operations can only affect non-transparent areas; the edges and empty areas are maintained.

Combining Channels

Another way to be conservative is to use combinations of channels. By saving building blocks of selections, they can be used in tandem by adding them together, subtracting one from another, even using their intersections. Channels can be combined using either the Load Selection dialog box or with keyboard shortcuts while clicking on the name of each channel.

The following exercise provides a simplified example of how these ideas can work.

Channel Housekeeping

1. Open **Wine.TIF** from the **SF-Adv Photoshop** folder. Open the Channels, Layers, and Swatches palettes. Notice that 3 channels (other than RGB) already exist in this file. We'll use these to create a Library channel file. Choose Image>Duplicate and name it "Wine Channels.PSD".

2. In this Library file we don't need the RGB image. First convert to Multichannel mode (Image>Mode>Multichannel) then delete the Cyan, Magenta, and Yellow channels. (They automatically change from RGB to CMY.)

3. But we do need to add a Gradient channel to the library. Click the New Channel icon, Press D for default colors and choose the Linear Gradient tool. Set the options to Foreground to Background. Drag the tool from left to right at a slight angle to create this gradient and name it "Diagonal".

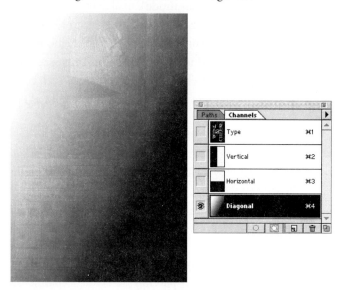

4. Save the file in Photoshop DCS 2.0 format, then select Single File DCS, No Composite and leave the window open off to the side. If you have enabled the automatic extension feature (Macintosh), Photoshop will automatically save the file as Wine Channels.EPS. Return to the original **Wine.TIF** file.

5. Our channels are still in this file. We'll see how to combine them here and with the channels in the library. Change the foreground color to cyan and the background color to magenta.

6. Command/Control-click on the Vertical channel to load it. Command-Option/Control-Alt-click on the Type channel to subtract it from the current selection, (Vertical). Press Shift-Delete (Macintosh) Shift-Backspace (Windows) to open the Fill dialog box. Set Use to Foreground color (cyan) and Opacity to 50%.

We save library channels with no composite because we're not going to print them. If a file is to be printed, it should be saved in one of the options with a composite preview.

7. Command/Control-click on the Vertical channel again. This time, choose Select>Inverse to select the other side. Command-Option/Control-Alt-click on the Type channel to subtract it from the current selection. Press Shift-Delete (Macintosh)/Shift-Backspace (Windows), but this time choose the background color (magenta) at 50%.

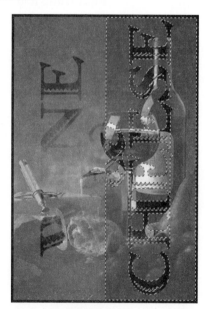

8. Command/Control-click on the Type channel, then choose Select>Load Selection. Choose Wine Channels from the Document pop-up menu and Diagonal from the Channel pop-up menu. Click the button to Intersect this with the current selection. Click OK.

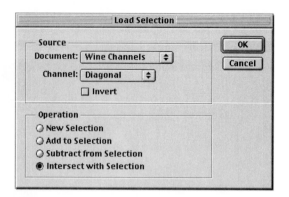

9. Press Shift-Delete (Macintosh)/Shift-Backspace (Windows) and Fill with the background color (magenta) at 40%.

10. Repeat Steps 8 and 9, this time check Invert in the Load Selection dialog box to get the lower right part of the type through the Gradient mask.

11. We won't need the Type, Vertical, or Horizontal channels any longer; they are stored in the Wine Channels file. Delete them here to save memory for a larger image.

12. Choose File>Place and Place **Banana Boat BW.EPS** from the **SF-Adv Photoshop** folder. Position it in the lower left corner, clearing the type. It is placed on a new layer once the Return key is pressed. In the Layers palette, duplicate the Logo layer, then click the Eyeball icon to hide the layer just created (Banana Boat BW.EPS copy) and activate the Banana Boat BW.EPS layer, which should be just above the Background layer.

13. We're going to use color from this layer to colorize the logo on top of it. Press Command/Control-Delete to Fill with the background color. Result: the entire layer is filled. That's not what we want. Press Command/Control-Z to Undo.

14. In the Layers palette, click Preserve Transparency for this layer. Press Command/Control-Delete again. It fills just the area occupied by the logo. Perfect.

15. With the Banana Boat BW.EPS copy layer active, click the Eyeball icon on the top layer to show it and set its mode to Screen.

16. Close both files without saving.

Special Purpose Channel Modes

Photoshop uses the unique capabilities of channels to enable Duotones (although it does not display a visible channel for them), bump plates, varnishes, and spot color. Using Spot Channels and Multichannel mode to pixel-edit PMS images can open up a variety of possibilities and effects for certain segments of the print industry to apply to their art. Making it work isn't difficult but requires some attention to the procedure and to saving files correctly for output.

The following two images will provide a chance to see what can be done and to which techniques to pay special attention.

Creating a Bump Plate

Adding varnish or a 5th color to a printed image can make the difference between just a picture and something good enough to eat.

1. Open the file **Berries.TIF** from the **SF-Adv Photoshop** folder. Among the blueberries are a few raspberries that need to pop off the page.

2. With the Magic Wand tool (Tolerance = 32, Anti-Alias on), click on a bright area of one of the raspberries. Choose Select>Similar, then choose Select>Grow, then Select>Modify>Smooth: 4 pixels. This provides a distinct selection of the Raspberry shapes. Select>Save Selection so we can reuse it. Name it "Raspberries".

The name of the channel will appear on the negative to indicate which spot color ink should be used to print.

3. Adding a spot red this way would blot out most of the dimple detail. We'll temper it by using the information contained in the Red channel to boost, not obliterate, those juicy berries. Duplicate the Red channel by dragging it to the New Channel icon. Double-click on the Red copy channel name to see Channel options. Choose Spot Color to change this to a Spot Channel. Click the swatch and then click the Custom button to choose a Pantone Coated color: Red 032. The channel is automatically renamed. Change Solidity to 25%. Click OK.

Solidity affects only the screen preview, not the output. It can be used to simulate the opacity of ink that will be used: e.g., 100% for a Foil Stamp, 0% for Varnish. Use 20–60% for spot colors depending on how dark and opaque they end up printing.

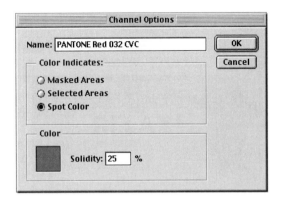

4. Everything on this channel that is black will print Red 032 ink. But we don't want to print red over the blueberries. With this channel active, choose Select>Load Selection Raspberries and check Invert to select everything but the raspberries. Feather the selection 2 pixels and press Option/Alt-Delete (Fill white).

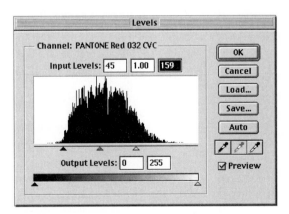

5. Often a bump plate is most effective as a highly contrasted image. With this channel active, choose Select>Inverse to return to the raspberries, then change the Levels setting as shown below.

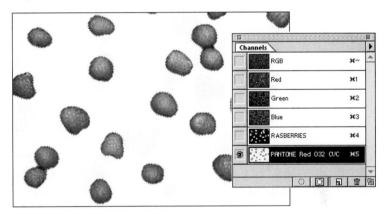

6. Click on the RGB channel to see the color image, then click the Eyeball icon next to the spot channel on and off to witness the effect.

7. Deselect and leave the file open.

Composites of spot channels can't be printed on desktop printers. The CMYK composite outputs normally, but each spot channel prints on a separate page.

Varnish Plate

Varnishes work well as allover coverage, just over the shape of certain subjects in the image, as drop shadows to those subjects, or even patterns and logos that overprint the entire image in clear varnish for a subliminal effect.

1. Make Raspberries the active channel. Select Command/Control-I to invert the channel.

2. Double-click on the name of the channel and rename it "Varnish". Choose Spot color to change it into a Spot channel. Click the swatch to define its color as anything in contrast to the image so that it can be distinguished from the image. Set the Solidity to 20%. Return to this dialog box and reset it to 0% once you are convinced the position is correct: varnish has no color.

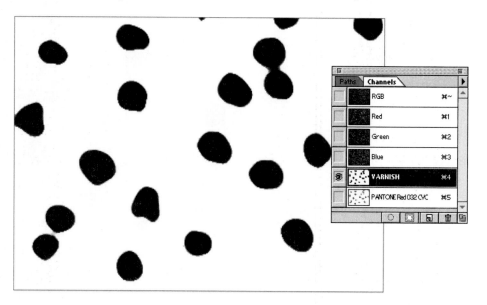

When using spot channels, always save to a DCS 2.0 file format and output to a PostScript level 2 or higher RIP. Use a Single or Multiple file, depending on your procedures. Macintoshes usually use Binary encoding, while output devices driven by Windows prefer ASCII. If problems occur, try ASCII anyway. Due to thier encoding, ASCII files take longer to print.

3. Convert the image to CMYK and save it as "Berries.EPS" in your **Work in Progress** folder using the Photoshop DCS 2.0 file format, Single File – Color Composite to retain the spot channels to be able to place it in a page layout program. (Multiple file may be required for your output procedure).

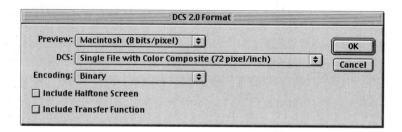

4. Close the file.

Spot Color Images

Spot channels make it possible to create original images in Photoshop or convert them from vector art while maintaining the separation and viewing the composite.

Creating Spot Color

Paths may be imported from Illustrator or drawn in Photoshop. Due to their nature, it was easier to draw these paths in Illustrator.

1. Open **Spot.EPS** from the **SF-Adv Photoshop** folder. It contains paths, copied from Illustrator, that will be used to screen-print a repeating pattern on ceramic and textiles. The image on a spot channel is made by painting that channel, filling a selection, pasting an image into the channel, creating type on it, and practically any way other images are generated in Photoshop, including using filters, as long as the desired "ink" channel is active.

2. Open the Channels, Paths, Layers, and Color palettes. If they are combined, drag each tab to a separate position. The image itself is blank. Load the Gold 15% tint path as a selection by clicking on the Load Paths as Selection icon.

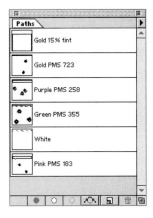

3. From the Channels palette menu, choose New Spot Channel. Click on the swatch to choose the ink that this channel will print and display.

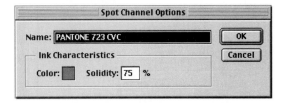

Pantone colors can be selected by typing the number.

Click the Custom button to choose from Pantone colors and select Pantone Coated 723 CVC (bottom of the slider). Click OK. The Channel is automatically named by the ink color. Change Solidity to 75% to simulate opaque inks. Click OK.

4. Notice that the selection is automatically filled with 100% color. But this area will be a light background for the pattern, only a 15% tint of Pantone 723. With

Channels can be filled only with percentages of black. One-spot channels appear in whatever color is defined for that channel.

the 723 channel active and the box selected, press Delete (white). Change the foreground color to 15% (black) via the Color palette. Press Option-Delete (Macintosh)/Alt-Backspace (Windows) to fill with foreground color. Then change colors back to default by pressing D.

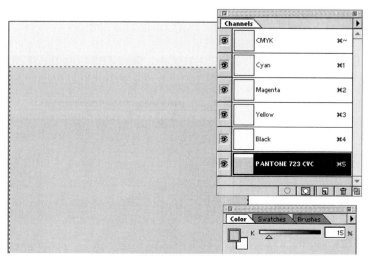

5. With the Pantone 723 channel active, load the path labeled Gold PMS 723 as a selection. Option-Delete (Macintosh)/Alt-Backspace (Windows) to fill with 100% color. While this channel is active, everything created will print gold. Deselect.

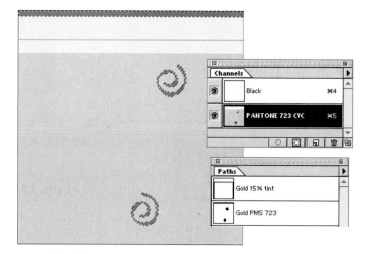

6. Choose New Spot Channel from the Channels palette menu again. This time choose Pantone 258 CVC (Purple) as the ink color. Go to the top of the Paths palette and Command/Control-click on the path named Purple PMS 258 to make it a selection. Leave the solidity at 75%. Option-Delete (Macintosh)/Alt-Backspace (Windows) to fill with color; it should appear purple on top of the gold. Deselect.

When creating type for spot color channels, use the Type Mask tool. The regular Type tool will add color to the RGB or CMYK channels.

Spot channels listed at the bottom of the Channels palette appear to cover those listed above. In reality, all channels overprint or print solid images (don't automatically knock out anything).

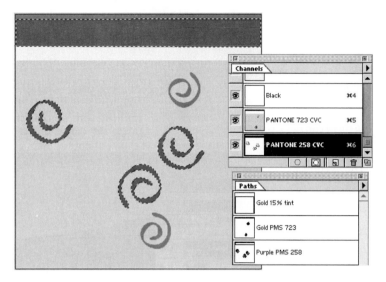

7. Repeat this process for a Green spot channel (Pantone 355 CVC). Fill the selection made from the Green PMS 355 path with 100% color. Then create a White spot channel. Since Pantone doesn't list white, use any light color, but be certain to rename it "White" so that it appears on the negative. Use the White path to fill small circles around the green squiggle. Create one more spot channel for Pink 183, and use the Pink path. When done, the image and channels should look like the ones shown below:

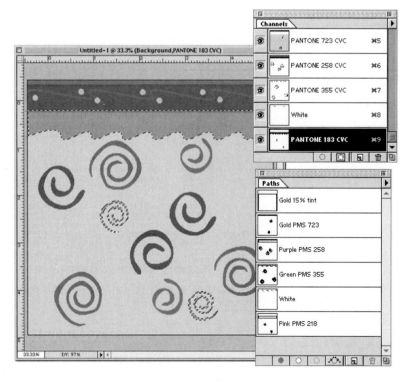

8. We'll add some type to be printed in white over the purple and pink bars. Activate the White channel and choose the Type Mask tool. Click on the left of the pink image at the crest of the waves. In the Type dialog box, use 36-point

ATC Yucatan and type: "Albuquerque, New Mexico". Position the type and fill. Don't deselect.

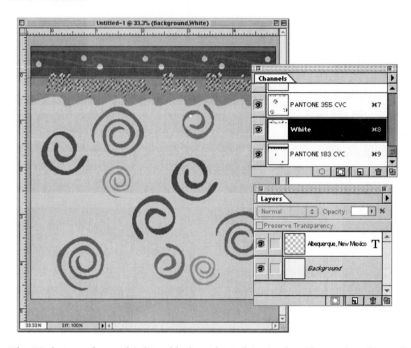

Type or any element can be on a separate layer as well as appearing on its correct spot channel. Be careful to select the layer, then reselect the spot channel to make certain that the correct pixels get edited.

As a general rule, decide which element to trap by thinking in terms of the darker color defining the shape. The lighter color usually overlaps either by spreading the shape or choking the hole.

9. The Pink spot channel is listed below the White in the Channels palette; therefore it blocks us from seeing the white type. Drag the White channel below Pantone 183 in the list.

10. Leave the file open for the next exercise.

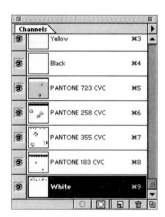

Trap Spot Color

Shifting the order of spot channels is only for display purposes. Spot channels do not knock out anything, but instead overprint just as the grayscale channel indicates. Manual knockouts and traps must be created. In this case, the type should knock out of the pink and purple where necessary, and slightly spread into the darker colors.

This image could be jazzed up by selecting the purple channel and adding a little noise (amount 50). Notice that it adds purple noise only. Filter effects can be applied to individual channels but do not merge colors of spot channels in their use.

Unless filter effects are to be applied, this type of job would almost always be done in a vector-based illustration program.

It's a good idea to convert spot color to Multichannel before saving. It conserves a substantial amount of disk space.

1. Use the current selection of the type and activate the Pantone 183 channel (Pink). Press the Delete key to create a pixel-perfect knockout. Activate the Pantone 258 channel and press the Delete key again to knock out that part.

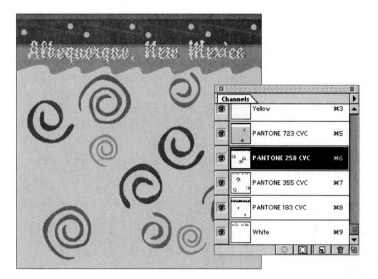

2. Return to the White channel for the spread. To create the overlap, we'll spread the selection. Choose Image>Trap. Select a width of 2 pixels. This automatically spreads light areas into dark ones. (As a rule of thumb, expand 1 pixel for every 100 pixels of resolution.) Notice the overlapping effect here and between color bars at the top. This is a trap.

3. Choose Image>Mode>Multichannel. This works well when no composite channels are needed.

4. Recombine the Layers, Channels, and Paths palettes by dragging their tabs into one another.

5. There is no need to save this file, but if it was intended for output it must be saved in the Photoshop DCS 2.0 file format. Close the file without saving.

Notes:

ADVANCED SELECTION TECHNIQUES

CHAPTER OBJECTIVE:

To understand the different ways in which selections can be made and used; to study multiple tool selections. By completing Chapter 6, you will:

- Become familiar with the methods for creating selections.
- Understand using selections, and have studied difficult selections.
- Become familiar with the Magic Wand tool, and understand how to adjust the Magic Wand's selection sensitivity with the Tolerance setting.
- Learn how to use Density Masking.
- Learn how to create custom Mezzotints using Density Masking.
- Understand the Color Range command, and realize its power.
- Understand how to use Quick Mask.

PROJECTS TO BE COMPLETED:

- Pokey Creek Book Cover
- Retouching the Jones Family Portrait
- Head in the Clouds Ad
- Baby Shower Invitation
- Farm Fresh Logo
- Photomat
- The Fix is in

Advanced Selection Techniques

Selections can be made in a number of different ways; and the resulting selections can be used in many more ways. Among the Photoshop methods for creating selections are:

✔ Rectangular Marquee tool

✔ Oval Marquee tool

✔ Lasso tool

✔ Polygon Lasso tool

✔ Magnetic Lasso tool

✔ Single Row Marquee tool

✔ Single Column Marquee tool

✔ Pen/Freeform Pen/Magnetic Pen tools (path converted to selection)

✔ Color selection

✔ Type Mask tool

✔ Painting in Quick Mask mode

✔ Painting in a Layer mask or Alpha channel

✔ Edit>Select All

Selections can be accomplished with a single tool, or by using a combination of tools to add to and subtract from a selection. During this process the selection can be saved to an Alpha channel or to a Layer mask, which can be updated as the selection is further refined.

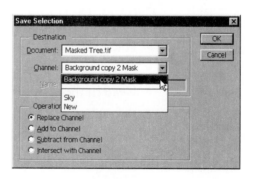

Each of these methods, with the exception of Select All, can generate a mask that protects the unselected pixels from change.

Add to a selection by holding the Shift key while drawing a new selection marquee; subtract from an existing selection by holding the Option/Alt key.

A selection can be Inversed, changing the unselected pixels to be selected, and the formerly-selected pixels to be unselected.

Using Selections

Once a selection is made, a localized effect or transformation can be applied without affecting the rest of the image. The hue, or color, of a model's sweater can be changed from blue to red without changing her skin tones. The Dust & Scratches filter can be localized to just the damaged portion of the image. The background portion of an image can be deleted to silhouette an object. A selection can be used to define an edge for the application of an airbrushed shadow.

Difficult Selections

Rarely will you encounter a natural image that does not require the use of more than a single tool and/or technique to produce a high-quality selection.

In this chapter, we will explore some enhancements to the standard selection methods based on emphasizing density and color differences to more clearly define a tonal edge for our selection tools.

At times, simply grabbing the Lasso tool and painfully executing a selection just will not work. Examples abound in the real world, but two in particular exemplify the problem: hair and foliage. Both are so random in nature and so prone to creating an impossible-to-draw edge that creating silhouettes of such elements is difficult to do well.

We're going to make a selection involving foliage. Hair — or anything else that presents complex edges — would work the same way. But first let's review the controls for adding to, and subtracting from a selection.

Multiple Tool Selections

1. Select New from the File menu, and set the options for an Untitled document window as follows; then press OK.

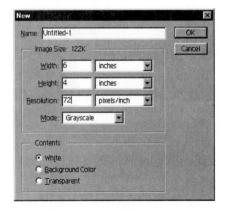

2. Press M to select the Rectangular Marquee tool. If necessary, rotate through the marquee tools by repeatedly pressing Shift-M until the correct tool is active. Draw two non-overlapping rectangles by holding Shift as you draw the second rectangle.

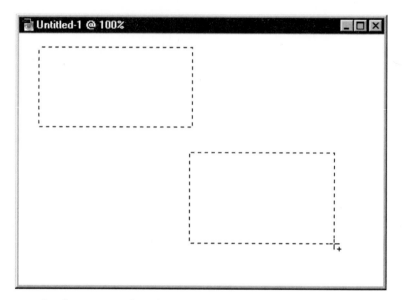

3. Press L for the Lasso tool; and if necessary, rotate to it by pressing Shift-L. Hold the Shift key and draw a small looping selection that intersects a corner of each rectangle.

4. Press Shift-M to select the Oval Marquee tool. Hold the Option/Alt key and draw a small oval within the first rectangle. This will subtract from the selection.

5. Begin subtracting another oval shape within the second rectangular selection, then add the Shift key in addition to the Option/Alt key. This will subtract a circle. Be certain to wait until you've started dragging with the Option/Alt key selected or this will not work.

6. Open the file **Market Oranges.TIF** from your **SF-Adv Photoshop** folder. Press Command/Control-A to Select All; Command/Control-C to Copy the image; Command/Control-W to Close the Oranges image.

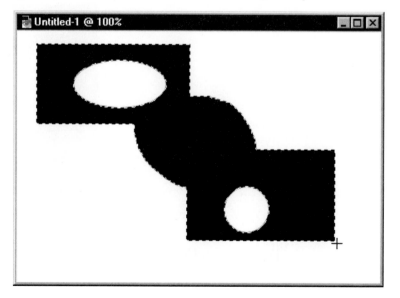

7. With the Practice Selection window open, choose Paste Into from the Edit menu.

8. Close the Practice Selection window without saving.

The Magic Wand Tool

You are probably already familiar with the Magic Wand tool. If so, consider this a refresher. The Magic Wand's selection sensitivity is adjusted with the Tolerance setting, in units of tone levels. For example, if the Tolerance setting is 10 levels, the Magic Wand selection will spread from the point of selection to include up to 10 adjacent tone levels both toward the lighter and darker ends of the scale.

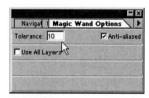

Double-click on a tool in the Tool palette to access the Options palette for that tool.

Consider the complete tonal range from black to white as covering 256 levels. This is the case for 8-bit grayscale images; we will ignore color for the moment. This is illustrated by a grayscale ramp in the following figure. When the Magic Wand tolerance setting is 3, the selection spreads from the point of clicking the tool on the gradient to include tone levels that are 3 levels above and below the initially selected level. In the example of Tolerance = 10, the selection covers a total of 20 levels around the initial point; 50 generates a 100-level selection; and a Tolerance setting of 128 will select the entire image if the initial point of selection is in the center of the gradient.

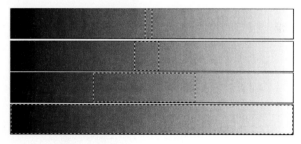

Using the Magic Wand Selector

1. Open the image **The Tree.TIF** from your **SF-Adv Photoshop** folder. Zoom into the edge of the foliage where it meets the sky. Notice how detailed the edge is between the tree and the sky.

You can supplement the Magic Wand tool with the Select>Similar menu function. This command will extend the selection to include areas of similar tone levels in other parts of the image that are not contiguous with the initial selection.

2. Zoom out so that you can see the entire image on your monitor. Double-click the Magic Wand tool, and set the Tolerance level to 16. Click in the sky anywhere except in the rainbow.

3. Deselect the area. Set the Tolerance to 64, and click in the blue portion of the sky. When the selection appears, choose Select>Similar; this will select all of the sky including some small areas totally surrounded by foliage.

With some minor cleanup you could probably get away with the selection mask we've created so far; however, there are even more accurate ways to make complex selections.

4. Leave the image open for the next exercise.

This is a technique that will yield variable results based on the characteristics of the individual image. At times, as in the case of the Tree image, a simple contrast adjustment to one of the color channels will generate a nearly perfect mask. Using the Density Masking approach rather than the Magic Wand tool will save you clicks and time. In other situations you will have to experiment with Brightness and Contrast — and even the mixing of channels using the Calculate commands.

Using Density Masking

1. Continuing working in the same image. Press Command/Control-D to deselect the current selection.

   Since each channel of an image contains the primary component of the particular color (red, green, and blue, for example), you would think that the most tone in this file is contained in the green channel. And so it is. Activate the Channels palette, and select and examine the Green channel.

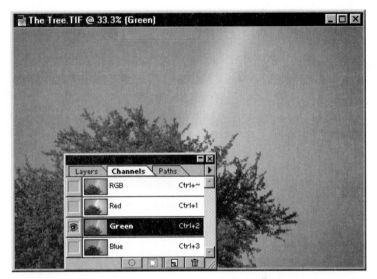

   There is a good range of tones in the Green channel, showing a generous amount of detail in the shadows and midtones.

2. Now look at the Blue channel. There's a good amount of contrast but not much detail in the tree.

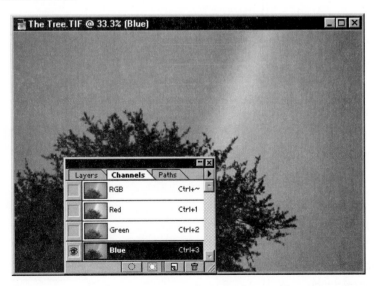

   This is the channel we're going to use, because for masking purposes we don't want a range of tones; we need edges.

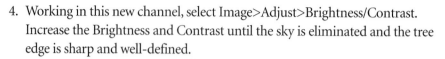

3. Duplicate the Blue channel. Rename it "Sky".

4. Working in this new channel, select Image>Adjust>Brightness/Contrast. Increase the Brightness and Contrast until the sky is eliminated and the tree edge is sharp and well-defined.

Duplicate a channel by dragging it to the New Channel icon at the bottom of the Channels palette.

5. Return to the Composite channel and load the Sky selection.

6. Save the image as "Masked Tree.TIF" in your **Work in Progress** folder. Keep the image open for the next exercise.

Overlay Image

A fun technique to try is using a density mask as an overlay image on a layer. Since the shape of the mask exactly matches the sky background, you can get some dramatic painting effects in the sky while retaining the image qualities of the tree.

Creating Custom Mezzotints Using Density Masking

If you drop the Contrast to -100, you'll have a perfectly neutral gray. Then simply increase the brightness until the sky disappears.

1. Activate the Layers palette, and drag the Background layer onto the New Layer icon to create a copy of the layer.

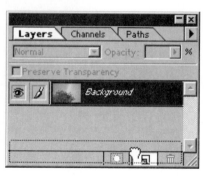

Mezzotints are considered by many graphic arts historians as the first "halftones," since they were an early attempt at reproducing tonal density — shadow, midtone, and highlight — by grouping tiny marks on a stone litho plate. Shadow areas would contain the greatest density of marks; highlights the least; with midtones represented by intermediate densities of marks.

Often, threshold adjustments can isolate the edges of images whose contrast has been increased. Try this to generate line art from black-and-white photographs — especially product shots or other images containing lots of lines and curves.

2. The Background copy layer should be active with the Sky selection loaded. Select Image>Adjust>Brightness/Contrast. Adjust both sliders until you've overexposed the sky and removed most of its color.

3. Set the Blending mode of the layer to Dissolve, and set the Opacity of the layer to 40%.

   This produces a mezzotinted sky and rainbow, with the tree untouched by the effect. To achieve a mezzotint that includes the tree, reset the Blending mode to Normal and the Opacity to 100%.

4. Deselect the Sky selection.

5. Choose Image>Adjust>Threshold. Move the slider toward the right to create a darker mezzotint, to the left to create a lighter mezzotint. Experiment with it. A lighter effect will give the impression that there is snow on the tree. Click OK.

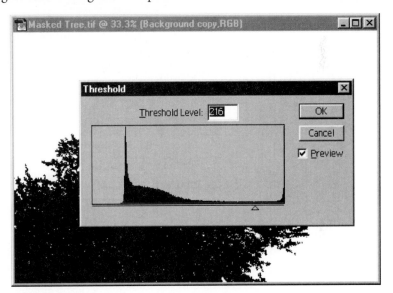

6. Set the Blending mode of the layer to Dissolve, and set the Opacity of the layer to 40%.

A moiré is an artifact generated by pairs of dot or line patterns that fall in a regular, repeating, reinforcing sequence resulting in the appearance of a series of parallel and/or crossed lines.

7. Save the image to your **Work in Progress** folder as "Masked Tree.PSD"; then press Command-E (Macintosh) or Control-E (Windows) to flatten the image.

   Note that the mezzotint may appear to change, depending on the zoom factor currently active for your image. This is simply a screen artifact; the data is unchanged.

8. Choose Filter>Blur>Blur, then choose Filter>Sharpen>Sharpen. This is to eliminate any moiré patterns created by overlaying the dissolved Threshold layer on the Background image. Look closely at the image.

   Using variations on this theme, you can create all types of textures, resulting in some excellent mezzotint and patterned effects. You may see an undesirable patterning in the image you have created. In spite of this, the exercise is useful to demonstrate the components of the process.

9. Revert the file, then change the Layer Blending mode of the Background Copy Mask layer back to Normal. Select Filter>Pixelate>Mezzotint; use Fine Dots. Is that better?

10. Close the file without saving.

Using the Color Range Command

The Color Range command is similar to the Magic Wand tool, but it's considerably more powerful. This brief exercise will help familiarize you with how it works.

Creating Masks Based on Color Range

1. Open the image **White Vanda.TIF** from your **SF-Adv Photoshop** folder.

2. Double-click the Eyedropper tool in the Toolbox. On the Options palette, set the Sample Size to Point Sample.

3. We want to make a selection that includes only the white flowers, eliminating the background and the orange flowers on the right side. Choose Select>Color Range.

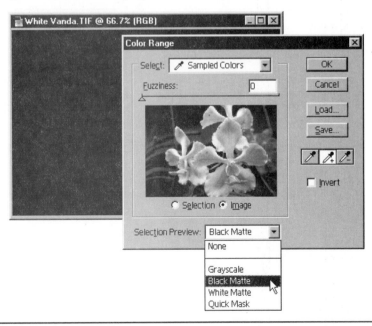

Set the following options in the dialog box: Select = Sampled Colors; Fuzziness = 0; Selection Preview = Black Matte. Click the Image radio button. When you choose Selection Preview = Black Matte, the image itself turns black. This indicates that no portion of the image has been selected at this point. The "Matte" covers any non-selected regions.

4. Select the plus (+) Eyedropper in the row of Eyedroppers. Working in the Preview window, click inside the foremost white flower as shown below.

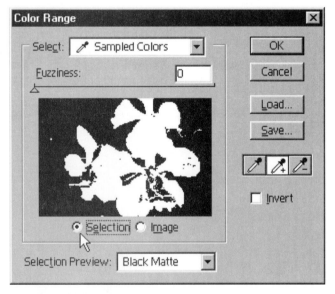

5. Look at the Image window behind the dialog box. Since we have Black Matte chosen as the selection preview, when we added that one tone it "peeled" the matte away from that area.

6. Continue to use the plus Eyedropper to select portions of the flower. Every time you do, the selection will grow accordingly. Watch as the matte is peeled away,

In general, you will have to clean up your selections. In certain situations, a simple click may grab everything you want. Experiment with the Fuzziness control. This increases the tolerance of the Eyedroppers, and it extends what is already selected to match the new tolerance. The Pop-up menu at the top of the dialog box provides for selection of specific color channels (red, green, blue) and tonal ranges (highlight, midtone, shadow).

and click in regions of the preview that correspond to areas in the image where the matte remains.

7. Click the Selection radio button at the bottom of the Preview window. Since the preview can sometimes be too small to work in, you can turn the Dialog window into a selection preview and click directly in the image itself to fine-tune the selection.

The Save option in the Color Range dialog box will save a selection of colors that can be reloaded and applied to another image.

You will find that some colors selected into the range will also be present in the background. In each case you must decide whether to include or exclude that particular color. The decision should be based on where it will be easier to touch up the selection later.
Notice the orange color in the center of the white flowers; that color is also present in the orange flowers at the right side of the background.

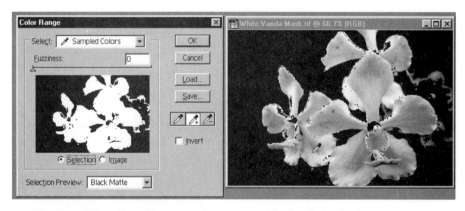

If you accidentally select tones that are outside the desired selection area, you can remove them using the minus (-) Eyedropper, which subtracts rather than adds tones to the region.

8. Continue to develop the selection mask until you're happy that it's as close to perfect as you're going to get it. Don't make yourself crazy while you're still in the dialog box. We're going to use another of Photoshop's features to clean the mask once we've gone back to the main image. Click OK and look at your work.

9. In the Eyedropper Options palette, change the Sample Size to 3 × 3 Average. Keep the image open and the selection active for the next exercise.

Using Quick Mask Mode

Quick Mask mode allows you to create or edit selections with Photoshop's standard painting tools. This can be extremely useful when creating complex selections.

Painting Selections in Quick Mask

1. The **White Vanda.TIF** image in which you created a Color Range selection should still be open from the previous exercise.

2. At the bottom of the Toolbox are two dotted Circle icons. The second (a small filled dotted circle) changes the mode of Photoshop from Normal to Quick Mask. Click it once, or press Q, and see what happens.

If you are having trouble distinguishing the Quick Mask color from the orange flowers in the background, change the Mask color to dark blue by double-clicking on the Quick Mask icon and selecting a new Mask color.

The masked areas (outside the selection) have been covered with the digital equivalent of Rubylith — showing you exactly where you have to fix the selection. The Quick Mask feature has the ability to clearly display your selection as you are refining it. The paradigm of painting and erasing the selection is conceptually more comfortable for some users, rather than the idea of looping pixels.

3. Select a small, hard, preferably angled brush. With Black as the foreground color, begin to paint over areas that should have been left out of the selection. As you paint, the Rubylith grows to cover the painted regions.

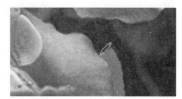

4. Select the Eraser tool, and paint areas where you wish to remove selection regions. This often happens when you use Color Range, since a small amount of a tone within a portion of the image might be inadvertently selected because it is within the selected range.

As an alternative to using the Eraser to remove a mask, you may switch the Foreground and Background colors while using the Brush tool: Press "D" to set the default B/W colors and "X" to swap them back and forth.

5. Complete the selection using Quick Mask mode. Click the Normal mode button (the left button) to leave Quick Mask mode and turn the mask into a selection.

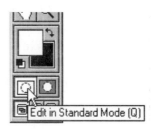

When you're done, save the selection into its own Alpha channel, then save the image as "White Vanda Mask.TIF" to your **Work in Progress** folder.

Selections and Paths

As you know, paths can be used to generate vector-based selections. They are similar to paths used in Illustrator and Freehand. When dealing with very complex selections, channels are the way to go. When creating simpler selections, however, compared to Alpha channel selections, paths keep the file size smaller. In addition, paths offer the distinct advantage of being able to create long smooth curves.

Paths can be exported with an image and used as a clipping path. When an EPS file with a clipping path is placed into a page layout program such as QuarkXPress, the area outside of the path is clipped to transparent.

Paths may be converted to or from selections. In some cases, they result in much smoother selections than may be achieved using conventional selection tools.

Using Paths as Selections

Paths are not constrained to follow individual pixels. In fact, a path will typically cut through pixels, especially in images that are relatively low in resolution. If used as a clipping path in an EPS image, the silhouetted image will output with a sharp crisp edge often without the soft Anti-Aliased edge seen in the Photoshop document window. When converted from a path, the selection edge will necessarily follow pixel edges.

1. If it's not already open, Open the image **White Vanda Mask.TIF**.

2. Load the selection you saved when learning about Quick Mask mode. Activate the Paths palette, and from the pull-down menu off the black triangle, select Make Work Path.

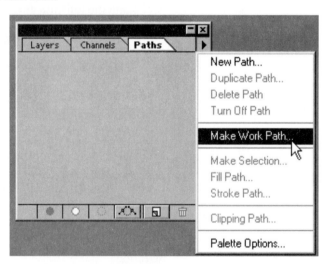

3. Enter a value of 1.5 pixels in the dialog box. Large values create fewer points and less accurate selections; smaller values generally create accurate selections, but with too many points. You have to strike a balance with each selection you convert. Click OK. The path points may not appear until the path is clicked on with one of the Pen tools.

Use the modifier keys with the Pen tool to achieve a much higher level of path-editing efficiency.

Command/Control temporarily changes the Pen tool to the Arrow tool.

Option/Alt temporarily changes the Pen tool to the Convert Point tool.

Moving the Pen tool to a path segment changes the tool to the Plus Pen tool (add anchor point).

Moving the Pen tool to an anchor point changes the tool to a Minus Pen tool (remove anchor point).

4. Double-click the name Work Path in the Paths palette and rename the path "Outline".

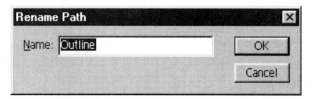

5. Zoom in on the path and use the Path Selection tool (the pointer) on the Pen palette to select and adjust points for a more accurate selection. (Click and hold the Pen tool to activate the pop-up cells, if the Path Selection tool is hidden.)

Look at the Pen tool flyout palette in the Tool palette.

To add points, use the Add Point tool (the Pen tool with the plus sign). To subtract points use the Remove Point tool (the Pen tool with the minus sign). To change a curve point into a sharp corner, click on the point with the tool on the far right of the palette (the Convert Point tool). To adjust the position of path segments and anchor points use the Arrow tool.

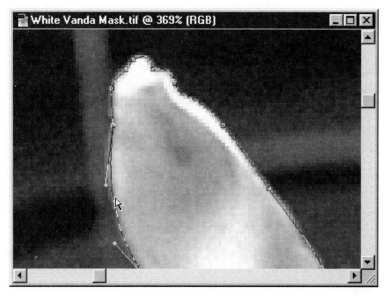

6. When you are satisfied that the path is as close as you can get it, drag the path down to the third button at the bottom of the Paths palette (Make Selection icon).

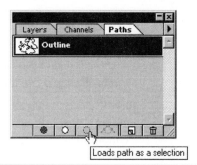

Paths can be scaled in Photoshop. Select the path with the Arrow tool (Press A), and select Edit> Transform.

On the Macintosh, all available image formats can save an included path. On Windows systems, a path can only be saved in EPS, JPEG, TIFF, PDF, or Photoshop native format.

If you use Adobe Illustrator or Macromedia FreeHand, you will find that your effort in learning to draw with the Pen tool also applies directly to that program.

7. Save the selection that is created to a new channel. Press Command/Control-D to drop the selection. Compare the channel you created with Quick Mask to the channel you created using paths. Note that the selection generated from paths is Anti-Aliased.

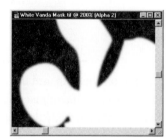 

*Color Range/*Quick Mask *channel and the channel created using Paths.*

8. Delete both channel #4 and channel #5. Use Save a Copy to save the file as "White Vanda Path.PSD" in your **Work in Progress** folder. Continue with the same file for the next task.

Use the Pen or Lasso?

Unfortunately, the decision whether to use the Pen tool or the Lasso tool — actually, any non-pen selection tool or technique — often comes down to "How can I avoid using the Pen tool?" Too many of us have never mastered the drawing techniques that make using the Pen tool enjoyable and effective.

If you need to create an EPS silhouette of an image or you wish to create a smooth, flowing selection, the Pen is your tool of choice. A clipping path is not limited to Selection borders, and can cut across pixels. As you develop a path, it can be saved in the Paths palette, along with other paths that you may have created in the image file.

Multiple selections can also be saved in an image file as Alpha channels; and these can be used to generate complex masks for a number of special effects. There are some valid reasons for using a selection tool; not just because you don't like to use the Pen tool.

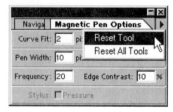

Magnetic Aids to Selections

The Magnetic Lasso and the Magnetic Pen tools incorporate a level of programmed intelligence that can identify an edge or shade step between an object and background. Of course, the intensity and contrast will vary in different images; and there are several option settings that allow you to tune the magnetic tools to suit the conditions.

Use the Palette Options menu to reset the tool to its default values as a starting point for optimizing values.

When creating a magnetic border, you can press "[" to decrease and "]" to increase the tool width by 1 pixel.

The fastening points that are produced as you draw with the Magnetic Pen tool are not equal to the final anchor points on the path.

Option Settings

Double-click on the Magnetic Lasso tool or the Magnetic Pen tool to display the Tool Options palette.

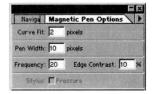

Width

This setting is the detection width around the cursor, set from 1 to 40 pixels, which limits the distance from the cursor that the tool looks for an edge to follow. To follow a well-defined edge, you can use a quick tracing movement with a higher width value; for a softer edge, use a smaller width value with a precise tracing technique.

Frequency

This determines the rate at which fastening points will be set. Increasing the value between 0 and 100 increases how quickly the Path/Selection border will be fixed in place. To follow detail more precisely, use a higher frequency.

Edge Contrast

This setting, from 1% to 100%, specifies the sensitivity to the edge you are following. Raising this value will cause lower-contrast edges to be ignored. Lowering this setting will allow the Magnetic tool to follow edges lacking in sharpness.

General Magnetic Techniques

To begin, click a starting point on the edge. You can release the mouse button as you move the cursor tracing the edge. When the Selection border begins to go astray, back up and press the Delete key as many times as necessary to remove the last fastening point(s). Move the cursor more carefully along the edge, clicking fastening points as necessary to control the shape of the Selection border.

For a sharp edge with good contrast, use a higher width value and more Edge Contrast and follow the edge rapidly; but if the edge is less distinct, use a lower width value, less Edge Contrast, and follow the edge more carefully.

To make better use of the Magnetic Lasso and Pen tools, change the cursor preferences for Other Cursors from Standard to Precise. This makes the on screen display the same as the tool's pen width setting.

Refer to the tips in the previous paragraphs as you make the Magnetic Selection border.

Close the Selection border by one of the following procedures:

✔ Move the cursor over the first fastening point and click when you see the Close Selection Border icon — the tool icon with a small circle to the lower right.

✔ Close the selection with a freehand magnetic segment by double-clicking or pressing Return (Macintosh)/Enter (Windows).

✔ Close the selection with a straight line segment by holding Option/Alt and double-clicking.

Once the selection or path is created, you can use the standard techniques to modify its shape. We will now use the Magnetic Pen tool to silhouette the single foreground orchid blossom.

Magnetic Pen Drawing

1. Continue working with the **White Vanda Mask.TIF** image.

2. Double-click on the Magnetic Pen tool and reset the tool options from the Palette menu.

3. Click on the edge of the flower to start creating the Selection border. A corner may be a good place to start, but it is not necessary. Release the mouse button and follow the edge with your tool around the edge of the flower.

4. When you return to your starting point, look for the small circle beside the Tool icon indicating that you can close the path with a click.

To make the selection directly, use the Magnetic Lasso tool to trace the Selection border.

5. From the Paths Palette menu, Make Selection, Anti-Aliased, with a Feather Radius of 2 pixels.

6. Press L to select the Lasso tool, and touch up any part of the edge that did not form accurately. (Check the bottom of the blossom where it is cropped at the lower edge.)

7. With the Lasso tool still selected, Control-click (Macintosh)/Right-Click (Windows) and choose Layer Via Copy from the contextual menu. This will place a copy of the blossom in a new layer with a transparent background.

8. In the Layers palette, turn off the display of the Background layer by clicking off the Eye icon. You can now see the blossom on a transparent background.

9. Rename the layer "Blossom".

10. Switch to the Move tool. Command/Control-A to Select All and press one of the Arrow keys one time. Notice that the Selection border changes from a rectangle enclosing the entire layer to a Selection border that follows the non-transparent pixel outline of the blossom.

11. To clean up the edge of the blossom, choose Select>Modify>Border. Set the width to 2 pixels.

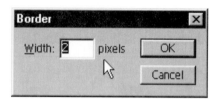

12. To get a visual check on the effect of deleting a 2-pixel border around the blossom, press Command/Control-H to hide the edges — the marching ants — of the selection. The selection is still active, so when you press the Delete key, 2 pixels are trimmed off the blossom edge. If that is too much to suit your taste, Undo (or go back in the History palette) and reset the border selection to 1 pixel.

13. To create an ethereal feeling, we will apply a soft glow to the blossom by selecting Layer>Effects>Outer Glow. Set the options as shown here: Mode: Screen, Opacity: 80, Blur: 30, Intensity: 30; click on the color swatch to change the color of the glow to match the purple of the flower center. Pick the color from the image itself, using the Eyedropper. Click OK.

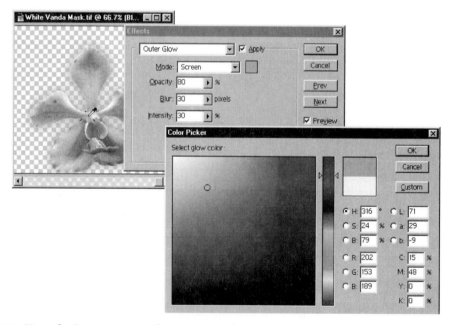

14. Keep the image open and continue to the next exercise.

We will create a composite image, selecting and moving the blossom to a different position and using a Layer mask to select the portions of the underlying image that will blend into the final image.

If you paste the entire image of the Old Man into the White Vanda image, you can pan-crop the Old Man layer. The additional part of the image that is not visible will be discarded when you flatten the layers.

Matching the Selection Size

1. Continue working with the **White Vanda Mask.TIF** image. Choose Open Image>Image Size and note the pixel dimensions of the current image.

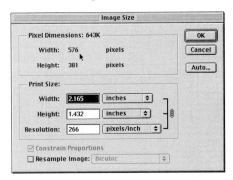

2. Press M or Shift-M, if necessary, for the Rectangular Marquee tool. Set the tool options to Style: Fixed Size, Width: 576, and Height: 381. This will allow us to copy an equally sized image from another file.

3. Open the file **Old Man2.TIF** from your **SF-Adv Photoshop** folder and click the Rectangular Marquee tool on the man's face. Move it to capture his eyes and mouth. Press Command/Control-C, Command/Control-W (to Copy and Close the image); and then Command/Control-V (to Paste the copied image into the White Vanda image).

4. The image is pasted into a new layer; drag this new layer between the Background and the Blossom layers.

5. Activate the Blossom layer. Move the blossom silhouette to center over the tip of the old man's nose.

6. Activate the Old Man layer and click the Add Layer Mask icon at the bottom of the Layers palette; turn on the display of the Background layer, although you will not be able to see it since it is below the old man's face.

Select a tool by pressing a single letter, and then rotate through the tool variations by holding the Shift key and pressing the letter.

Making a layer image, like the old man's face, into a layer mask allows you to select which parts of the underlying image will show. All of the painting tools are available for use in manipulating a layer mask, so that subtle blending effects can be achieved, as well as sharp-edged windows. Try to develop a counterplay between the deep lines on the old man's face and the leaves in the underlying image.

The Orchid Man is a composite of three layers. The top layer is a silhouette of a Vanda bloom with a soft glow around it. The middle later is the tightly cropped face copied from the Old Man image. A layer mask is used to softly blend parts of the underlying image, which is the original White Vanda image. A specular — zero dot — highlight has been added with a Twinkle brush to make the composition feel friendlier.

7. Click on the Layer mask to activate it. Airbrush the old man's face with a 100 pixel, soft-edged brush at 20% to reveal some of the underlying Background image on the sides. Stay away from his eyes, though. Be certain to reset your Foreground and Background colors to Black and White. Exchange them so Black is in the foreground. If you accidentally removed too much of the man's face, exchange the Foreground/Background colors so that White is in the Foreground. Brush some of the face detail back into view.

8. As a special touch, add a twinkle in the old man's eye with application of a Sparkle brush (100% white). In the Brushes palette menu, select Load Brushes, and open the Assorted Brushes.abr file in the Photoshop 5>Goodies> Brushes folder. Press Load. Select the Paintbrush tool, and find the Sparkle brush that looks like a small starburst. Press D for default colors (Black & White) and X to swap White to the Foreground color. Add a layer above the Face layer in the Layers palette. This way, the sparkle can be moved precisely into position. Position the brush on the corner of his eye and click once.

9. Close the file without saving.

Creative Techniques

If you modify the suggested steps above, your composition could look quite different from what is pictured here. Techniques covered elsewhere in this course, especially the chapters on Layers and Special Effects, will provide more ideas for creative expression. Experiment with the Selection and Blending effects to see where it can take you.

As is the case when creating realistic drop shadows under type, or generating Highlight and Shadow masks, these are techniques that you should try to keep at the forefront of your arsenal. You can only do that through practice and use of these procedures. Learning to create complex selections takes time — it is not a skill that just comes to you when you see it for the first time. Whenever you have to make a complex selection, consider using the masking techniques covered here.

CHAPTER 7

LAYERS

CHAPTER OBJECTIVE:

To understand the power and flexibility that layers bring to the design and modification of images; to learn the inherit strategies for using layers. By completing Chapter 7, you will:

- Understand when it is to your best advantage to use layers on your images.
- Know how to make changes to a layered image.
- Learn how to blend layers.
- Learn about Layer masks, and know how to use them to create composites.
- Understand the use of Clipping groups, and learn how to use them to link multiple layers.
- Study Adjustment layers and Layer Effects.

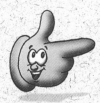

PROJECTS TO BE COMPLETED:

- Pokey Creek Book Cover
- Retouching the Jones Family Portrait
- Head in the Clouds Ad
- Baby Shower Invitation
- Farm Fresh Logo
- Photomat
- The Fix is in

Layers

Layering is a powerful technique that allows flexibility in the design and modification of an image. Layers can use up system resources very quickly; therefore, you should plan your documents carefully before working on them.

Below are some considerations in planning a composite or photo manipulation involving layers. The answers to the following questions will determine how many layers you will use, how many layers you will maintain at one time, and how many layers you will keep. To avoid costly delays at the end of a project, it is important to answer as many of these questions as possible before you begin working.

Strategies for Using Layers

- What is the largest final use of this image? Before you begin, you should be certain that all of your source images are suitable for the final size of the piece you are working on. Otherwise, you may end up degrading image quality by enlarging or stretching too much. This strategy also helps you to avoid creating an entire composite, only to discover that it is too small to print correctly.

- Will you keep the individual parts of a composite or layer group available in a separate file for later changes? Once you have worked on a composite, you could flatten the image to save space; this is common with an image that is going to be used only once. However, you may want to save the original image in Photoshop format, and save a copy in a printable, flattened format. This gives you the ability to make modifications later on, or if the image will be used in several printed or on-line pieces. This is especially true in Photoshop 5, which allows you to edit text in a special text layer, or to edit layer effects, such as drop shadows.

- How much scratch disk space and memory are available? The more RAM and free disk space you have, the more layers you will be able to use. Photoshop will sometimes request as much as five times the size of the file in scratch disk space, regardless of how much RAM is available. Many users even have an entire hard drive set aside as Photoshop's scratch disk. Photoshop 5 allows you to specify up to four separate drives as scratch disk space. However, be aware that some filters run entirely in RAM. If enough actual RAM is not available, the filter simply won't run.

- Can the image be flattened as you work? You can conserve resources by merging certain layers together once they require no more changes. Using this technique, you might find that you use ten layers to create a final document, but only two or three layers were active in the document at any given time. Editable text and effect layers cannot be flattened and retain their editability.

- How much long-term storage space is available? Sometimes you'll find that even though you have enough immediate resources — RAM and scratch disk space

These strategies are presented as general guidelines. However, sometimes it may not be possible to consider all of these aspects in advance.

— you don't have enough storage space to archive all of your files. In this situation, you may choose to flatten the image once it is finished, simply to conserve hard drive space. If it is imperative that you keep all layers intact, you can separate the layers into individual flattened documents with the layer transparency and masks saved as channels, and save the documents as JPEG or compressed TIFF files. When you need them, simply reassemble them into the original file. Be aware that JPEG can cause a loss of image quality. Also, to do this with editable text and effects layers, you must first render or transform them to a non-editable state.

- How much time is available? The less time that you have available, the more important it is to pick the quickest way to create an image. Working in layers is not always the fastest way to accomplish an immediate, simple project.

Why Use Layers?

Consider the following example:

Suppose we want to put type in the center of the beach scene. The layout calls for a "ghosted" box, or lightened area, on the image where the type will be set. In this case, some of the type has been added in PageMaker, but the ghosted box must be created in Photoshop.

Doing this with a traditional flat image would require us only to select the area to ghost, fill it with white at 80%, and resave the image. Unfortunately, if any changes in the intensity of the ghosting were necessary, or any other modifications were required, the entire file would need to be recreated. Instead, you can create a layered file to accomplish the same goal, and more.

Creating a Layered Document

1. Open the image **Sandy Beach.TIF** from your **SF-Adv Photoshop** folder.

2. Click the New Layer icon — the small page at the bottom of the Layers palette.

3. Using the Rectangular Marquee tool, select an area on the center of the image covering parts of the sand, water, and sky. Choose Edit>Fill. Fill the square with 100% white; leave the Blending mode at Normal.

4. Reduce the Opacity of the layer to 80%.

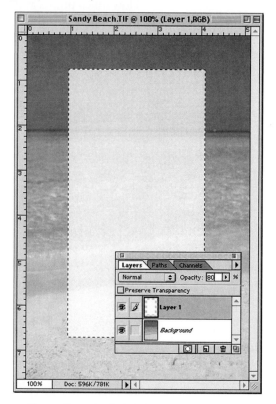

5. Deselect. Save as "Layer Practice.PSD**"** into your **Work in Progress** folder. Keep the image open; we'll be using it in the next exercise.

Making Changes to a Layered Image

It took a few more steps to produce this effect than it would have taken in a document without layers. However, let's assume that your client has decided he would like a headline filled with the original, unaltered image inside of the ghosted box. He would also like to see a little more of the image detail in the ghosted area.

If you had created this file in a traditional manner, you'd have to start over again with a fresh copy of the scan. Not so, with layers.

The Type Mask tool creates type-shaped selections, not editable type. The new Type tool in Photoshop 5 allows you to edit your text later on. To turn editable type into a selection, select the type layer with either the Command key (Macintosh) or the Control key (Windows) held down.

Modifying Layers

1. If it is not already open, Open the image **Layer Practice.PSD** in your **Work in Progress** folder. Make certain that Layer 1 is active.

2. Select the Type Mask tool.

   Click the tool at the top of the ghost box. Using 45-point ATC MaiTai Bold, type "RELAX!". Click OK.

3. Adjust the type so it is centered at the top of the box. Use the Type Mask tool, not the Move tool to adjust the placement of the type. Choose Select>Save Selection to save your selection as a new channel. Name the channel "Relax".

4. Press the Delete key and Deselect. The words are now punched out of the lightened area of the image, allowing the original image to show through.

5. In the Layers palette, adjust the Opacity of Layer 1 to 50% to allow a little more of the image to show through.

   Unlike a flat counterpart, this image is now available for quick changes and revisions. The Opacity of a layer is just one of the many options that you can adjust.

6. Save the image before closing.

Layer Options

You can change the name of a layer, its Opacity, and the Blending mode, as well as control how one layer interacts with the layer directly underneath, all from within the Layer Options dialog box. Each layer has a unique set of options. As you're aware, the Blending modes and Opacity settings in the Layer Options dialog box work just like the Blending modes for channels and painting tools.

Blending Layers

Photoshop can blend two layers in a document based on the brightness values of pixels in each layer, measured either in gray or in one of the color channels. The Blend If part of the Layer Options dialog box defines which pixels within the layer are affected by the Blending mode and Opacity selected.

There are two control bars to control the way one layer is blended into another. One controls the layer itself; the other controls the layer underneath.

For each layer, the bar represents the full color range, from dark to light, of the channel selected in the Blend If pull-down menu. The sliders control the range of color that will be included in the blend for a particular layer. Option-clicking (Macintosh) or Alt-clicking (Windows) the triangles causes them to split apart, allowing soft fades in all areas of transition. To reunite the triangle's halves, simply slide one half back to the other; the triangle will reattach.

Understanding Layer Option Blending

1. Create a New RGB document called "Layer Options Test"; the document should be 2″ square and 72 ppi. Set the Contents to White.

2. Make certain that your Background color is set to White. Click on the Foreground color swatch and change the Foreground color to 255 Blue; Green and Red should be set at 0. Double-click the Linear Gradient tool. On the Gradient

Options palette, set the Gradient to Foreground to Background; make sure Opacity is set to 100%. Hold down the Shift key while creating a gradient from right to left.

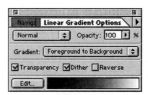

3. Click the New Layer icon to create a new layer. Change the Foreground color to 255 Red, with no Green or Blue. On the new layer, Layer 1, hold down the Shift key and create a left-to-right gradient. Make certain that both layers are visible; the Red gradient will obscure the Blue gradient.

4. Double-click Layer 1 to activate Layer Options. Change the name of the layer to "Red". Make certain that the Preview box is checked, and click OK.

5. Double-click the Red layer to activate Layer Options again. Change the Opacity to 50% and the Mode to Multiply. Notice that the bottom layer is partially visible, blended with the new Opacity of the top layer. Move the dialog box to view the image, if necessary. Select Cancel. The Mode remains Normal, the Opacity remains 100%. Layer Options allows you to test various Opacity and Blending mode settings, without affecting the current settings.

6. Activate Layer Options for the Red layer again. Select Green from the Blend If pull-down list.

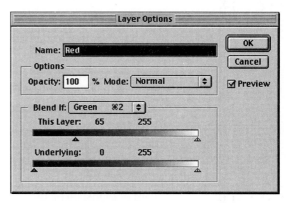

Remember that RGB is an additive color mode; each pixel in a color channel is measured with a value from 0 (no color) to 255 (100% of the color in question). Black, or no color, is created when R, G, and B all equal 0. White is created when all three values equal 255.

Blending options that are defined on the bottom layer, with no Background layer, will blend to transparency. When flattened, the transparent areas are filled with the background color.

Move the Black slider on the left of This Layer until it reads 65. Notice that some Blue gradient is showing through on the left side of the image.

7. Make certain that the Info palette is visible. Drag the cursor over the red area in the image, just before the red cuts off. Notice that the value of green measures 66 or above.

8. Now try adjusting the highlights. Move the White, Right slider on This Layer until it reads around 150. Now the Blue gradient is visible again, this time on the right side of the image.

9. Right now the edge where the blend begins is abrupt, but a smooth transition is as easy as it is desirable. Option-drag (Macintosh) or Alt-drag (Windows) the right side of the left triangle of the This Layer bar to 115. The triangle splits apart and a second number appears above the control bar. Adjust the slider until the blend is smooth. Repeat with the White slider to smooth further.

10. Save the file as "Layer Options.PSD" to your **Work in Progress** folder for later use, then Close it.

Practical Usage of Layer Options

The previous example, though not likely to occur as such in nature, highlights a few important properties of blending layers using Layer Options. With experimentation, you'll discover many uses for Layer Options. For example, in a photo such as a product shot with a white background, you can isolate the image against another background without using selection tools or masks. Layer Options are also great for creating textural backgrounds and special effects.

The basic rules for the Layer Options sliders are:

- In the channel selected for blending, any pixel with a brightness value below the target number on the black This Layer slider on the left does not participate in the blend. It simply disappears from the composite.

- Any pixel with a value above the target number on the white This Layer slider on the right isn't included in the blend either; it disappears from the composite, too.

- If you move the sliders on the Underlying Layer bar, the effect is the opposite of moving the sliders on the This Layer bar. The Underlying slider protects the values outside the triangles on the layer below from the effects of the blend. In our example, the blue on the underlying layer would show through because it would not be included in the blend defined on the red layer.

- In both instances, the values between the triangles are the ones that blend.

The left half of the split triangle indicates the beginning of a transition. The right half defines where the blend ends.

You cannot define Layer Options for a background. A background can, however, be converted into a normal layer.

Layer masks are used to control how different areas of a layer are hidden or revealed. A Layer mask is similar to a Grayscale channel, except that it affects only a single layer.

- Blended edges are smoothed by Option-dragging (Macintosh) or Alt-dragging (Windows) the sliders. The space between the split sliders indicates the range of brightness values that will be smoothly blended.

Layer Masks

Layer masking is a faster and more flexible way to make complex composites. Layer masks combine the advantages of Photoshop's layers with the power of masking. Like selection masks, it is possible to edit a Layer mask with any of Photoshop's painting tools. Since Layer masks are Grayscale channels, you can use both partial masking and feather masking techniques.

Usually you will add a mask to a Photoshop layer manually. However, when using the Edit>Paste Into command, a new layer is created with the pasted data, and a mask is added to the layer in the shape of the selection.

With Layer masks you can create very complicated blends between many photos quickly and easily. The effects of a Layer mask are temporary until you decide to permanently merge the mask with the layer. Because you can edit a mask independent of the layer itself, it is easy to change a composite and see the results before committing to the change.

The following exercise will show you how to combine two separate images, using a Layer mask, to form an interesting composite result.

Creating a Layer Mask

1. Open the files **CD Photo.TIF** and **Couple Lunch.TIF** from your **SF-Adv Photoshop** folder. We are going to position the image of the CD in the upper left corner of the composite.

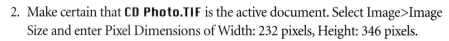

2. Make certain that **CD Photo.TIF** is the active document. Select Image>Image Size and enter Pixel Dimensions of Width: 232 pixels, Height: 346 pixels.

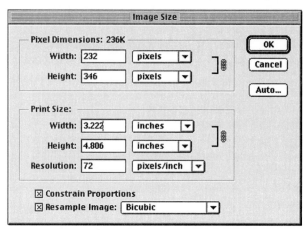

3. Make certain that both images are completely visible. With the Move tool, click and drag the CD image Background Layer onto the image of the couple. (Without the Move tool, you must drag the actual name of the CD layer to the image of the couple.) When you release your mouse button, a new layer, Layer 1, will be created. Close **CD Photo.TIF** without saving.

4. Make certain that the Layers and Channels palettes are both visible. If they are both in the same palette window, drag the tab of the Channels palette out and drop it on the desktop.

5. With Layer 1 selected, click the Layer Mask button at the bottom of the Layers palette. A preview of the mask will appear alongside the layer's preview. The Layer Mask channel will also appear in the Channels palette. Each layer may use only one mask.

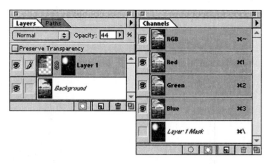

For Layer masking, it is best to have Layer Previews turned on in the Layers palette. To turn them on, select Palette Options from the pull-down menu in the Layers palette, then select the size of the preview you prefer. Remember that larger preview sizes use more memory.

6. Click to the left of the Mask preview on the Channels palette to make the Layer mask appear as an Alpha channel, just as if you were turning on a channel. You can change the color and opacity of the mask by choosing Layer Mask Options from the Channels palette when the masked layer is active in the Layers palette. Activate the Channels pull-down triangle, and select Layer Mask Options. Leave the Opacity setting at 50%. Click on the Red color swatch to change the mask color to blue. This is to remind you that you are editing a Layer mask, not a regular channel.

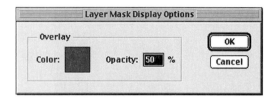

By default, Layer masks are linked to their layer. To unlink a Layer mask, simply click on the link icon between the two thumb-nails. This allows you to move the layer and its mask separately.

7. Click again on the Layer Mask eye icon in the Channels palette to turn the Layer Mask off. In the Layers palette, click on the layer image preview to continue editing the layer normally. Notice that there is an icon between the eye and the thumbnail previews that indicates whether painting is on the image layer or the mask.

 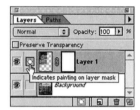

8. Move the CD-ROM image into the upper left corner of the document.

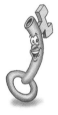

9. To edit the Layer Mask, click on the mask thumbnail. The Layer Mask Painting icon appears, indicating that the Layer Mask is active. To see the results of your changes to the Layer Mask in the next step, in the 50% blue "Overlay Color," hold down the Option (Macintosh) or Alt (Windows) and the Shift keys, while clicking on the mask thumbnail.

10. Make an elliptical selection around the CD-ROM. Make certain that your colors are default black-and-white. Then choose Select>Inverse, Feather the selection by 18 pixels, and use the Paint Bucket tool to fill the selection.

Holding down the Shift and either the Option (Macintosh) or Alt (Windows) keys while clicking on the Layer mask thumbnail, allows you to see all of the image elements, with the Layer mask shown in its "Overlay Color."

Holding down Option or Alt without the Shift key while clicking on the Layer mask, allows you to see (and modify) the Layer mask as a grayscale image.

Holding down only the Shift key, while clicking on the Layer mask, disables the Layer mask.

 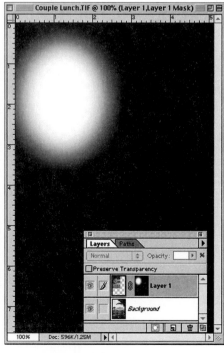

Editing a Layer mask can be confusing at first. Be certain that you have the correct layer selected, and that the Layer Mask icon (not the Paintbrush icon) is visible. Otherwise, you will be painting over actual image pixels!

Be careful when you drag the Layer Mask icon to the trash. If you drag any other part of the Layer icon bar to the trash, you will delete the entire layer, mask and all!

11. To view the file without the effects of the mask, select Layer>Disable Layer Mask (or hold down the Shift key while clicking the mask thumbnail). With the Layer mask disabled, change the Opacity of the layer to 44%, as shown below.

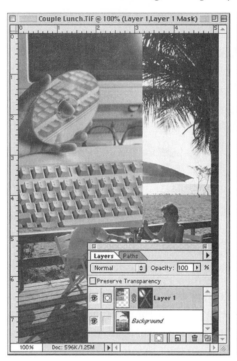

12. If you wish, you may also use various soft-edged paint brushes to modify the shape of the mask. By default, painting with black hides (or masks) the layer, allowing areas of the underlying image to show through; painting with white allows areas of the layer to show. As you paint, you will be able to see the effects of the mask.

13. Another way to view the mask over the layer is to turn on the Eye icon for the mask in the Channels palette, or to turn off the Eye icon for the RGB channels, and edit the mask as a channel by itself.

14. If you are satisfied with your mask, Save the image as "Masked Layers.PSD" to your **Work in Progress** folder.

15. A mask can be either removed or applied permanently to its layer. Select Layer>Remove Layer Mask (or drag the Layer Mask icon into the trash can at the bottom of the palette).

16. A mask may be either discarded or applied permanently. Click Apply. At this point, you could create another Layer mask to isolate other portions of the image.

17. Drag the Channels palette back over the top of the Layers palette to recombine the palettes.

18. Close the file without saving.

Complex Composites Using Layers

It's time to explore the real advantage of Layer masking. Using Layer masks, we are going to create several versions of a composite, while keeping an original Photoshop file available for later editing.

Using Layers in Composites

1. Open the files **Sandy Beach.TIF** and **Lovers In A Pool.TIF** from the **SF-Adv Photoshop** folder. With the Move tool, drag the image of the lovers onto the beach image. Make certain that the couple covers the whole image area; adjust it with the Move tool if necessary. Double-click Layer 1 and rename it "Lovers". Close the **Lovers In A Pool.TIF** image.

2. Click the first icon in the Layers palette to add a Layer mask to the Lovers layer. The brick is pretty unattractive for a romantic beach image. We want the happy couple as far away from that nasty brick background as we can get them. Let's experiment with a few different settings.

3. Activate the Paths palette. Use the Pen tool to make a tight path selecting the brick background. Leave a bit of room around the couple's hair. If the Pointer or one of the other path tools is visible in the Toolbox, click and hold the tool to make the Pen tool available for selection, or press P until the Pen appears on the Tool palette. Double-click the path and rename it "Couple Path".

   Adjust the path until you're satisfied with it, then drag it to the third button at the bottom of the Paths palette to create a new selection. Activate the Mask channel, and Fill the selection with black.

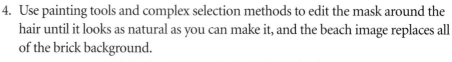

Using paths is tricky at first, but it can be a tremendous time saver. Practice!

4. Use painting tools and complex selection methods to edit the mask around the hair until it looks as natural as you can make it, and the beach image replaces all of the brick background.

5. Open the file **Oranges.TIF** from the **SF-Adv Photoshop** folder. Drag the oranges Background layer into the beach image. Make certain that the oranges cover from the top of the image to below the couple in the pool. Rename the layer "Oranges". Close the **Oranges.TIF** image.

6. In the Layers palette, position the Oranges layer so that it is between the beach and the lovers, and the oranges are blocking out the beach.

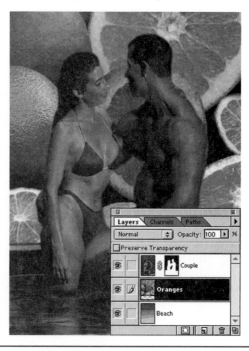

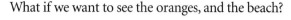

What if we want to see the oranges, and the beach?

7. Add a Layer mask to the Oranges layer. Activate the Gradient tool and create a gradient from black to white, bottom to top, that allows the oranges to fade in just below the horizon on the beach.

Experiment by beginning and ending the gradient in different areas of the image; hold down the Shift key to constrain the gradient to a vertical axis while you draw. When you are satisfied, save the file to your **Work in Progress** folder as "Beach Ad.PSD".

8. Select File>Save a Copy and save a copy of this image as a TIFF file; name it "Beach Ad.TIF". The TIFF will be flattened, and ready for printing, but our layered image is unaffected. Only visible layers will be included in the new TIFF.

9. Open the image **Masked Layers.PSD** that you created in the last exercise. Copy the Background layer (the couple having lunch) onto the beach image. Name the layer "Lunch Couple" and position it above the Lovers layer. This will allow you to fade the new layer into the Lovers without changing the Lovers mask.

10. Add a Layer mask to Lunch Couple to fade them into the right side of the image. Allow the umbrella to show through the lovers for an interesting effect.

Layers can be real space savers when creating repetitive graphics, such as buttons for the Web. You can view each button background in turn, and either File>Save a Copy of each flattened button, or Image>Duplicate with the Merged Layers Only option checked.

Always keep an unflattened version of your files, just in case.

If you have saved Alpha channels in your Photoshop document, make certain to check the option to Remove Alpha Channels when saving as a TIFF file. Some applications will not import a TIFF properly if it contains Alpha channels.

The Sample Merged check box, available on the Options palette for several painting tools, uses data from all visible layers, not just the current, active layer.

11. Save the image as "On the Beach.PSD" to your **Work In Progress** folder.

12. Experiment with turning layers on and off, adjusting the Opacity and Mode of each layer; try adjusting the order of the layers to understand how they're interacting.

13. Close the file without saving.

Clipping Groups

A clipping group is a collection of Photoshop layers that work together as a team. The bottom layer in a clipping group, known as the base layer, masks the images on all of the layers above it included within the clipping group. You can have as many clipping groups in one document as you like. Clipping groups are unique because the base layer uses its transparency as a mask for the other layers in the group, rather than adding the same mask to each layer.

You can use Blending modes with each layer in a clipping group, but after the grouped layers are blended, the entire group takes on the Blending mode of the base layer.

Using Clipping Groups

1. Open **Layer Practice.PSD** from your **Work in Progress** folder.

2. Click the New Layer icon in the Layers palette to create a new layer; the name will default to Layer 2. Choose Select>Load Selection, and load Relax, which you saved when creating a type mask.

3. Using the Lasso tool, drag the word "Relax!" selection. Position it slightly above and to the left of the knocked-out text. Fill the text with 100% black. Deselect.

4. Activate the Background layer. Use the Rectangular Marquee tool to select an area of water at least as large as the headline. Press Command/Control-C to copy your selection to the clipboard.

5. Paste your selection and Layer 3 will be created. Make it the top layer and position the selection so that it completely obscures the headline.

6. With Layer 3 selected, choose Layer>Group with Previous. The water will take on the shape of the text on Layer 2.

7. Using the Move tool, change the position of the water. Notice that moving the water doesn't affect any of the other layers, but it does change the way the water shows through the text.

8. You've just created your first clipping group. A clipping group is indicated in the Layers palette by a dotted line between the grouped layers. The base layer for a clipping group is designated by an underlined layer name.

You can add as many layers to a clipping group as you want. However, each layer dramatically increases the file size of the image.

To add or remove layers from a clipping group, hold down the Option (Macintosh) or Alt (Windows) key while clicking on the line separating the two layers.

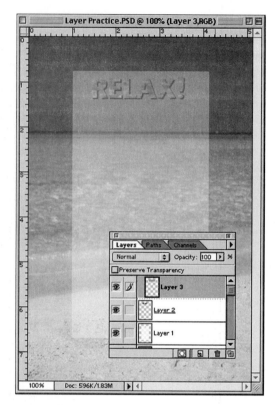

9. Save the image; keep the image open for the next exercise.

Properties of a Clipping Group

Clipping groups allow you to link multiple layers. The base layer acts like a mask to all of the layers in the group. Wherever there is image data on the base layer, it interacts with the other layers in the group. Wherever the base layer is transparent, the other layers in the group are masked out. This makes it possible to edit many elements of a picture independently, without disturbing the whole image.

Manipulating Clipping Groups

1. Open the file **Layer Practice.PSD**, if it's not already open.

2. Activate Layer 2 and press Command/Control-G to activate the Group with the Previous Layer command. This makes Layer 1 the base layer of the group. Notice how the composite has changed. Layer 1 becomes the mask for all the layers in the group, and Layer 2 no longer masks Layer 3.

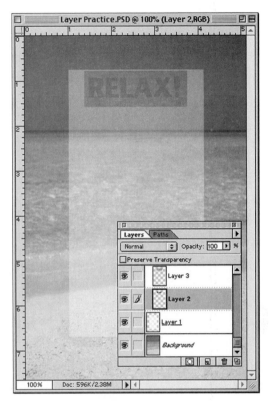

Each base layer's name is underlined in the Layers palette. To define how a group interacts with the rest of the image, Photoshop uses the Mode and Opacity setting of the group's base layer. However, within the group, each layer's Opacity setting affects how it interacts with its base layer.

3. With Layer 2 selected, choose Layer>Ungroup, which will also ungroup Layer 3. Then select Layer 3 and choose the Layer>Group with Previous option. This returns the composite to its correct form.

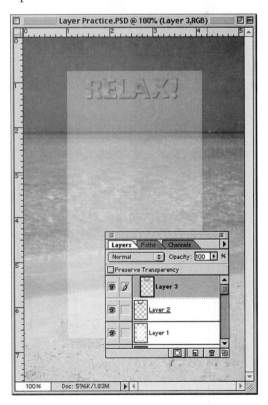

When you apply adjustments, such as Levels or Curves, directly to an image, the pixel data are changed permanently. When you use Levels or Curves adjustment layers, the original data are retained until the image is flattened. This allows you to "redo" an incorrect image adjustment.

4. Activate Layer 1. Open the image **Orange Slice.TIF** from the **SF-Adv Photoshop** folder. Activate the Paths palette, and drag the existing path down to the dotted circle button on the palette to create a selection. Copy the image of the orange. Close **Orange Slice.TIF** without saving.

5. In the Layers Practice file, Paste the orange to create Layer 4.

6. If necessary, drag Layer 4 to the position just above Layer 1. Press Command/Control-G to make Layer 1 and Layer 4 a clipping group. Position the orange so that it gives the composite a special "tropical" flavor. Notice that Layer 4 is using the Opacity setting of the base layer, Layer 1.

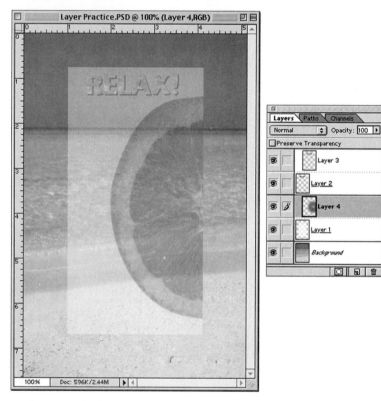

7. Save the image before closing.

Adjustment Layers

Adjustment layers are a special type of Photoshop layer. They contain no image data; instead, Adjustment layers allow you to apply color adjustments, such as Curves, Levels and Hue/Saturation to layers or layer groups. The specification for each command may be edited at any time, until the layer is permanently merged into the layers it is affecting.

Each Adjustment layer contains a Layer mask. You can paint on the mask as you would a regular Layer mask or Alpha channel. Instead of hiding or showing portions of the image, however, an Adjustment Layer mask determines which portions of the underlying layers are affected by the color correction command included in that layer.

Adjustment layers allow you to isolate portions of an image for correction, and adjust that layer separately. They're terrific for correcting a color cast in a blue lake, for example, when the blue sky is acceptable without changes. They are also great for experimenting with corrections such as Levels or Curves without overcorrecting the image. Rather than attempting to reapply new adjustments to a previously modified image, you can edit the existing Levels or Curves Adjustment layer.

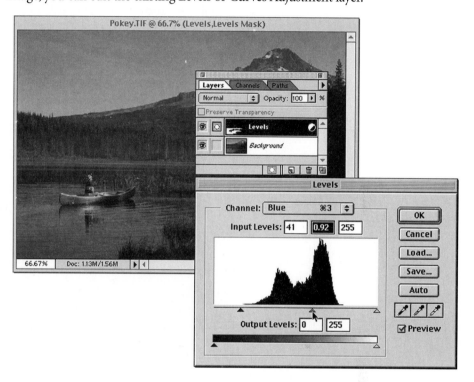

If a selection is active when an Adjustment layer is created, the selection is automatically converted to the mask for the Adjustment layer. Adjustment Layer masks may be saved or loaded just like any mask or Alpha channel.

Many of the commands available from the Image>Adjust submenu may be used as an Adjustment layer. The exceptions are Autolevels and Desaturate, which may be achieved using Levels and Hue/Saturation respectively; Replace Color and Variations, because they require real-time interaction with the image; and Equalize.

You can change the Opacity, order, or Blending mode of an Adjustment layer, just like a regular layer. However, you cannot merge one Adjustment layer into another.

Using Adjustment Layers

1. Open the image **Lemon.TIF** from your **SF-Adv Photoshop** folder.

2. Create a selection which includes just the lemons, then choose New Adjustment Layer from the Layers palette pull-down menu.

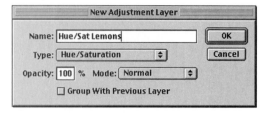

3. Change the Name of the layer to "Hue/Sat Lemons" and change Type to Hue/Saturation. Leave the other settings at their defaults and click OK.

4. Slide the Hue slider around to recolor the lemons; make them any color that looks fun or interesting to you. Notice that though there is not a selection border visible, only the lemons are changing color. Click OK.

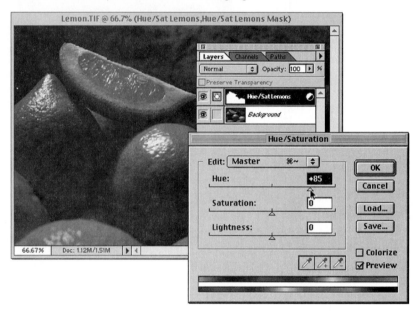

5. Choose Select>Load Selection and load Hue/Sat Lemons Mask; click the Invert check box.

6. Choose New Adjustment Layer to add another Adjustment layer to the image. Make it a Hue/Saturation Adjustment layer called "Hue/Sat Background". Click OK.

7. In the Hue/Saturation dialog box that appears, click Colorize. Colorize the background in a bright color that contrasts well with the lemons. Click OK.

8. Add another Adjustment layer. This time change Type to Curves and let the Name default to Curves. Click OK. Adjust the individual color channels in the Curves dialog box so that the color in the image shows some fairly dramatic changes. For example, you could push the red curve much higher and bring the green curve much lower. Click OK.

9. In the Layers palette, drag the Hue/Sat Background layer down below the Hue/Sat Lemons layer. Nothing changes in the image, because the two layers have no unmasked data in common.

10. Drag the Curves layer down below the Hue/Sat Background layer. The colors in the image change, because now the curves are being applied after the Hue change.

11. Add a new layer to the document. Position it just above the Background layer and paint it with some bright colors; the colors won't appear as they do on the swatches because they are being affected by the Adjustment layers.

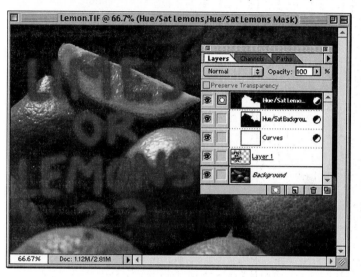

Group the Adjustment layers with the new layer by selecting each Adjustment layer and then selecting the Group with Previous option from the Layer menu.

12. Notice that Layer 1 is still affected by the Adjustment layers, but the lemons have returned to their original hue. Drag Layer 1 into the trash.

13. To see how the image would appear without the results of an Adjustment layer, simply click on the Eye icon to the left of the layer thumbnail. Turn off different combinations of Adjustment layer views and note the results. Then be sure to reset all Adjustment layer views to visible.

14. Adjust the Opacity of the Hue/Sat layers; notice how the effect changes, the closer the Opacity of the layer is to 0 (zero). Essentially, an adjusted version of the image is being blended with an unadjusted version. Using this method you can soften the effect of a Curves or Levels command. Return all Opacity sliders to 100%.

15. Double-click any Adjustment layer. A dialog box with your original settings for that command will appear. You can make changes as desired and click OK to change the command specifications. Note that double-clicking an Adjustment layer with the Invert command will bring up the Layer Options dialog box, as there are no settings for this command — it's either on or off.

16. Close the file without saving.

Adjustment Layers allow you to experiment with a variety of effects, and to return to the original condition of that layer without having to revert or revert to a History state.

Layer Effects

Before the introduction of Photoshop 5, special effects such as drop shadows could be created by the creative use of standard layers. For example, a drop shadow could be created by Command/Control-clicking a layer (which selects the layer's contents) then creating a new layer, feathering, and filling the shape with black, and positioning the results appropriately. Photoshop 5 has made this process obsolete.

Photoshop's Layer Effects include Drop Shadow, Inner Shadow, Outer Shadow, Outer Glow, Inner Glow, as well as Bevel and Emboss. Once any of these effects are applied to a layer, they can be modified at any time provided that the layered Photoshop file is retained.

Using Layer Effects

1. Open the file **Layer Options.PSD** from your **Work in Progress** folder. Change the Foreground color to a medium gray (R = 150, G = 150, B = 150).

2. Select New>Layer from the Layer menu. Then, with a hard-edged paintbrush, draw a shape on the new layer.

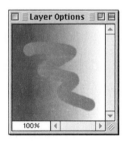

3. Choose Layer Effects>Drop Shadow. If the Preview option is checked, you will immediately see the results of the effects.

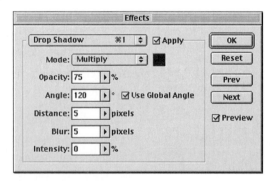

4. If you want to change the drop shadow's color, click on the square below the Apply check box. Experiment with other settings, such as the angle of the drop shadow, and observe the results. When you are finished, click OK.

Both text and layer effects can be edited after they are created in Photoshop 5.

5. Notice that the new layer has a special icon, indicating that one or more Layer Effects have been applied.

To edit the Layer Effects, simply double-click the Layer Effects icon, and the Effects dialog box will appear, with the current settings for that layer.

6. Change the Layer Effects to Inner Shadow, Bevel and Emboss, or any other effect by selecting the Apply check box. Using multiple effects for the same layer is usually not a good idea. Experiment with various settings for each effect.

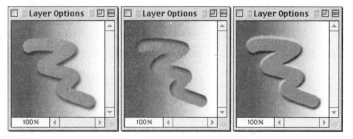

7. After applying a Layer Effect, paint additional strokes on the layer. Note that the Layer Effect is applied to the new work.

8. Add type to the file, using the Text tool. The text will automatically appear in a separate layer. Apply a Layer Effect to the text. Note that the text remains editable, as well as the desired special effect.

9. Save and close the file.

Layer Alignment

Another aspect of Photoshop layers is the fact that they can be aligned or distributed, once they have been linked together. This allows you, for example, to align the top edges of the contents of two or more layers, as shown below.

Aligning Layers

1. Create a New Photoshop file, approximately 3.5″ × 3.5″, at 72 ppi, in RGB color. Name it "Layer Align".

2. Create three new layers, and create a different colored object on each one. Link the layers together by clicking on the space to the right of the Eye icon. Notice that linked layers can be moved simultaneously.

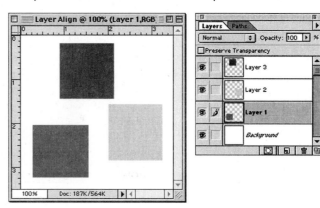

3. Select Layers>Align Linked>Top. Notice the effect on the three objects. Select Undo and experiment with the other alignment and distribution commands.

4. Close the file without saving.

CHAPTER 8

RETOUCHING

CHAPTER OBJECTIVE:

To understand the many methods of retouching an image; to learn how to use the various methods to rebuild, repair, or remove elements in an image. By completing Chapter 8, you will:

- Learn how to master the techniques of the Rubber Stamp tool functions.
- Learn how to analyze and implement the proper method to retouch an image.
- Know how to approach repairs in a structured manner.
- Become familiar with the tools and brushes used for retouching and repairing an image.
- Learn how and when to use filters for retouching.

PROJECTS TO BE COMPLETED:

- Pokey Creek Book Cover
- **Retouching the Jones Family Portrait**
- Head in the Clouds Ad
- Baby Shower Invitation
- Farm Fresh Logo
- Photomat
- The Fix is in

Retouching

The word "retouching" has several different meanings. It can mean simply removing dust spots, scratches, or other impurities that have been picked up in the scanning process. It can also mean extensive work restoring old photos or compositing images into new and unique visuals.

Usually, retouching means repairing. Most original images need some fixing. The White Vanda flower image that we'll be using later as an example has a slight case of an airborne fungus known as Botrytis, which causes spotting on the petals. Those spots needed to be eliminated for its use in a catalog or brochure to give the impression of a perfectly healthy, fungus-free product.

There are several approaches to retouching an image. Most are manual efforts using portions of the image itself as the "paint" to cover-up problem areas. Another approach is to use special filters for the job. The best method for a particular image can only be determined through analysis of the original scan and some experience.

The Rubber Stamp Tool

The photos that you will be using in your designs are often imperfect. It may be necessary to rebuild, repair, or remove elements in the image; for example, wiring, scaffolding, or part of the studio floor that the photographer could not avoid in the shot. Another instance occurs when everything about the photo is perfect except for a few real life factors that can't be helped. Unfortunately, those factors hinder the usefulness of the image for certain purposes. What if an athlete in the image is wearing a jersey with the competition's logo on it? Not good. These are all examples of retouching to change part of the content captured during the original shot.

The Rubber Stamp tool excels in reconstructing details that would have been in the image had the problem not existed. It simply recreates photographic details and color already in the image that are impossible to create convincingly. The first click of the tool (holding Control/Alt) designates which pixels the tool is to sample. The second click paints on the image with those pixels. The Rubber Stamp tool functions easily, but since it duplicates everything, mastering the techniques requires practice. The examples in this chapter will provide some practice and tips.

Painting with Portions of an Image to Repair Flaws

1. Activate the Brushes palette and create a hard, flat, Horizontal brush by clicking on an empty area of the palette. If a blank space isn't available, enlarge the palette or select New Brush from the Brushes palette menu. Enter Diameter: 25 pixels, Hardness: 75%, check the Spacing box and set it to 25%, Angle: 0°, Roundness: 20%.

Changing work doesn't make it yours. Always be certain that your retouching efforts don't infringe on someone else's intellectual property rights. There are many horror stories about designers removing labels or logos from a product shot without having permission to do so. Obtain the appropriate rights to reproduce and alter all of the source images used. Legislation today even requires that certain types of images be labeled as modified when they are retouched for publication.

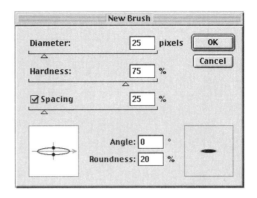

2. Select New Brush from the Brushes palette menu to create three more brushes: a vertical one (90° Angle) and two diagonal brushes (one at 45° and one at -45° Angles) with the values left the same. When done, four new brushes should be available that are particularly useful for retouching tasks in addition to round brushes and others developed for specific jobs.

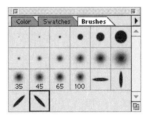

3. Open the image **Bishop's Harbor.TIF** from the **SF-Adv Photoshop** folder. This is one of the few remaining live-aboard marinas in the Florida Keys. A few of the boats show the effects of having been in the water for a long time, serving as home and castle for some of the planet's most unusual residents.

4. Double-click the Rubber Stamp tool in the Toolbox to activate the Options palette for this tool. Like other Paint tools it offers Blend Mode and Opacity settings. Opacity is frequently helpful to avoid patterns of cloning and to finely blend repairs into the image so that they look more natural. For the time being, leave the Opacity at 100%.

When working on a layered image, check "use all layer" if the Sample point should include pixels and effects from other layers to complete the effect (visible layers only). Leave it unchecked to sample from only the active layer.

To Align or not to Align, that is the question. If the objective is to clone the same part of the image over and over, uncheck Aligned. If maintaining the sample point's relative position to the area being painted is more useful, check it. Click to check it now for Step 5.

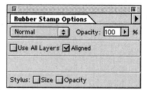

5. Zoom in on the stern of the boat near the lozenge-shaped opening. Select the new Vertical brush from the Brushes palette. Option/Alt-click on the opening, then move to the right as shown below, and paint to clone the area.

The location of the first Option/Alt-click became the Source or Sample point for the Rubber Stamp tool; the place painted becomes the Destination or Target area.

6. Release the mouse button. With the Hand tool (while pressing the Space bar) move the image to the left. Click the Rubber Stamp tool again and start painting to the right of the first bumper (the rubber thing hanging off the side of the boat). Do not reselect a different Sample point.

Remember, double-clicking any tool in the Toolbox will automatically access its Options palette.

Be cautious when using the Rubber Stamp tool on computer systems with less than (24-bit) 16.7 million colors. Retouching may look great on screen, yet become blatantly obvious when output.

The crosshair (pixels being sampled) followed the cursor. The Tool icon (target area being retouched) paints whatever image is under the crosshair. When Aligned is checked, the Sample point tags along, keeping the same distance and relationship established by the first two clicks. To sample "in front," rather than behind the tool, Option/Alt-click again and start painting to the left, above, or below that point. Aligned is useful for fixing things like this weathered paint job.

7. Uncheck Aligned in the Rubber Stamp tool's Options palette. Option/Alt-click on the first rectangular porthole, and paint another one immediately to its left.

8. Release the mouse button. Paint somewhere in the sky. Release the mouse button again, and paint another window somewhere else on the image. Do it a third time. Non-Aligned anchors the Source or Sample spot so that it doesn't tag along. With each new mouse click to paint, it sources the exact point originally sampled, not a relative position. If this is the intent, watch the crosshair closely to capture just the areas of the sample that are desired. It can easily stray beyond if one doesn't pay close attention to the crosshair.

9. After experimenting, close the file without saving.

Here's a short list of things to keep in mind when approaching a retouching or repair job. Key issues include: make certain that you don't miss anything, select the proper size brush, select a sample location (Option/Alt-click) close enough to grab the perfect tone but not so close as to clone and reclone identifiable patterns of pixels, and make certain that the edges of the brush are soft enough to blend the repair into the image itself; use the Rubber Stamp's Opacity control to help with this.

Approaching Repairs in a Structured Manner

In this section, take the opportunity to retouch an image using the skills we covered. Don't be hesitant to experiment and develop some experience using the Rubber Stamp and custom brushes to fix flawed areas in an image. Keep these tips in mind:

- Examine the entire image with a 1:1 aspect ratio. It's easy to become too critical and waste time when very high magnifications are employed; it may, in fact, do more harm than good. Keep a reasonable perspective.

- To analyze where retouching is needed, start in the upper left, and work horizontally across the image. At the corner, travel back to the left, carefully repeating the analysis and repairs. The technique of randomly searching for flaws rarely ensures catching every mark; attack the image with an organized strategy.

- Consider the file's resolution when choosing a brush size and the distance between Sample point and Target area. High-resolution files require bigger brushes than low-res images. Adjust brush sizes to fit the project. Change the brush shape and size frequently to suit the image and blend changes. If the brush is too big and the distance between sample and target area too close, pixels repeat themselves in an obvious pattern sometimes called railroad tracks.

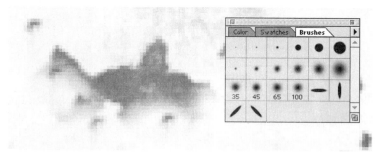

An example of undesirable railroad tracks.

- Use a soft-edged brush to create a gradual transition between repairs and the background. If the brush is set to 100% hardness, there will be no transition, often making the repair stand out. If the brush is too big and soft, it will look as though your repair area is smudged or not sharpened correctly.

This takes practice. It isn't something anyone learns overnight. Keep in mind that every image is unique, and will need to be approached differently. Remember to create custom brushes (or load a personally created set saved from previous retouching sessions). Also experiment with the distance and relationship between the Sample point and the spot being painted.

When removing an object, also retouch the area around it to avoid ghost images. They stick out like "patched-jeans" in the output. To check for this possibility, use the Eyedropper tool and the Info palette to watch for abrupt dropoffs in color.

- Experiment with the Rubber Stamp tool's Opacity and Blend modes. In tight spots where there isn't much to sample from, vary the opacity to mix the tone values applied for retouching and re-retouching. Careful (not a license to scrub) use can save much time and improve the repair job.

- Match tones carefully. If a shadow, tone, or pattern falls in the area to be repaired, align the sample and target to continue the shadow, pattern, or tone. Otherwise, the repair sticks out like a sore thumb.

- When repairing an edge or other line such as a table edge or boat mast, the Sample and Target points should be aligned in exactly the same relation to the pixels creating the edge. For example, sample on the top pixel of the "good" edge, then start painting on the top edge of the line to be repaired. The image below shows deleting a tree while maintaining lines in the sky. Control/Alt-click the Sample point sitting on the wire, then click to paint also "sitting" exactly on the wire and paint in the direction of the line.

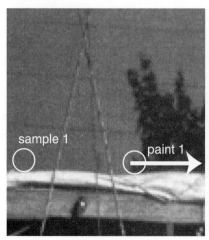 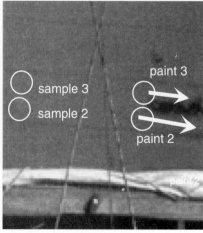

- When attempting to remove a large flaw, work from the outside in, all the way around. Working from only one side is actually more difficult because there are fewer varied pixels to sample. The result is usually railroad tracks and a tendency to clone the image that's being removed. Note that here we're using a very small brush, and choosing a Sample point very close to where we paint. Work carefully, and keep your eye out for "artifacts" — things that shouldn't be there (bumps, repeating pixel patterns, edges inadvertently picked up from the sample region, etc.).

Other Retouching tools

Both the Brush and Rubber Stamp tools have two special incarnations in the form of a History brush and Pattern Stamp tool respectively. Each provides some unique possibilities for artistic and practical retouching.

The History brush works like a regular brush, except that it paints with an historical version of the file. During experimentation or intense retouching, a particular area may have looked perfect about 10 steps ago. By selecting that "step" in the History palette (click to the left of the step's name, not on the name) the tool will recreate what the image looked like at that point wherever the History brush is dragged.

In the White Vanda image, after applying several artistic and color affects, we painted only the center of the flower with the History brush. We chose a less distorted version of the image by sourcing its appearance several steps back. Choosing the brush size and amount of softness is as important here as when using the Rubber Stamp tool. In this case, the surrounding image appears hand painted while the flower's center is taken more directly from the photograph.

The Pattern Stamp is a specialty tool, since its main function is to paint with tiles of a Defined Pattern taken from a selection in the image. The first step is to marque an area (rectangular selection), then Edit>Define Pattern.

The History brush cannot paint from a version of the image that occurred before an image size, crop, or Color mode change.

After defining the pattern, switch to the Pattern Stamp tool, hidden with the Rubber Stamp tool. Choose a brush tip and paint. The tiles will align perfectly.

Fixing the Flower

Open the **White Vanda.TIF** image from the **SF-Adv Photoshop** folder. The petals are quite spotted from that fungus mentioned before. Repair them using the tools and techniques discussed. There are more flaws in this image than first appear at a casual glance. Make believe this is your brochure and your flower. There is no need to save this image when complete.

Using Filters for Retouching

The conditions under which a transparency or print is stored, handled, and scanned can have a dramatic affect on its quality.

In this short exercise, we're going to explore a specialized blur filter designed to remove dust and scratches from an image — just the type of flaw that's found in images that have been improperly stored, or scanned without being cleaned first.

To track down some imperfections when retouching, examine the individual Color channels. Sometimes the flaws are more noticeable there, particularly on low-color systems.

Keep slides and prints properly stored and the scanning area clean! The lengths that professionals go to in these areas (including gloves) would astound the average agency or publisher. Keep a can of compressed air around to clean images and equipment if you intend to do your own scans.

Even when limiting the application of the Dust & Scratches filter, you may need to sharpen the image selection area afterward.

Running the Dust & Scratches Filter

1. Open **Trident.TIF** from the **SF-Adv Photoshop** folder. Look at the sky behind the wake. We must remove some fairly large dust particles that were scanned as small splotches on the image.

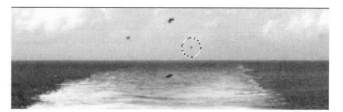

2. Select one of the defects, making certain that your Lasso tool has a Feather setting of 1–2 pixels. As with many of the settings we use in the practice exercises, this setting would be proportionally higher for a higher resolution image. The purpose of making this selection first is to limit the application of the filter and to blend its effects into the surrounding pixels of the image.

3. Press Command/Control-H to hide the selection border so that we can compare selection and background pixels more easily. Remember that the marquee indicates the 50% position of any feathered selection; a few more pixels outside will be slightly affected.

4. With one of the defects selected, choose Filter>Noise>Dust & Scratches.

5. Adjust the magnification of the thumbnail selection inside the Dust & Scratches dialog box by clicking the Plus (+) and Minus (-) buttons in the dialog box. We find that it is helpful to have the thumbnail selection set to a higher magnification than the file image (use it to keep perspective of the effects).

Move the cursor outside the Dust & Scratches dialog box and click on the image. It will turn into a little square which corresponds to the Preview window. Position the square over the dust marks in the sky to shift the preview over the area being affected. Set Radius to 1 and Threshold to 0 for starters.

6. Make certain that the Preview box is checked. Adjust the Radius slider until the dirt disappears; this determines how far the filter searches for differing pixel values.

7. The Threshold slider determines how different the pixels must be in tone to be affected. The higher the Threshold, the greater the tonal difference must be to effect a change. A setting of 0 will affect all isolated pixels or pixel groups as specified in the Radius setting. Increase the Threshold from 0 until the defect reappears, then back off a little. When satisfied click OK.

   Higher Radius settings combined with lower Threshold settings increase the possibility of blurring the selection too far.

8. Drag another selection around a "spot" and use the filter again, testing the settings appropriate for this patch. Do this for each blotch; it will provide an opportunity to optimize the control settings for a variety of defect and background pixels.

9. Low-res files, like this one, lose significant sharpness when employing the Dust & Scratches filter. To demonstrate this, make a selection around the sailors on the bridge. Apply the Dust & Scratches filter with the Radius set to 2 and increase the Threshold to 10, then click OK.

10. Now apply the Unsharp Mask filter to get some of that lost detail back. Sharpening will reverse the negative effects of the Dust & Scratches filter only somewhat. It usually doesn't reintroduce the artifacts obliterated by the filter, but get familiar with how drastically Dust & Scratches can be used before Unsharp Masking can't return the image to adequate sharpness.

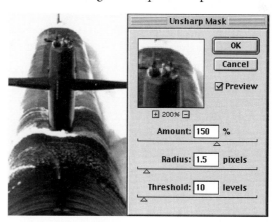

11. Close the file without saving.

Complete Project B: Retouching the Jones Family Portrait

Notes:

REVIEW 1

CHAPTERS 1 THROUGH 8:

In Chapters 1 through 8, we learned about Photoshop's color modes, advanced image adjustment, practical color correction, how to transform images, advanced channel operations, advanced selection techniques, layers, and retouching. Through this series of discussions, extensive hands-on activities and exercises, you should:

- Understand how to access the Mode setting for an image. You should be familiar with the eight different color modes supported by Photoshop, know how to change an image from one mode to another, and understand how to check the color channels in any Photoshop image.

- Understand Levels and Curves, and realize how they affect the overall control of the tonal range of your images. You should also know how to use Levels for effects, and understand the relationship between Curves and Levels.

- Know the difference between RGB and CMYK images, and understand how an image may look good on screen, yet not reproduce with the color quality you expect.

- Know the three ways to use the Transform commands, and understand how the ensuing transformation applies to layers. You should also know how grids and guides are used for precision image alignment.

- Know how to create depth in your images. You should know how to create special Alpha channels and combine them to create special effects or complex masks. You should also understand how to mix an image's channels with the Channel Mixer.

- Know the different methods for creating and using selections. You should know how to use the Color Range command, and understand the Quick Mask mode.

- Have built a solid understanding of layers; when it is to your best advantage to make changes to a layered image; and know how to blend layers.

- Understand the many methods of retouching an image, and know how to approach repairs in a structured manner.

CHAPTER 9

BLURRING AND SHARPENING IMAGES

CHAPTER OBJECTIVE:

To learn how to use the Blur and Sharpen Filter sets to save bad scans or damaged photographs; to understand and use the Focus Adjustment Blur filters, which allow you to blur similar colors while maintaining images. By completing Chapter 10, you will:

- Learn how to use the Gaussian and Smart Blur filters, the most important Blur filters available to you.
- Learn about the Special Effects Blur filters — Motion Blur and Radial Blur.
- Learn how to use the Sharpen filters, paying close attention to Unsharp Mask (USM), the most powerful Sharpen filter.
- Understand Sharpening with Luminosity Only.

PROJECTS TO BE COMPLETED:

- Pokey Creek Book Cover
- Retouching the Jones Family Portrait
- **Head in the Clouds Ad**
- Baby Shower Invitation
- Farm Fresh Logo
- Photomat
- The Fix is in

Blurring and Sharpening Images

The Blur and Sharpen Filter sets provided in Photoshop are true workhorses for anyone faced with the challenge of saving bad scans or old damaged photographs. Blur can help reduce moiré patterns, which are interference patterns created when scanning printed material that contains a halftone screen. Sharpen can save those old fuzzy photos of your first birthday. However, don't overlook some of the creative uses of these filters.

In a professional prepress environment where digital images have become the norm, it is clear that understanding the need for sharpening images cannot be overemphasized.

The Blur Filters

All of Photoshop's Blur filters work essentially the same way: they average the brightness values of contiguous pixels to soften the image.

The Blur filters could be categorized either as "focus adjustment" Blur filters (filters which simulate the effect of an unfocused camera lens), or "special effects" Blur filters, which blur pixels in more unusual ways.

Focus Adjustment Blur Filters

The first two filters in the Blur **submenu** are Blur and Blur More; they work just fine, but offer no control over the amount of blurring. The champions of this group of Blur filters are Gaussian Blur, which you may have already used, and Smart Blur which allows you to blur similar colors while maintaining edges.

Gaussian Blur allows you to define the amount of blurring to be applied to the image. The strength of the blur is specified in pixels in the Radius field. Photoshop uses this value to average the brightness of a pixel with that of the surrounding pixels. A setting of 1 or below can soften an image. (Blur and Blur More are roughly equivalent to 0.3 and 0.7 radius values, respectively.) Greater values can add atmosphere to an image, or make the contents difficult to recognize. Remember that the higher the resolution of the image, the higher the Radius value must be to achieve the same effect.

Smart Blur filter, which works in Grayscale, RGB, and Multichannel modes, allows you to blur tones closely related in value without affecting the edge quality of an image. You can set a Radius for blurring, just as you can with the Gaussian Blur filter. The Smart Blur Threshold setting, however, allows you to determine how closely pixels must be related in tone before being blurred. Settings can range from 0.01 to 100; the higher the value, the more the image is blurred. Setting a fairly low Radius with a high Threshold produces smooth, broad areas of color with distinct transitions between tones.

Look carefully at the Smart Blur filter. It will definitely come in handy.

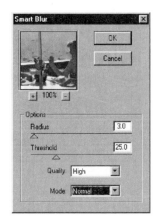

You can specify a Quality setting, or change the Mode setting so that the filter isolates only the edges according to the current settings. You can also set the Mode to Overlay Edges. With this option, the image is blurred, and the edges are outlined in white.

Using Gaussian Blur

1. Open **Couple Lunch.TIF** from your **SF-Adv Photoshop** folder.

2. To give the image a romantic feel, select an oval section in the photo surrounding our guests using the Elliptical Marquee tool.

Switching to the Quick Mask mode is only necessary to visualize the softening of the selection edge in this exercise.

3. Switch to Quick Mask mode by clicking on the icon in the lower right of the Toolbox.

4. Select Filter>Blur>Gaussian Blur. Set the Radius to 32 pixels to soften the edge of the selection. Click OK.

The Gaussian Blur has practical, in addition to artistic, uses. When a blend must cover a long distance relative to the change in percentage of color, a Gaussian Blur can prevent or minimize banding. Many production specialists introduce a Gaussian Blur in this situation as a matter of course.

5. Click the icon in the lower left of the Toolbox to return to Normal mode and turn the Quick Mask mode back into a selection. We want to blur the background, not the couple, so choose Select>Inverse to turn the selection inside out.

6. Select Filter>Blur>Gaussian Blur again and set Radius to 8 pixels. Notice that the work we did in the Quick Mask mode has softened the edge between the blurred and unaffected part of the image. The result should be a soft vignette around the couple for an other-worldly effect.

7. Close the file without saving.

Special Effects Blur Filters

The other two options on the Blur menu are Motion Blur and Radial Blur. These filters are generally used only for special effects.

Motion Blur has a wheel for changing the blur angle, and a Distance value to specify the number of pixels to blur. Motion Blur can create a convincing sense of motion by duplicating an image in the Layers palette, blurring the bottom layer and using the Eraser tool to remove parts of the top image. This will allow the portions that indicate motion to show through, such as the rear bumper of a moving car.

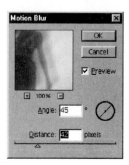

Radial Blur either Spins the pixel around the center point of the image, or Zooms, which blurs in a spoked fashion for the amount specified. The further the pixel is from the adjustable center point, the more it will be blurred. Draft, Good, and Best Quality options are available to improve filter performance. To enhance performance, test the filter in Draft or Good mode; when you find a setting you like, Undo, then reapply the filter in Best Quality mode.

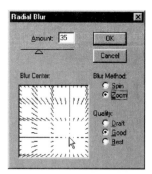

Using Motion Blur

1. Open **Pineapple.TIF** from your **SF-Adv Photoshop** folder.

2. With the Lasso tool, select a portion of the image to blur. Choose Filter>Blur>Motion Blur.

3. Set the Angle of motion by click-holding on the turn wheel and dragging it to 30 degrees, or enter the angle manually in the adjacent box. Set Distance to 60. Click OK.

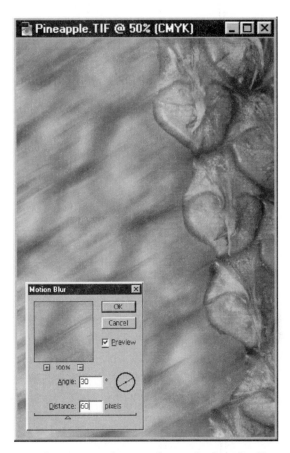

4. Undo the Blur with Command/Control-Z, and select the filter again. This time, try a smaller Distance such as 10. The image keeps a lot more texture.

5. Select the original Snapshot in the History palette to restore the image to its original state; leave the file open for the next exercise.

Using Radial Blur

1. With the **Pineapple.TIF** image still open, select Filter>Blur>Radial Blur.

2. Click the mouse pointer in the dialog box to set the relative center of the blur. This will be the point from which the blur radiates or the center-point of the spin, depending on whether you choose the Spin or Zoom methods.

3. Select an Amount of 35, Zoom Method, and Good Quality. Click OK. If you use Best Quality, rendering may take a few minutes, depending upon the speed of your computer.

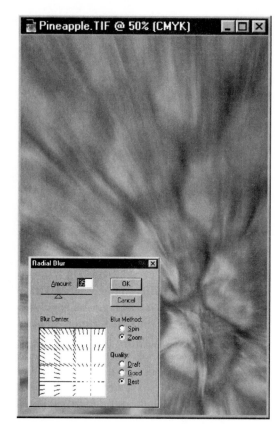

4. Close the file without saving.

The Sharpen Filters

Photoshop offers three preset Sharpening filters: Sharpen, Sharpen More, and Sharpen Edges. The first two operate about as well as their counterparts in the Blur submenu. Although you can apply a filter as many times as you like to produce the effect you want, this can be particularly time-consuming, and generally not as effective as using the other Sharpen filters.

Sharpen Edges operates only on areas of high contrast. It uses the brightness value of a pixel to determine where the edges are, then sharpens only those areas.

Unsharp Mask

The most powerful and useful Sharpen filter is Unsharp Mask (USM) — a special topic that deserves much more than casual interest. This filter, named for a conventional color trade shop scanner method of sharpening, allows you to control the magnitude of sharpening, the width of the sharpened edge. and which pixels are sharpened.

All scanned images share a common defect — softening of detail that exists in the original object or image. The manufacturers of conventional color trade shop drum scanners recognized the need for sharpening transparencies scanned on their equipment, and incorporated Unsharp masking into the process of generating color separations.

Sharpening is achieved by first identifying which edges will be sharpened (the Threshold). The Amount setting determines the magnitude of the contrast, and the Radius setting specifies the width of contrast enhancement. A Threshold setting of 10 means that any two neighboring pixels must have a brightness value difference of at least 10 levels in order for the filter to apply to those pixels.

To set the Threshold value, push the Amount up high and increase the Threshold gradually until sharpening of grain or dust is eliminated. Next, set the Radius for a halo width that will not be obtrusive. Finally, reduce the Amount to the maximum acceptable setting.

The Amount setting is calibrated, for some strange reason, as a percent from 0 to 500; there is nothing especially good about using 100%. In fact, we want to push the Amount as high as possible while avoiding the artifacts discussed below. An appropriate amount of sharpening will depend upon the individual image.

Unsharp Masking does not actually restore focus to an image; that would be an impossible task. Instead it artificially creates the impression of increased focus by finding the border between two pixels that meet the Threshold amount, then, within the specified radius, darkening the darker pixel and lightening the lighter one. The example that follows shows an unsharpened, properly sharpened, and oversharpened image.

It is not always possible to eliminate unwanted sharpening of grain or dust without loosing the ability to sharpen soft edges in an image. Other strategies would apply sharpening only to channels that do not contain the grain, select localized areas for USM, or use the Sharpen tool on specific areas.

The key to using the USM filter is to apply as much as possible without creating some other problem. The typical problems that result from misuse of the USM filter are:

- Obvious halos that are clearly visible and recognizable as not being a component of the image. The illustration above is an example of obvious halos.

- Distracting color shifts in the sharpened areas.

- Sharpening of unwanted detail such as scratches, even though the detail may actually be part of the image.

- Intensification of Noise or Grain.

Localized sharpening can be applied with careful application of the Sharpen tool.

Understanding Unsharp Mask

1. Open **Shell.TIF** from your **SF-Adv Photoshop** folder.

2. Select Filter>Sharpen>Unsharp Mask.

3. Check the Preview option. Enter an Amount of 300%, a Radius of 5, and a Threshold of 0. The woman is sharper, but the excessive white halo makes her appear positively saintly. (We have it on good authority that she isn't.) If you click on the clouds with the mouse, notice how grainy they are in the Preview window. (A setting of 5 is actually too strong for an image of this resolution, but it will help you see the effects.)

   Change the Threshold gradually, observing the unwanted graininess of the clouds and the desired graininess of the beach sand in the foreground.

4. Change the Threshold setting to 20 levels. Since the pixels in the clouds are similar in brightness, they aren't sharpened. Reduce the Radius to 2 pixels, and the Amount to 250%. This is still fairly extreme USM, but it demonstrates the use of the filter. Click OK.

5. Press Command/Control-Z a few times to compare the image before and after.

As a rule of thumb, the following parameters may be followed for print images:

Threshold: 2–10
Radius: 0.5% of resolution (ppi)
Amount: enough to enhance the edges without a noticeable halo.

Image before sharpening.

In most images you will seek a compromise in the USM settings, attempting to increase sharpness in the detail while minimizing unwanted effects.

Image after USM. Note the woman, palm trees, and sand.

6. Close the image without saving.

Sharpening with Luminosity Only

Sometimes the application of the Unsharp Masking filter to the entire image will produce a color shift along the sharpened edge. This can be minimized by applying USM to the Luminosity channel of a L*a*b image, or by following the USM filter with the Fade filter, set to 100% Luminosity.

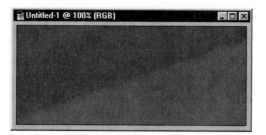

Image before USM.

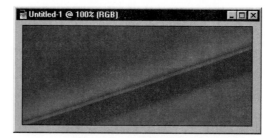

Color shift generated by USM.

Reduction of color shift by applying Fade Filter with 100% Luminosity.

Complete Project C: Head in the Clouds Ad

THE REMAPPING COMMANDS

CHAPTER OBJECTIVE:

To learn how Photoshop's Remapping commands map or recolor pixels; to learn how this group of commands is dynamically editable through the Adjustment layers. By completing Chapter 10, you will:

- Learn how the Invert command creates the photographic negative of an image.

- Learn about the Equalize command, and understand how it reads the brightness level of each pixel in each channel to remap and calculate every pixel in an image to redistribute the brightness values along a curve.

- Understand how the Threshold command converts images to black-and-white pixels to give you control over how much detail is retained.

- Understand the Posterize command, which is similar to the Threshold command, except that it maps color rather than black-and-white.

PROJECTS TO BE COMPLETED:

- Pokey Creek Book Cover
- Retouching the Jones Family Portrait
- Head in the Clouds Ad
- Baby Shower Invitation
- Farm Fresh Logo
- Photomat
- The Fix is in

The Remapping Commands

Photoshop's remapping commands "map" or recolor pixels according to the rules (formula) associated with each command. All the commands under the Image>Adjust menu are remapping commands. This chapter focuses on the group that includes: Invert, Equalize, Threshold, and Posterize. The same group is available as dynamically editable commands through the Adjustment Layers: Layer>New>Adjustment Layer command.

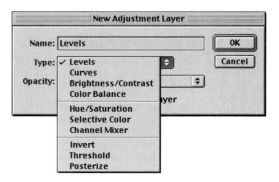

Press Command-I (Macintosh) or Control-I (Windows) to Invert a file.

Invert

The Image>Adjust>Invert command creates the photographic negative of an image. In Bitmap, Grayscale, RGB, and L*a*b* modes you get a very realistic negative. If you use this command in CMYK mode, the result may not be what you expect, as the inverted Black channel will overpower everything else.

Original RGB Image

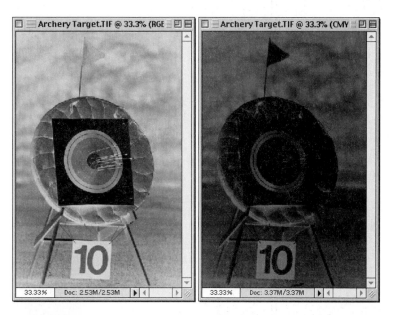

Inverted RGB image.   Inverted CMYK image.

Equalize

The Image>Adjust>Equalize command reads the brightness level of each pixel in each channel. It remaps the pixels with the brightest value to white, and the pixels with the darkest value to black; it then recalculates every pixel in the image and redistributes the brightness values along a curve. The Equalize command is not available as an Adjustment layer.

Original image.

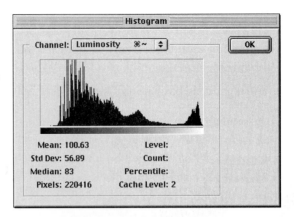

Histogram for the original image.

Image after the Equalize command.

The Equalize command should be used only in special circumstances. By its very nature, it changes the effect that may be built into an image by remapping to a full spectrum, rather than the range that may have been intended by the creator of the image.

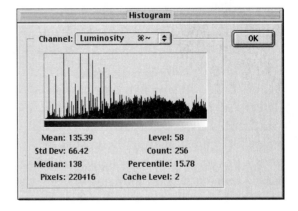

Histogram after the Equalize command.

The effect is to increase the contrast and saturate the color. If you use only a selected portion of an image when equalizing, Photoshop provides an option to map only the selection, or to map the entire image based on the Brightness values included in the selection.

Threshold

By selecting Image>Adjust>Threshold or Layer>New>Adjustment Layer>Threshold you will be provided with a means of converting the image to black-and-white pixels only (no grays), while giving you control over how much detail is retained. The Threshold command offers a single slider below a Histogram of the image. Moving the slider to the right causes increasingly dark pixels in the image to become black. Moving it to the left causes increasingly light pixels to become white. Using the Adjustment Layer option allows the Threshold value to be edited at any time based on the original image data.

The Threshold command is a quick way to preview the location of the brightest and darkest pixels in a file. This can help guide you to set the highlight and shadow areas in a file to optimize tone and color.

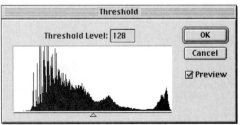

Pixel distributions before and after applying the Threshold command.

The slider determines the Brightness value that will be used as the mapping point for the entire image. Pixels having a value brighter than this point will all be turned white, and pixels having a darker value will change to black.

Using the Other>High Pass filter with a value of 20 or 30 before running Threshold can dramatically improve the amount of detail retained.

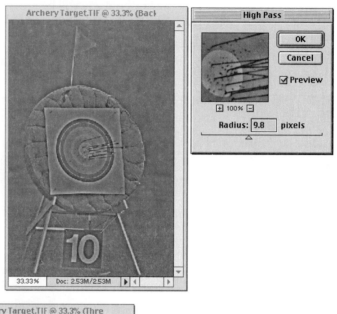

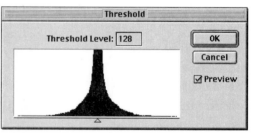

Image after a High Pass Filter command followed by the Threshold command.

Posterize

Posterize is similar to the Threshold command, except that it maps colors rather than black-and-white. When you apply Posterize to an image, Photoshop evenly divides the 256 levels of brightness into the specified number of Levels that you enter in the dialog box. This bands the colors, so the smooth transition between colors is replaced by hard-edged blocks of color. The lower the value you enter, the fewer the colors left in the image.

A great way to make images look hand-colored is to duplicate the image into a new layer; desaturate the bottom layer; posterize the top layer; and set the Blending mode of the upper layer to Color and adjust the opacity as desired.

If you are using Adobe Streamline to vectorize a posterized image, and it does not seem accurate enough, try using the Straight Lines Only option. It creates a much more accurate vectorization, though with a lot more points than using Streamline's curve.

The Posterize command is available as an Adjustment layer or as an Image>Adjust command. The Adjustment Layer option allows you to edit the Posterize settings at any time in the future based on the original image data.

Running the Dust & Scratches filter after posterizing helps remove single pixels of color, rendering an image suitable for tracing in a program such as Adobe Streamline. If you use the High Pass filter before running Posterize, the edge definition will sometimes be improved, but a definite loss of color will result. The Posterize command can also assist in wonderful special effects.

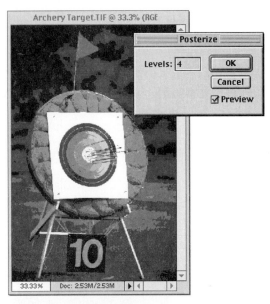

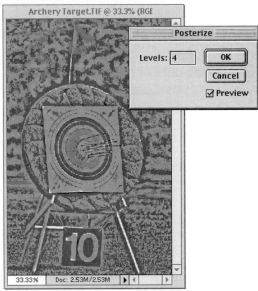

Posterize command and Posterize command after a High Pass Filter command.

Posterizing Images

1. Open **Shell.TIF** from the **SF-Adv Photoshop** folder. Press C to activate the Cropping tool. Crop the image so that only the shell is showing.

2. Select Layer>New>Adjustment Layer. For the Type, Select Brightness/Contrast. Set Brightness to -30 and Contrast to +30. Click OK.

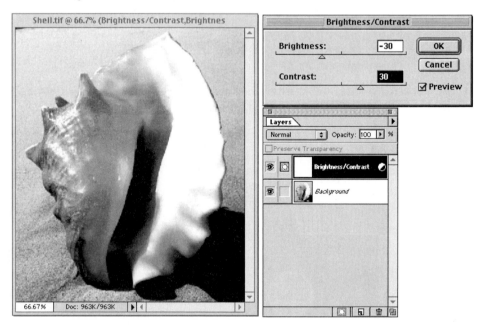

3. Select Layer>New>Adjustment Layer. For the Type, Select: Posterize; set Levels to 4. Click OK.

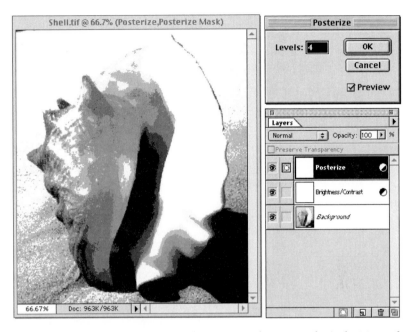

4. Click on the Background layer in the Layers palette to make it the Target layer. Then run Filter>Noise>Dust & Scratches, with Radius set to 4 pixels. Click OK. This is a posterized image. The image in this state is well prepared to vectorize in a program such as Adobe Streamline. We're going to spice up this image as an illustration. Having the remapping commands in the form of Adjustment layers means that you can double-click on the layer in the Layers palette and edit the settings at any time.

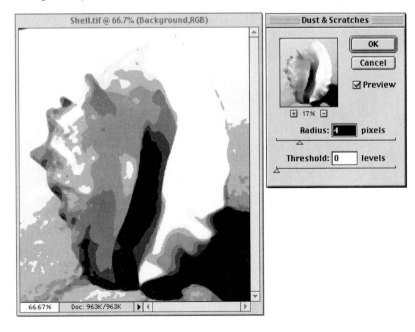

5. Select the entire Background layer. Copy the layer as it appears by running Edit>Copy Merged (this will copy the selected area as it is seen rather than as it is in the Target layer).

6. Select Edit>Paste. A new layer (Layer 1) is created. Move Layer 1 to the top of the Layers palette by clicking and holding on the layer and dragging it to the top of the stack.

7. On the Layer 1, select Filter>Pixelate>Crystalize; set the Cell Size to 4 pixels, then click OK.

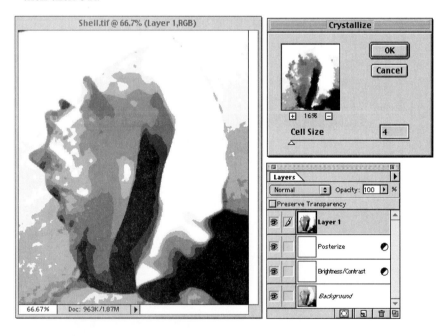

8. Blur the resulting image using Filter>Blur>Gaussian Blur with a width of 2.0 pixels. Run the Filter>Stylize>Find Edges filter.

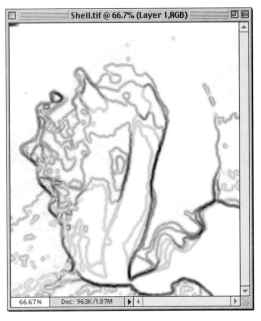

Some filter operations are only available in RGB mode.

9. Select Image>Adjust>Desaturate. From the Image>Adjust>Levels dialog box, set the Black Point slider to 175.

10. Activate Filter>Sharpen>Sharpen More. Press Command/Control-F two times to run the filter repeatedly on the image.

Some filter operations require real RAM to be available; they will not run with scratch disk virtual memory. One workaround is to apply the filter to each of the Color channels separately.

11. Change the Layer Blending mode from Normal to Darken.

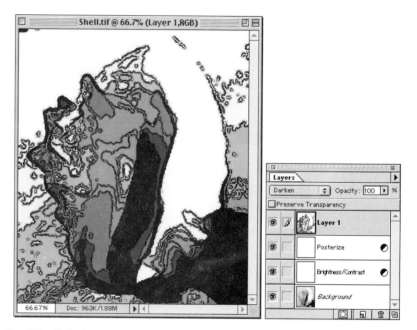

The Desaturate command removes all Chromatic values and renders the image as neutral lights and darks.

12. Double-click the Zoom tool to view the image at 100% to see the detail. Close the file without saving.

SHADOWS AND OTHER LAYER EFFECTS

CHAPTER OBJECTIVE:

To learn how to apply dimension to images and parts of images with Photoshop's Layers feature; to learn how to add special effects to layers. By completing Chapter 11, you will:

- Learn how to apply a drop shadow and inner glow to a Type layer.
- Understand how to create Multimedia buttons.
- Learn how to apply Soft Embosses and Glows.
- Understand how the Layer Effects allow you to easily make dynamic effects.

PROJECTS TO BE COMPLETED:

- Pokey Creek Book Cover
- Retouching the Jones Family Portrait
- Head in the Clouds Ad
- Baby Shower Invitation
- Farm Fresh Logo
- Photomat
- The Fix is in

Shadows and Other Layer Effects

In addition to managing the look and feel of two-dimensional images themselves, Photoshop allows us to give dimension to images and parts of images using its powerful Layers feature, and adding special effects to the layers. Layer effects are easy to apply, they are editable and reversible. As with all other features of Photoshop, the image's resolution and ultimate application must be taken into consideration before applying the effects.

The effects may be applied to images or type, and are not exclusive. Multiple effects may be applied to the same layer. If the same effect is applied over itself the results may not be as you anticipate — but they can be easily undone.

Drop Shadows

The effect most often used is the Drop Shadow. Its concept is easy to understand (we've been looking at our shadows since we were kids), and it gives substantial depth and realism to an image. Shadows can be combined with other effects to heighten the interest of an image, or to enhance its realism. Care should be taken not to overuse these effects, thus reducing their value to each image.

Applying a Drop Shadow

1. Open **Shell.TIF** from the **SF-Adu Photoshop** folder.

2. Select the Type tool, and pick a color from one of the pink tones in the shell. Type "SEA" in 72-point ATCMaiTai Bold.

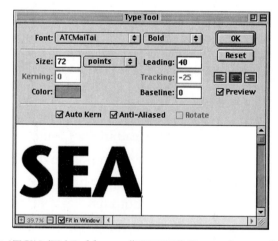

3. In 42-point ATCMaiTai Bold, type "SHORE". Center the two layers of type on one another.

4. With the Info palette visible, and using the Measure tool, measure the angle of the shadow of the shell. Measure toward the shell to find the angle. You'll find it's around 154°.

The Global Angle check box allows you to determine a shadow angle once for the entire image, and simply use it consistently. Check Global angle when you type an angle in and it becomes the default for that image.

Particularly when creating shadow effects, pay attention to the details of the photograph you're working on. Shadows should flow in the same direction and should be the same approximate density as shadows in the photograph. When that doesn't happen, the image looks artificial.

5. Select the SEA layer and apply Layer>Effects>Drop Shadow with an Opacity of 60, an Angle of 154, a Distance of 20 pixels, and a Blur of 5 pixels. Click Use Global Angle. Leave the Mode set to Multiply.

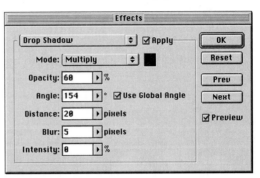

6. The type on the SHORE layer is considerably smaller. Keep the same settings, except set the Distance to 12 pixels and the Blur to 3 pixels.

Notice that the Type layers have acquired a new symbol, telling you that a Layer effect has been applied.

Bevel and Emboss Features

Beveled and embossed elements can be included as part of a photograph, and very subtly alter the overall effect of the original, or they may be individual elements, constructed for a specific use. More and more people are building web pages with snazzy buttons, and the Bevel and Emboss features are excellent for these uses.

Adding Inner Glow

7. The words look stark and out of place. Let's soften them a bit. Select one of the Type layers (we'll apply the same effect to both), then select Inner Glow. Select a brown tone from the shell. Set the Mode to Dissolve, Opacity at 50%, Blur to 5 pixels, and Intensity to 50%. Click the Center button. Apply the same effect to the other type layer.

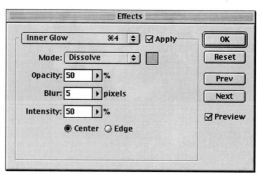

One of the wonderful things about Layer Effects is that they are applied to the layer, and not to the object on the layer. Let's see how elegantly this works.

8. Select the SHORE layer, and highlight the word. Replace it with the word SHELLS. All the effects have been added to the new layer data.

9. Save the file to your **Work in Progress** folder as "SeaShells.PSD". Close the file.

Creating Multimedia Buttons

1. Create a New RGB file with a width of 100 pixels, a height of 30, at 100 ppi. Make the background transparent. Name the file "Forward".

2. Set the Foreground to red and Fill the layer.

3. From Layer>Effects, select Bevel and Emboss. Set the Style to Inner Bevel and the Depth to 15 pixels. Accept the rest of the defaults and click OK.

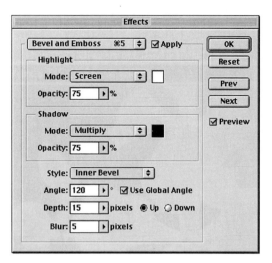

"Up" states and "Down" states of multimedia buttons are created as two separate graphics, then an action is applied in a separate program such as Fireworks, Shockwave, After Effects, and Image Ready — the coding must fit with the precise coding of the page. The difference in the artwork may be color, or how the "light" is perceived as striking the button.

Note that this is an "Up" button. The highlight comes from above, and as a multimedia element, this would be the "up" state of the button.

4. Create a New layer.

5. Select the Line tool and set its weight to 6 pixels, Anti-Aliased. Select the End Arrowhead, and set its shape to a width of 250% and a length of 300%. Click OK. Set White as the Foreground color and draw an arrow in the center of the button. (Press the Shift key to constrain the line to horizontal.)

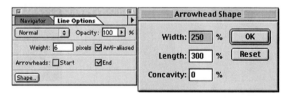

6. To give the illusion that the arrow is cut into the button, select the Inner Shadow Layer Effect. Set the Distance to 2 pixels and the Blur to 1 pixel. Click OK.

7. Save the file to your **Work in Progress** folder as "Forward Up.PSD".

8. Now let's create the depressed, or "down" state of this button. Go to Layer 1 and change the Bevel and Emboss effect. Click the Down radio button.

9. On Layer 2, change the Distance to 3 pixels and the Blur to 2 pixels.

10. Save the button as "Forward Down.PSD" in your **Work in Progress** folder.

Forward Up and Forward Down buttons.

Soft Embosses

1. Open **Beach Boy.TIF** from the **SF-Adv Photoshop** folder.

2. Select the Type tool, and, using ATCMaiTai Bold, set the size to 10 points, and select a blue from the Background as the color.

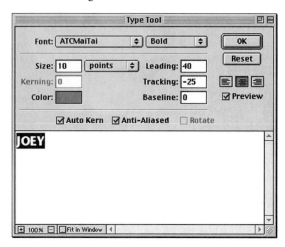

3. Type "JOEY", and place it centered on his hat.

4. From Layer>Effects, select Bevel and Emboss. Set the Opacity for both Highlight and Shadow to 50%, Style to Pillow Emboss with a Depth of 2 pixels and a Blur of 3 pixels. Accept the rest of the defaults.

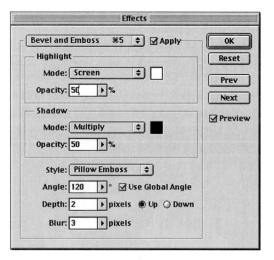

This results in a soft "smooshed into the layer behind" look, giving almost a quilted effect.

5. Close the file without saving.

Glowing in the Dark

Sometimes it is useful to be able to create a soft, glow effect, such as might be seen on a sign at night. Since the lights may be "off" on the original image, it may be necessary to create the entire effect from scratch. This used to be difficult. Now it's a Layer Effect.

Creating the Glow

In this exercise, we're going to add a neon glow to a sign.

1. Open **Bakery.TIF** from the **SF-Adv Photoshop** folder.

2. With the Pen tool, create a path of just the neon tubing on the word BAKERY. It should be close, but doesn't need to be perfect.

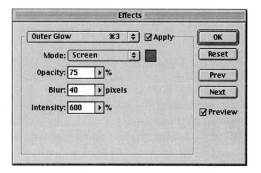

3. Name the path "Bakery", Convert it to a Selection, and Save the selection.

4. Select a red from the BAKERY letters for the Foreground.

5. Create a New layer and load the selection to that layer. Fill the selection with the Foreground color.

6. From Layer>Effects, select Outer Glow, and apply an Opacity of 75%, Blur 40 pixels, and Intensity of 600%. Set the Mode to Screen and the color to pure red. Click OK.

7. On the Background layer, make a loose selection around the word BAKERY, Feather it 6 pixels, then, from Image>Adjust>Hue/Saturation, adjust Hue to 50, Saturation to 50, and Lightness to -75. Deselect.

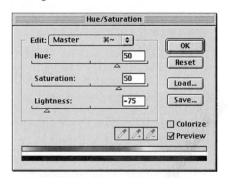

8. From Image>Adjust>Curves, drag the Highlight to an Output level of 63.

The sign appears to glow in the dark. Close without saving.

Summary

The Layer Effects make creating interesting effects relatively easy. When there is sufficient resolution to output these effects, they can add strikingly to the image. However, effects should be used to enhance an image, not purely for the sake of using the effect. When they are used sparingly, Layer Effects will make images look more dynamic. If used flagrantly, the images will often assault your audience's sensitivities.

Complete Project D: Baby Shower Invitation

CREATING PATTERNS AND TEXTURES

CHAPTER OBJECTIVE:

To learn how to easily create unique, project-specific tiles and textures as backgrounds for brochures, posters, web pages, or for almost anything you want to enhance. By completing Chapter 12, you will:

- Understand how the method that you use to create tiles depends on what type of tile you're creating.
- Learn about basic tiling and alternating tiles.
- Understand how to create Offset Graphic tiles.
- Understand how to create Rubber Stamp tiles.
- Understand how to create Mirrored tiles.
- Understand how to create Textured and generic backgrounds.

PROJECTS TO BE COMPLETED:

- Pokey Creek Book Cover
- Retouching the Jones Family Portrait
- Head in the Clouds Ad
- Baby Shower Invitation
- **Farm Fresh Logo**
- Photomat
- The Fix is in

Creating Patterns and Textures

Often a designer needs to add a pattern or texture to a project, whether for use as a background or to be composited with type or images. While there are many companies offering stock photography suitable for backgrounds, Photoshop allows you to easily create unique, project-specific tiles and textures.

Pattern Definition

Patterns are texturally interesting as backgrounds for brochures, posters, web pages, or just about anything. Photoshop's patterns tile horizontally and vertically, repeating a square or rectangle. There are third-party plug-ins available, however, that will allow you to automatically create pattern tiles in hexagonal, triangular, and other shapes. There are also plug-ins that create random textures and "weld" them together to make tiles.

There are many types of tiles that can be made *without* special software; the method you choose to create a tile depends on what tile you're making. For text, a simple offset tile will usually do; for photographs, more complexity is needed.

Basic Tiling

1. Open **Paradise.TIF** from the **SF-Adv Photoshop** folder.

2. Press Command/Control-A to Select All and then choose Edit>Define Pattern.

3. Create a New document named "Tiles.PSD". Make the new image 5″ × 5″ in RGB mode, 100 ppi, with Contents set to White.

4. Choose Edit>Fill, and select Pattern in the Use pull-down menu. Make certain that Blending is set to 100% and Normal. Click OK.

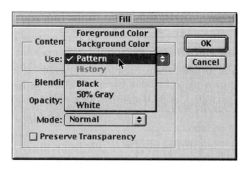

5. This is a simple repeating tile. Let's get a little more complex. Save **Tiles.PSD** to your **Work In Progress** folder. Leave it open for the next exercise. Close **Paradise.TIF** without saving.

Paradise   Paradise   Paradise   Pa
Paradise   Paradise   Paradise   Pa
Paradise   Paradise   Paradise   Pa
Paradise   Paradise   Paradise   Pa
Paradise   Paradise   Paradise   Pa
Paradise   Paradise   Paradise   Pa
Paradise   Paradise   Paradise   Pa
Paradise   Paradise   Paradise   Pa
Paradise   Paradise   Paradise   Pa
Paradise   Paradise   Paradise   Pa

Alternating Tiles

Taking a careful look at a background tile pattern may reveal that the tile it produces will be boring and repetitive. When that is the case, an alternating tile will spice up the effect with very little additional work.

1. Create a New document, 150 pixels wide × 150 pixels high, Resolution 100 ppi, with a Background of White. Select Edit>Fill, to Fill the document with your previously defined pattern.

2. Select the middle line of text with the Rectangular Marquee tool. Be certain to select from edge-to-edge to include the White background of both sides of the type.

3. Choose Filter>Other>Offset, and set the Horizontal Offset Value to 50 pixels. We have three lines of type, and this is one-third of the width of our image. Set the Vertical Offset Value to 0 and click the Wrap Around radio button. Click OK.

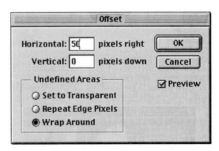

4. Now select the bottom line of text with the Marquee tool. Choose Filter>Other>Offset. This time, set the Horizontal Offset Value to 100 pixels; leave Vertical at 0. Click OK.

5. You now have three different offset versions of **Paradise.TIF**. Select All and choose Edit>Define Pattern.

6. Activate **Tiles.PSD**. Add a New layer. Choose Edit>Fill, and Fill the area with the newly defined pattern.

Paradise Paradise Paradise Pa
ise Paradise Paradise Paradise
radise Paradise Paradise Parad.
Paradise Paradise Paradise Pa
ise Paradise Paradise Paradise
radise Paradise Paradise Parad.
Paradise Paradise Paradise Pa
ise Paradise Paradise Paradise
radise Paradise Paradise Parad.
Paradise Paradise Paradise Pa

7. Save **Tiles.PSD**. Close the new pattern document without saving.

Offset Graphic Tiles

1. Open **Tiles.PSD** if it's not already open.

2. Create a New RGB document. Set both Height and Width to 100 pixels; set Contents to White and Resolution to 100 ppi.

3. Select Filter>Noise>Add Noise and set the Amount to 300. Make the Noise Monochrome and Gaussian. Click OK, and Gaussian Blur the image 1 pixel.

4. Choose Filter>Distort>Pinch. Set Amount to 100, and click OK. Press Command/Control-F ten times to reapply the filter.

5. Choose Filter>Distort>Twirl. Set Angle to 200 and click OK.

6. Choose Filter>Other>Offset. Change both Horizontal and Vertical to 50; make certain that Wrap Around is selected. Click OK.

7. Choose Pinch from the Filter>Distort menu. Distort the image with the Amount set to 100. Repeat the filter action by pressing Command/Control-F ten times.

8. Apply Filter>Distort>Twirl again, only this time set Angle to -200.

9. Select All and, in the Edit menu, define a New pattern. Activate the **Tiles.PSD** document. Create a New layer and Fill the layer with the tile.

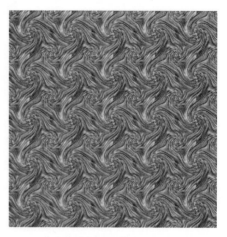

Patterns such as this are especially good for colorizing with the Image>Adjust>Hue/Saturation command.

10. Save **Tiles.PSD** before closing. Close the latest Pattern document without saving.

Rubber Stamp Tiles

1. Open **Rock.TIF** from the **SF-Adv Photoshop** folder.

2. Choose Filter>Other>Offset. Set Horizontal to 100 and Vertical to 50; note that this is precisely half of the height and width of the image. Make certain that Wrap Around is selected.

3. Distinct lines will be apparent where the offset occurred. Use the Rubber Stamp tool to clean up the edges; *don't get too close to the edge of the image.*

4. Press Command/Control-F to Offset the image back into place. Select All and Define Pattern.

5. Open **Tiles.PSD** from your **Work in Progress** folder. Create a New layer, and select Edit>Fill to Fill with the current pattern.

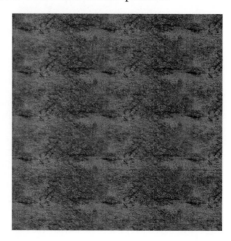

6. If the Edges don't seem perfect (that is, if you can see them) in the tiled layer, return to the **Rock.TIF** image, Offset it again and do more touchup. If you offset a different amount this time (for example, setting Horizontal to 50 and Vertical to 25) it might make the flaws more apparent.

7. The very light and very dark areas spoil the illusion. Use the Rubber Stamp tool to even out the tones. You'll probably want to use Offset a few times while working, just in case you've messed up the edges. Remove the dark spots altogether. Select All and Define Pattern again. Refill the layer in the Tiles document.

8. Although the pattern is still somewhat apparent, the Fill is perfect for a multi-media background. Text and graphics overlaid on it will enhance the illusion of seamlessness. Virtually any textured background can be treated in this manner. Save **Tiles.PSD** before closing. Close **Rock.TIF** without saving.

Creating Mirrored Tiles

1. Open **Beach Boy.TIF** from the **SF-Adv Photoshop** folder.

2. Double-click the Rectangular Marquee tool to display the Options palette for that tool. Change Style to Fixed Size. Set both Height and Width to 50 pixels. Click the Marquee on the image to select as much of the boy's face as you can within the 50 x 50 pixel area.

3. Copy your selection. Create a New RGB document with a White background. Allow the image size to be the default size of your copied data. Select Command/Control-V to Paste the copied data into the new document. Close **Beach Boy.TIF** without saving.

4. Press Command/Control-E to Merge the layers. Make certain that your background color is white. Select Image>Canvas>Size. Click the upper right corner of the Anchor and enter 100 pixels for both height and width.

5. Double-click the Background layer to make it a normal layer. Click OK to let the name default to Layer 0.

6. Set the Blending mode of the layer to Darken, and duplicate the layer three times.

7. Click on the top layer. Choose Edit>Transform>Flip Horizontal.

8. Click on the second layer and choose Edit>Transform>Flip Vertical. Click on the third layer, choose Edit>Transform>Flip Horizontal and choose Edit>Transform>Flip Vertical.

9. Select All and Define Pattern. If the Tiles image is not loaded, open it now; otherwise, activate **Tiles.PSD**. Create a new layer and Fill it with the pattern.

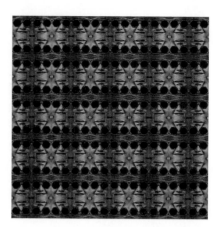

10. Save **Tiles.PSD** before closing. Close the image containing the tile without saving.

Textured Backgrounds

Pattern tiles are great backgrounds for many purposes. Sometimes, though, you need something a little more generic. Photoshop has the ability to create varied backgrounds quickly and easily.

We couldn't possibly begin to show you all of the possibilities for backgrounds here. The point is to show you a few so you get the idea, then let you experiment to create your own backgrounds.

Noise-Based Backgrounds

Many excellent backgrounds begin with the Noise filters. Blur, Sharpen, Emboss, and other filters make the options almost limitless. Here are a few for you to try:

Basic Noise Background

1. Create a New RGB document. Set the dimensions to 5″ square at 72 ppi, with a White background.

2. Select Filter>Noise>Add Noise. Set the Amount to 300. Make the Noise Gaussian and Monochromatic.

3. Duplicate the Background layer; name the layer "Basic". Select Filter>Blur>Gaussian Blur and set the Blur to 2.0 pixels. This is the most basic of textured backgrounds. Adjust Brightness/Contrast, then colorize as you wish using Image>Adjust>Hue/Saturation.

4. Turn off Basic and Duplicate the Background layer again. Name the layer "Leather". Select Filter>Blur>Gaussian Blur; this time set the Blur to 5.0 pixels. Colorize the image with Hue and Saturation with settings of Hue 30, Saturation 50, and Lightness 20. Select the Add Noise filter again; set Amount to 3. Be certain to check the Monochromatic box.

5. Turn off Leather and duplicate the Background layer. Name this layer "Stars". Select Filter>Stylize>Diffuse. Activate the Darken Only button, and click OK. Press Command/Control-F four or five times to repeat the filter, until the Background layer resembles a starfield.

The more you experiment with noise-based textures, the more variety you'll be able to put in your files. When you find one that you particularly like, be certain to save the steps so it may be reused. (Saving steps as an Action is described in Chapter 15.)

6. Turn off the Stars layer and duplicate the Background layer again. Name the new layer "Marbled Paper". Motion Blur the image at a 45° angle, for 20 pixels. Choose Filter>Distort>Ripple. Set Amount to -333 and Size to Large. Use Image>Adjust>Brightness/Contrast to bring out the detail. Colorize the image.

7. Create three unique backgrounds of your own using Noise. Try varying the Blur or Noise amounts, and using the Pixelate and Stylize filters.

8. Save the image as "Textures.PSD" to your **Work in Progress** folder.

Real-World Backgrounds

By experimenting with Photoshop's tools and filters, you can create textures that imitate patterns and objects in the real world.

Simulating Crumpled Foil

1. Create a New RGB document. Set the dimensions to 5″ square at 72 ppi, with a White background.

2. Choose Filter>Render>Clouds; then Filter>Render>Difference Clouds. Now, choose Filter>Stylize>Find Edges.

4. Press Command/Control-L to load the Levels dialog box, and click on the Auto button.

5. Run Filter>Sharpen>Unsharp Mask; set Amount to 200%, Radius to 1 pixel, and Threshold to 0.

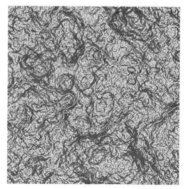

6. For gold foil, colorize with the Hue/Saturation dialog box. Select Image>Adjust>Hue/Saturation. Click Colorize. Set Hue to 40, Saturation to 75, and Lightness to -5.

7. Close the file without saving.

Creating Gingham Checks

1. Create a New document in RGB mode. Make it 20 pixels × 20 pixels, with a resolution of 72 ppi, filled with white.

2. Set the Foreground color to bright red. Double-click the Marquee tool. In the Options palette, change the Style to Fixed Size. Change Width to 10 and Height to 20. Select the left half of the image with the Marquee, and Fill it with red.

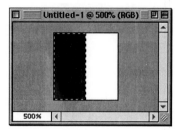

3. Press Command/Control-A to select the entire image, and choose Edit>Define Pattern. Close the document without saving.

4. Create a New RGB document. Set the dimensions to 5″ square at 72 ppi, with a White background.

5. Select Edit>Fill and Fill with the newly defined pattern.

6. Duplicate the Background layer. Select Layer>Transform>Rotate 90° Clockwise.

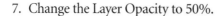

7. Change the Layer Opacity to 50%.

8. Close the file without saving.

Modifying Textures to Create New Textures

This is a nice, easy pattern. You could go completely crazy and create a plaid that would work equally well as a pattern fill. (Be certain to make your psychiatrist's reservation before you begin the project!) When creating patterns that imitate woven fabrics, remember that a "solid" is the overlap of two 50% layers.

1. Create a New RGB document. Set the dimensions to 5″ square at 72 ppi, with a White background.

2. Press D to make certain that you're on default colors. Select Filter>Render>Clouds.

3. Select Filter>Distort>Ripple. Change the Amount to 999 and the Size to Large.

4. Duplicate the layer. Rename the original layer "Water". Rename the new layer "Copper Mesh".

5. Activate the Copper Mesh layer and select Filter>Stylize>Find Edges. Press Command/Control-I to Invert the colors in the current layer.

6. Duplicate the Copper Mesh layer. Rename the new layer "Fur".

7. Select Filter>Blur>Motion Blur. Set the Angle to -45° and the Distance to 10 pixels.

8. Select Filter>Sharpen>Unsharp Mask. Set Amount to 100 and Radius to 2 pixels. Leave Threshold at 0.

9. Activate the Water layer and turn off the other layers. Select Image>Adjust>Hue/Saturation. Click the Colorize check box. Change Hue to 205, Saturation to 50, and Lightness to -10. Level the image to bring out bright highlights and deep shadows.

10. Activate the Copper Mesh layer. Select Image>Adjust>Hue/Saturation. Make certain that the Colorize check box is checked. Set Hue to 35, Saturation to 100, and Lightness to 0. Level the layer to bring out detail.

11. Activate the Fur layer. Choose Image>Adjust>Hue/Saturation again. Check the Colorize check box. Set Hue to 28, Saturation to 60, and Lightness to -35.

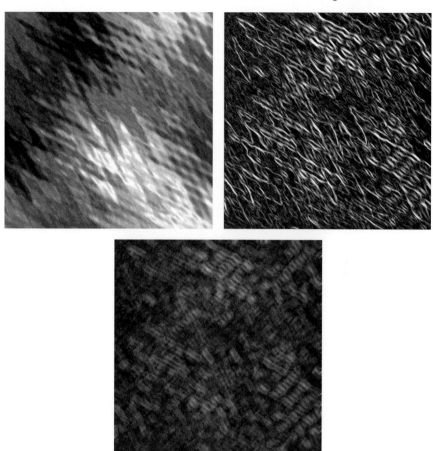

12. Close the file without saving.

Summary

Use the power and versatility of Photoshop to add variety to your images. These patterns and textures can be especially effective when used as backgrounds for other images, or for a combination of images and text, as is found on web pages. While a few effects have been presented here, the limitation on creating patterns and textures is bounded only by your imagination.

Complete Project E: Farm Fresh Logo

Notes:

THE RENDER FILTERS

CHAPTER OBJECTIVE:

To learn how the Render filters can be used for the creation of specialized blending patterns and entire lighting schemes for images. By completing Chapter 13, you will:

- Learn how the Clouds and Difference Clouds filters generate random color values based on the Foreground and Background colors.

- Learn how the Lens Flare filter simulates the refraction in a camera lens and creates "sunspots," which can add a sense of light, action, or motion to a photograph.

- Learn how to use the Lighting Effects filter to create light sources, set colors of light, choose types and styles of lighting, and apply texture to an image.

- Understand how to use the Texture Fill command.

PROJECTS TO BE COMPLETED:

- Pokey Creek Book Cover
- Retouching the Jones Family Portrait
- Head in the Clouds Ad
- Baby Shower Invitation
- Farm Fresh Logo
- Photomat
- The Fix is in

The Render Filters

The Render filters offer some of the most powerful and interesting special effects in Photoshop. They allow the creation of specialized blending patterns and entire lighting schemes to apply to images.

Clouds

You have already used the first two options in the Filters>Render menu, Clouds and Difference Clouds, when you were creating textured backgrounds. These two filters generate random color values based on the foreground and background colors. As their names suggest, these effects simulate cloud patterns. The Clouds filter has no transparency; if you apply it to an image, it will obscure everything.

The Difference Clouds command is similar to Clouds, but it won't overwrite transparent areas of a layer. The filter is applied as if you were overlaying clouds on the image in Difference mode. Applying the filter on a white layer repeatedly creates the marble-like texture, which is wonderful as a colorized background. Pressing the Shift key while applying either Clouds filter will make more highly defined clouds.

Lens Flare

The Lens Flare filter simulates the refraction in a camera lens when a bright light shines into it. It creates "sunspots," which can add a sense of light, action, or motion to a photo. The Filter>Render>Lens Flare dialog box allows definition of the brightness of the flare, movement of the center of the flare, and specification of a lens type. This filter works only with RGB images.

Using Lens Flare

1. Open **Sandy Beach.TIF** from the **SF-Adv Photoshop** folder.

2. Select Filter>Render>Lens Flare. Experiment for a moment with Brightness, Lens type, and Lens position. Move the crosshair in the Preview window to move the Flare source. Notice that the Brightness setting is sensitive in this image; high values turn the image mostly white. On a dark background, higher settings work better and give you all kinds of interesting lens highlights.

3. Change Brightness to 121 and Lens type to 105mm prime. Move the Lens near the upper right corner of the image. Click OK.

If you are working on a Macintosh, and the model you are using has no math coprocessor, you will not be able to use this filter.

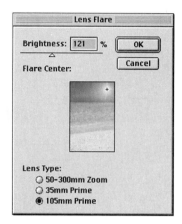

4. Close the image without saving.

Lighting Effects

The Lighting Effects filter is one of the most dynamic filters in Photoshop. It allows for creation of light sources, setting colors of light, choosing types and styles of lighting, and application of texture to an image. This filter will work only in RGB images, but the effects are incredible.

Because of the complexity of this filter, the dialog box can be a bit overwhelming. To clarify its uses, we'll go through the functions one by one.

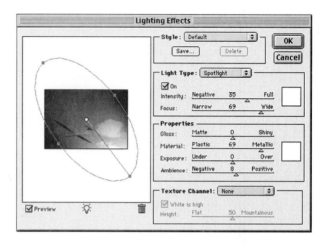

- The Preview window allows you to see the effect of the filter on a thumbnail image as you are making changes in the dialog box.

- In the Preview window, you can move lights by clicking on their center circle and dragging, change the size of a light by moving the points on the outer circle, and change the direction that a light is shining by moving the point at the end of the Direction line.

- Add new lights by clicking on the light bulb at the bottom of the Preview window and dragging it into the frame. Delete lights by either clicking on their center circles and pressing the Delete key, or by dragging them into the Trash Can at the bottom of the window.

- The Style pull-down menu provides a predefined list of light settings. You can use the presets as defined, or experiment by changing one or more options. Once you find a style you want to keep, you can add it to the list by clicking the Save button.

- Light Type allows you to choose one of three types of light: Spotlight, which is a focused beam; Omni, which radiates from the center equally in all directions, and Directional, which creates a Light source that is not focused on a particular spot, similar to diffused sunlight.

Spotlight

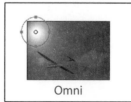

Omni

Directional

Lighting filters can create the effect of directional lighting which causes specific highlights and shadows, or it can create an overall lighting effect for your piece, almost like gallery lights shining on a painting in a museum. Experimentation will help you create just the effect you're attempting to achieve.

- You can change the Color of light and ambience by clicking on one of the small boxes on the right side of the dialog box.

- Intensity changes light from brightest to darkest. Negative settings actually remove light from an image, turning it very dark.

- Focus changes the width of the light's Focus point.

- Gloss sets the amount of reflection. The slider can be adjusted from dull Matte to Shiny gloss.

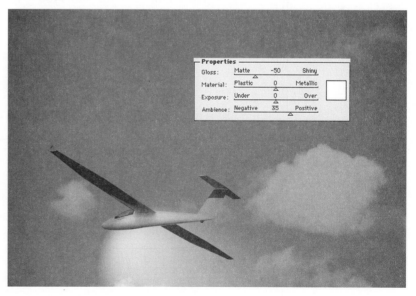

- Material determines which color of light is reflected: Plastic reflects the color of the light; Metallic reflects the color of the object.

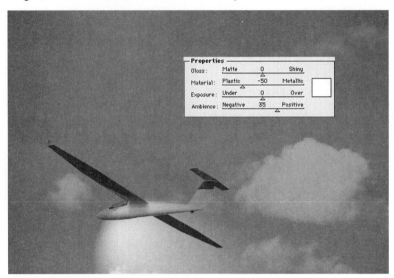

- Exposure values add to Light intensity if Positive, or subtract light when set to a Negative value. A value of 0 is neutral — there is no change in Light quality.

- The Ambience slider adjusts the light in the image *before* the Light effect is applied. It softens shadows and highlights when positive, or intensifies highlights and shadows when negative.

- The Texture channel allows you to use a channel as a "bump map." A bump map specifies which portions of the lighted image will appear embossed or debossed.

- The White Is High check box controls which portions of the Texture channel will appear raised. Checking this box sets the light areas in highest relief. Height controls the level of relief.

Fortunately, you don't have to memorize all that — and after you've experimented with it, you'll find that working with lighting effects is not only a lot easier than it sounds, but it's fun, too.

Creating Hammered Copper

1. Open **Gardening Panel.TIF** from the **SF-Adv Photoshop** folder.

2. Select Image>Mode>Lab Color.

3. Activate the Channels palette. Duplicate the Lightness channel. Gaussian Blur the channel 2.5 pixels. Rename the new channel "Texture".

4. Choose Image>Mode>RGB to convert back to RGB Color mode.

5. Select Filter>Render>Lighting Effects. Play with the settings until you get a feel for how they are affecting your image. Make certain that the Texture channel is specified as the Texture channel, then adjust the settings as noted below.

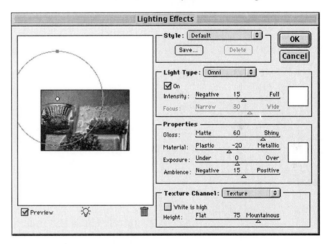

6. Click the Save button and name the settings "Emboss"; click OK twice to apply the filter to the image.

7. This is an excellent way to do a color emboss, but we want a Copper effect. Choose Hue/Saturation from the Image>Adjust menu. Click the Colorize box, and adjust the colors so that the image looks like copper. We used Hue 25, Saturation 55, and Lightness -10.

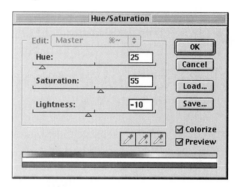

8. Close the file without saving.

Type and Lighting Effects

You've already learned a couple of ways to emboss type, but the Lighting Effects filter can produce some truly impressive results. Instead of merely embossing the type, the filter adds highlights and shadows that look incredibly real.

The following exercise is only a hint of what is possible using the Lighting Effects filter with type.

Putting Your Name in Lights

1. Open the **Textures.PSD** image from your **Work in Progress** folder.

2. Activate the Channels palette; click the New Channel icon to add a new channel to the image.

3. With the Type tool, click in the middle of the image. When the Type dialog box appears, click on the Centered button, and select a Font and Size. A fairly heavy typeface is a good choice for this effect — don't pick an especially thin typeface.

4. Type your name in the box. You may have to experiment with size, since it depends on the length of your name! If you're not certain, start with about 72 pixels and adjust up or down from there. If you don't get the correct size the first time, don't worry. Just Undo, and choose another size.

5. Gaussian Blur your name 2 pixels. Activate the Layers palette and select one of the background textures you created. Turn off all other layers.

6. Run the Lighting Effects filter. Make certain that the Texture channel is set to Alpha 1. Change the Style to Emboss. Play with the settings until you see something that you like; click OK.

7. Run the filter on the rest of the layers, one at a time. Vary the settings to try to achieve as many different looks as possible. What happens if you run the filter on the same background again, this time with one of the color channels selected as the Texture channel? By the time you finish this exercise, you should be confident in your ability to manipulate the Lighting Effects filter.

8. Close the file without saving.

The Texture Fill Command

When the Type tool is used in a channel, the resulting type is not editable. Instead, it creates a type-shaped selection, cut out of the Channel mask.

The Texture Fill filter loads an image into a channel in the current document, generally for use as a bump map. The image must be a grayscale saved in Photoshop format. If the Texture image is smaller than the current image, the texture is repeated like a pattern within the channel, which makes Pattern tiles a natural for this command.

1. Open **Sandy Beach.TIF** from the **SF-Adv Photoshop** folder. The lack of busyness in this photograph will allow us to readily see the effects of the Texture Fill.

2. Create a New channel. Allow it to default to the name Alpha 1.

3. From Filter>Render>Texture Fill, select **Orangepulp.PSD** from the **SF-Adv Photoshop** folder.

4. Activate the composite RGB channels to see the effect you have created.

5. Return to the Alpha 1 channel and Invert the effect. Re-inspect your work by viewing the Composite channel again.

6. From the Image menu, adjust the curves so that the Output Shadow value is 100.

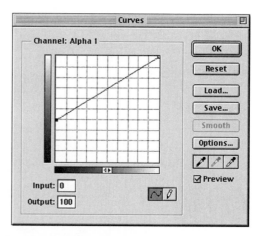

7. Apply a Gaussian Blur in the amount of 4 pixels to the Alpha channel to soften the effect.

8. Revert the file, and reapply the texture fill, but this time apply it to the Blue channel. Note the radical results you achieve.

9. Close the file without saving.

If you find a bump map you especially like, you can save it to a separate file so that you can easily access it as a Texture channel for other images. You may wish to create a separate folder for Texture fills.

Summary

Render filters cause Photoshop to create very specific effects, over which the user has varying degrees of control. Working with each of the filters, and experimenting with running the filters on individual channels as well as on the composite image will give even more variety to the documents you create. Especially when working with complex filter settings, be certain to write them down. Ideally, you'll want to include before and after examples so you know exactly what happened — not just that you obtained a "cool" result.

CHAPTER 14

*I*MPORTING AND *E*XPORTING

*C*HAPTER *O*BJECTIVE:

To learn how to import an Illustrator or Freehand file into a Photoshop document; to understand the two different file formats for images on the World Wide Web, and to know which format to use, depending on the type of image that you're creating. By completing Chapter 14, you will:

- Learn how to save files in JPEG and GIF formats.

- Learn about filters with a range of color.

- Learn how to save a file with Transparency.

- Understand that creating images for the Web is different than creating images for print production.

*P*ROJECTS TO BE *C*OMPLETED:

- Pokey Creek Book Cover
- Retouching the Jones Family Portrait
- Head in the Clouds Ad
- Baby Shower Invitation
- Farm Fresh Logo
- Photomat
- The Fix is in

Importing and Exporting

As you've learned, information comes to Photoshop from many different sources, and Photoshop's own layered images aren't compatible with most other applications. For example, most desktop publishing programs prefer TIFF or EPS files for importing. Most formats are easily accessible using the Save As and Save a Copy As commands from the File menu. There are certain situations, however, that require actions that are somewhat trickier than simply opening or saving a file.

Working with Adobe Illustrator Files

By now you have experience in opening vector-based documents and placing EPS files into existing Photoshop files. In addition to these methods, however, you can import an Illustrator or FreeHand file by copying a graphic from within a drawing program, then pasting the files into a Photoshop document. The advantage of using this method is that you may paste the image as a rasterized image (which is similar to placing an EPS file), *or* you can specify that the graphic be pasted as a path, which will add it to the Paths palette. This is an excellent way to create custom clipping paths for images to be saved as EPS files.

The File>Export>Paths to Illustrator command allows you to export paths created in Photoshop for use in Illustrator. This is a great way to accurately wrap type around an irregular shape or create a trap for an image which includes a clipping path.

Images for the World Wide Web

There are two types of images commonly used on web pages — GIF and JPEG. Both of these compressed file types offer substantial savings of load time (and disk space) over typical print-oriented formats such as TIFF files. The main drawback is that both compression algorithms have their limitations.

Which format should you use? — it depends on the type of image you're converting. JPEG is generally used for photographic images. GIF files are preferable for computer-generated artwork, especially those containing large, flat areas of color. GIF89a should be used for images that require transparency.

JPEG images allow the user to specify the level of compression required. The resulting file contains 24 bits of RGB data, yielding high-quality photographic results in most instances. However, compressing an image reduces its quality. More compression equals lower quality. When saving a JPEG image, you also have the option of saving the paths associated with the image (but not clipping paths), though a JPEG saved with paths may cause some browsers to choke.

GIF images contain 256 colors or less, as defined in the Index color mode. Any colors not contained in the Color palette may be remapped to another color in the palette. For more photographic results, the converted file can be dithered. Using this compression scheme, if a color does not exist in the palette, dots of different colors in the palette are placed closely together to achieve the illusion of the missing color. Dithered GIF files are more photorealistic, but are usually larger than undithered files.

The color palette used in a GIF file may be the standard System palette from Macintosh or Windows-based systems. A 216-color Web palette includes only the colors common to both Macintosh and Windows, so graphics will be viewed with relative consistency cross-platform. The Adaptive palette draws on the most commonly used colors in the existing image to define its color group. Custom Color palettes may be loaded and saved to ensure consistency among graphics on a web page.

JPEG and GIF files may be saved *interlaced* (GIF) or *progressive* (JPEG). This means that if the browser supports it, the image will appear in stages, beginning with a low resolution image and then "filling in the blanks" until the image is at full resolution. The purpose is to give the viewer a framework of the image early on, instead of waiting for the entire image to paint before it is displayed. An indexed color file may be exported with a certain color or colors designated as transparent, in GIF89a format.

Saving a JPEG File

1. Open **Sailboat Beach.TIF** from the **SF-Adv Photoshop** folder.

2. Select File>Save a Copy. In the Format pull-down, select JPEG. Name the file "Sailboat1.JPG" and Save it in your **Work in Progress** folder.

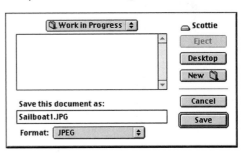

3. Note the various options available to you:

Although a JPEG image can be compressed very small, the compression method used is "lossy" — the more the file is compressed, the more data the compressing mechanism throws away or "loses." Use only as much compression with JPEG images as you need to, or you will begin to see artifacts and a loss of detail within the image.

Image Options allows you to specify the level of quality you want in the image. You can enter a number from 1 to 10, adjust the slider, or select a quality factor from the pull-down list.

Format Options lets you specify Baseline ("Standard"), a format recognized by most browsers; Baseline Optimized, which optimizes the color quality in a file and will produce slightly smaller files — but is not supported by all browsers; or Progressive, which allows a JPEG to load into a Web browser in stages, creates a slightly larger file, and is not supported by all browsers.

4. Change Quality to 0 and set the Format Options to Baseline ("Standard"); click OK to Save your file.

5. Name another copy "Sailboat2.JPG". Change Quality to 5 and Save to your **Work in Progress** folder.

6. Save one last copy as "Sailboat3.JPG" and Save to your **Work in Progress** folder. Change Quality to 10.

7. Close the image. Select File>Open and click on each of the newly saved JPEG files. Note the file size in the Open dialog boxes.

8. Open all three files. Note the quality loss in the sky and the strange halo artifacts around the edges of objects in Sailboat 1 and 2. You'll need to experiment to find the perfect combination of quality and file size to suit your needs. When you are finished, Close the files without saving.

Saving a File in GIF Format

1. Open **Tropical Interiors.EPS** from the **SF-Adv Photoshop** folder. Make certain that Mode is set to RGB and Resolution to 100 ppi. Leave the dimensions at their defaults. Make certain that Anti-Aliased is checked.

2. Select Image>Mode>Indexed Color. Click OK to the Flatten Colors dialog box (you really have no choice). Notice that the Color palette tells you how many colors are in the file (60). Leave the palette at Exact and click OK. The image has acquired a white background.

3. Select File>Save As "Tropical Interiors.GIF" and select CompuServe GIF from the menu.

4. Save to your **Work in Progress** folder and select a Row Order of Interlaced.

5. Close the file.

Files with a Range of Color

While the Adaptive palette usually yields the prettiest results, the Web is not a color-controlled environment. Older monitors may not display 24-bit color, and the colors on the Macintosh are different from those in Windows. When it can't display the exact color specified, a browser will substitute a palette that works for the monitor being used. It will also dither the colors in the image. Dithering is placing pixels next to one another to simulate a different color.

1. Open **Spectrum.PSD** from the **SF-Adv Photoshop** folder.

2. To have more control over how the image is converted, you first need to convert the image to Indexed Color Mode. Select Image>Mode>Indexed Color. Click OK when you're asked if you want to flatten the layers.

3. For Palette, select Web. Set Dither to None. Notice the visible banding in the Color Wheel.

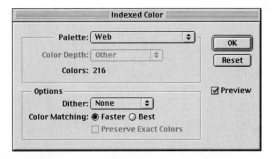

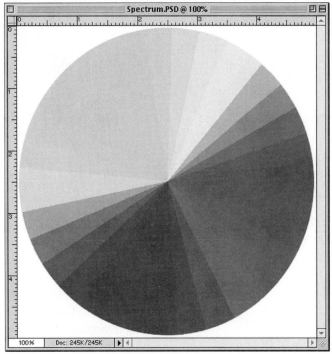

4. Now change Dither to Diffusion. Click OK. Notice that the image quality is tremendously improved. However, it's nowhere near what you'd get with a JPEG file. With continuous tone images, you're much better off with lossy compression than with banding.

5. Close the file without saving.

Saving a File with Transparency

1. Open **Broadway.EPS** from the **SF-Adv Photoshop** folder. Make certain that Mode is set to RGB and Resolution is set to 100 ppi. Leave the dimensions at their defaults. Click on Anti-Aliased.

   This logo comes in with a white background, which is not desirable for the background we're going to lay it over. The GIF89a Export filter gives us the tools to define transparency in a GIF image.

2. Convert the file to Indexed with an Adaptive palette and a color depth of 8 bits per pixel, and diffusion dither.

3. Select File>Export>GIF89a Export. From the palette, select white to be transparent. (The white swatch is on the bottom row. Do you see a problem here?)

4. The Transparency filter immediately shows us that we're not only going to lose the background — we're going to lose all the white elements if we follow this route.

   There's an easy solution to the problem. Click Cancel to exit the window.

5. With the Magic Wand tool, select the White background and Invert the selection (Command/Control-Shift-I) and apply a Quick Mask mode. When creating transparency from Indexed Color, the filter blocks out the masked portion.

Neither JPEG nor GIF can save a file with transparency. The GIF89a Export Filter must be used to achieve a transparent effect. Although they are often used on web pages, animations with transparent areas often have rough edges and contain artifacts that blend in poorly with the background.

6. Choose File>Export>GIF89a Export, and select Transparency from Quick Mask.

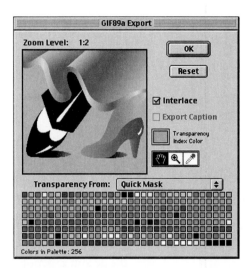

Notice that the background to become transparent displays as neutral gray. This is "Netscape gray," the default Netscape browser background color. You can change the background color by clicking on the Transparency Index Color swatch in the GIF89a Export Options dialog box. It doesn't matter what color you choose, except that it should be easily identifiable. The background will be transparent, not the color displayed.

7. Click OK to close the Preview window and the GIF89a Export window, then name the file "Broadway.GIF". Save it to your **Work in Progress** folder. Close the original file without saving.

The Myth of RGB GIF

Occasionally we hear that an RGB file can be saved as GIF, leaving the impression that it's somehow different from an indexed color GIF. Let's take a closer look at the process and its results.

1. Open **Orange Slice.TIF** from the **SF-Adv Photoshop** folder. This is an RGB file with a predefined path.

2. Convert the path to a selection. Invert the selection, and apply a Quick Mask.

3. Choose File>Export>Gif89a Export.

4. Click Preview. Hold down the Option/Alt key, and click on the Zoom tool, then click on the orange so that you can see that it has a transparent background. Click OK to return to the first GIF Export menu. Notice that the palette is Adaptive, and that there are 256 colors. Doesn't that sound familiar?

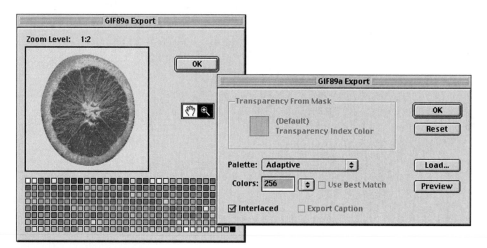

Choose Cancel to return to the file.

5. Deselect the Quick Mask mode and choose Image>Mode>Indexed Color. Leave the default selection of Adaptive palette and 256 colors. Notice how much better the image looks than it did when going straight to the Gif89a Export.

6. Invert the selection and apply a Quick Mask mode so that the background is masked.

7. Export the file through Gif89a.

8. Click Preview, then Transparency from Quick Mask. Zoom out to see the transparency.

9. Save the file as "Orange Slice.GIF" to your **Work in Progress** folder.

A Final Word About Web Images

It should be clear from the exercises we've done that creating images for the web is different from creating images for print production. Instead of exact color matches with infinitesimal nuances of color, we have a reasonable shot at an acceptable range of color, based upon the viewer's monitor settings and platform.

More important than exact color match is that pages load fast. It's important to pay attention to the details of numbers of colors in the palette, the resolution of the image, and the dimensions of the image. Remember, it's designed for screen resolution, so resolution greater than 96 ppi (on Windows-based systems; 72 ppi for Macintoshes) will be thrown away. The standard is 72 ppi.

For print output, the standard is 1.5–2 times the value of the line screen, usually around 300 ppi. If images will be used for print and for the Web, they should be manipulated at high-resolution. A high-resolution RGB file should be saved in Photoshop format. Save a copy of the file at high-resolution in CMYK for print, and a copy at reduced resolution for the Web.

The Web palette is comprised of the 216 colors common to both the Macintosh and Windows environment. Using other colors, particularly in GIF files, will often result in the color being far off from what is intended.

CHAPTER 15

WORKING SMARTER

CHAPTER OBJECTIVE:

To learn how to work efficiently when performing color correction and manipulation on large files or batches of files; to learn how to use the Auto Levels command and the Auto button. By completing Chapter 15, you will:

- Learn how the Actions palette allows the recording of a series of commands for playback and application to files or file groups.

- Understand how the History palette brings to you, the Photoshop user, the ability to revert up to 100 actions and steps backward to correct an image or task.

- Learn how to use the Contact Sheet.

- Understand the Conditional Mode Change.

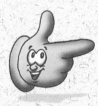

PROJECTS TO BE COMPLETED:

- Pokey Creek Book Cover
- Retouching the Jones Family Portrait
- Head in the Clouds Ad
- Baby Shower Invitation
- Farm Fresh Logo
- Photomat
- The Fix is in

Working Smarter

While performing color correction and other photo-manipulation tasks, file processing can really bog down. When you consider that an 11″ × 17″ poster printed at 150 lpi clocks in at about 57 MB, it's not surprising.

Here are a few suggestions for making the most of your time when performing color correction and manipulation on large files or batches of files.

- Do your initial corrections/experimentations on a low-resolution version of the file. Many dialog boxes, such as Curves and Levels, have options to save settings. Finding settings for corrections that work can be saved, then loaded and applied to the high-resolution file.

- For commands whose settings can't be saved, such as Photoshop's filters, keep a written log of the specific steps you used to produce the effect. Then apply the steps, in order, to a higher resolution file.

- Make certain that the White and Black Contrast point of the image are adjusted to maximize the overall contrast of the image. To save time in correcting the contrast of an image, Use the Auto Levels command and the Auto buttons in the Levels and Curves dialog box. An exercise showing how to set and apply the Auto Levels will be presented later in this chapter.

- When running a preset list of commands, turn off the Preview option in all dialog boxes before running the commands. This will save a lot of time on screen redraw.

- When running complex filter commands or editing colors, work on a single channel at a time. An RGB channel requires one-third the memory that working on the composite does. In a CMYK file, a single channel requires only one-fourth the memory. If the command in question is a filter, run it on each channel in the document in succession.

- Maintain a Photoshop (.PSD) file of all images that you send to a client, output vendor, or a web site. If alteration has to be done, you will save time maintaining a copy of the file that has not been saved for final use. Store the .PSD files in a separate folder, on your computer or a removable disk.

- Make certain that the scratch drive is defragmented. In addition, click on the triangle in the lower left corner of the screen and change it to "scratch size." Pay close attention to these numbers. The first is the amount of memory all open documents require. The second is available RAM. When the first number becomes larger than the second, the scratch disk is being utilized, and program operation will slow down.

The most important thing you can do to improve Photoshop performance is to have RAM, RAM, and more RAM! Some Photoshop filters run entirely in RAM.

There are graphics accelerator cards designed specifically to speed up Photoshop.

Don't use a compressed drive or removable disk for a scratch disk; it will degrade Photoshop's performance.

- To save time zooming in and zooming out when doing close-up work on an image, use Photoshop's View>New View command. This command produces a second window of the active document. Zoom into one window and use the Hand tool to move around the image. The second window will display all of the changes that you make in the first, giving you a view of the big picture without excessive zooming.

- Running in 256-color video mode (the image data will still contain full-color information) can speed up screen redraws considerably. Be forewarned: become familiar with correcting using readings from the Info palette before attempting to color correct in 256-color mode.

- Store extra channels and layers in a separate document. They're easy to bring back into the old image, provided the resolution and color mode are the same as the original file. Every channel you add to an image increases its file size. For example, a CMYK file with six additional channels would be 2.5 times the size of a regular CMYK document. If the channels aren't being used for the moment, why deal with all the extra file overhead? Save them into their own document, and load them back into the image when needed.

- If the file will be exchanged with others using previous versions of Photoshop, Save the file as a TIFF. Saving the file as a Photoshop 2.0 file will take longer and waste disk space.

- Turn off the Preview icons in the Layers and Channels palette. These icons, while convenient, use more Photoshop resources than you might think. Getting into the habit of naming the layers and channels according to the data they contain makes previews unnecessary.

- On Macintosh systems, quit any running applications or TSRs (Terminate-and-Stay-Resident programs — usually utilities which load automatically when you start your system), before loading Photoshop. Quitting these applications after Photoshop is loaded will prevent the available memory from being used.

- If there are commands or tasks that are repeatable in several images, use the Actions palette. The Actions palette can record, and then playback, repeatable tasks on many images with the same correctable needs, such as preparing images for web site placement. The Actions palette will be described later in this chapter.

- Use keyboard commands. All of Photoshop's tools and many of its menu items are available using keyboard commands. Many of Photoshop's menu items are two or three levels deep, so using the mouse for every command can become cumbersome. The more of these commands committed to memory, the more efficient working in Photoshop becomes.

- Don't wait for screen redraw when working on large files. For example, when zooming into an image twice, don't wait for Photoshop to redraw the image before clicking the Zoom tool a second time — better still, type in the Zoom percentage.

- Using the History palette will allow for the return to a previous level of correction for Photoshop images. A description of the History palette is shown later in this chapter. However, there are instances where the palette's overhead simply gets in the way. If it's not needed, lower the number of History states to 1 in History Options.

Keyboard Commands

Throughout this course you've learned many keyboard shortcuts for the commands and functions that Photoshop offers. In the manual that comes packaged with your Photoshop software, you will find these keyboard commands and shortcuts, as well as other shortcuts listed in a handy pull-out chart.

Some of the shortcuts listed have always been offered as commands in the form of Menu>Submenu>Command. Why? The uses of Photoshop vary widely from user to user; it's often easier to remember a less commonly used command via menus than it is an esoteric keyboard shortcut. When using a particular command over and over again, however, it's time to learn the shortcut. Don't underestimate the time-savings involved! It may seem like only a few seconds here or there, but knowledge of shortcuts often makes the difference between someone who merely knows Photoshop well and someone who can complete nearly any job quickly and efficiently.

Adobe supplies a Quick Reference Card for the most popular keyboard commands/shortcuts. Photoshop's on screen Help is set up to effectively provide help in finding the proper keyboard commands/shortcuts. Select Help>Keyboard to access a list of on screen help. These Help pages can also be printed.

Keep a copy of these commands nearby while working in Photoshop; while working and repeatedly using commands, make a concerted effort to memorize its shortcut where available.

Using the Auto Levels Command and the Auto Button

The Auto Levels command, located in the Image>Adjust pull-down menu, and the Auto button, Located in the Levels and the Curves dialog box, can speed the application of the proper White and Black points to an image. Using preset values in the Auto Option window, located in the Levels and Curves dialog box, allows you to set values for the White and Black points as dictated by the output vendor or application used, and apply these values to many images. The Auto Levels option will redistribute the intermediate pixels values proportionally.

When you realize you've been regularly using a menu command, look at the right-hand-side of the menu (where the prices are in restaurants). You'll discover the keyboard shortcut for each menu command for which a shortcut exists right before your eyes. Pretty soon you'll have memorized those that are important for the way you work.

Using the Auto Levels Option

1. Open **Work.TIF** from the **SF-Adv Photoshop** folder.

2. Select Image>Adjust>Levels to view the Histogram of this image.

3. As the Histogram shows, the concentration of the pixels is in the highlight and shadow areas, with very little distributed through the midtones on the image.

4. Hold the Option/Alt key down. The Auto button in the Levels dialog box turns into an Options button. Press the Options button to open the Auto Range Options dialog box.

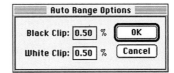

5. The Auto Range Options dialog box sets the value that the image will have in the White and Black Point set. Any pixels that have a value greater than these settings will be set to a representative, rather than an extreme, pixel value. The balance of the pixels will be redistributed throughout the image. For this example, maintain the 0.50% value for the White and Black Clip point. Select OK.

6. Select the Auto button in the Levels dialog box to apply the Auto Range Options values. The pixels in the image are redistributed in a more pleasing manner, as represented in the Levels Histogram.

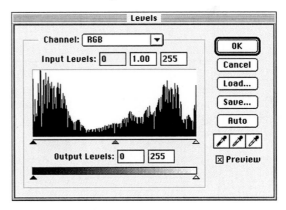

7. Close the file without saving.

The Auto Levels command is best used when similar images will be included in the same document. Be careful when images are drastically different, or will be used in different processes.

Using the Actions Palette

The Actions palette allows the recording of a series of commands that can be played back and applied to any file, or group of files, as needed. In addition, it gives the ability to add or delete commands from an action, edit existing commands, and insert "stops," which allow the pausing of the action to insert undefinable commands, such as creation of selections.

Using the Actions palette can automate special effects such as three-dimensional type, or batch-correct a group of files.

Using the Actions Palette

1. Open **Button1.PSD** from the **Buttons** folder inside your **SF-Adv Photoshop** folder.

2. Select Window>Show Actions to make certain that the Actions palette is visible.

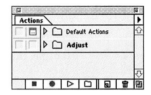

3. From the Actions palette pull-down menu on the upper right corner, select New Set.

The Photoshop CD includes a lot of great special effects Actions.

4. Name the new set "Web Files".

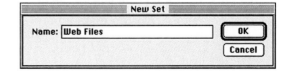

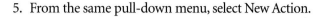

5. From the same pull-down menu, select New Action.

6. Name the action "GIF Files" and click Record.

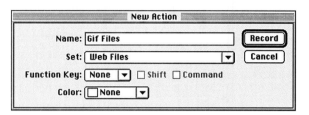

7. Choose Image>Image Size and change both Height and Width in Pixel Dimensions to 50 percent. Click OK.

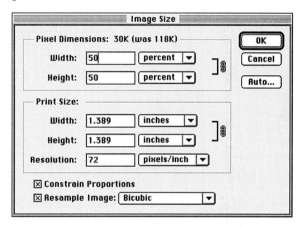

You can swap Actions between platforms, provided you name the action with a PC extension (.ATN) and that you change the items that are specific to a single platform, such as the Windows Window>Tile option.

8. Choose Image>Mode>Indexed Color. Flatten the image. Set the Palette to Web, Dither to Diffusion, and Color Matching to Best. Click OK.

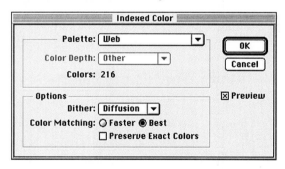

9. Save the image in CompuServe GIF format, allowing Photoshop to add the file extension "Button1.GIF". Save into your **Work in Progress** folder.

10. Close the file. Choose Stop Recording from the Actions Palette pull-down menu, or click on the black square at the bottom of the palette.

You can edit an individual step of an Action to customize it for your particular task.

If you set File>Preferences> Saving Files to Always Append File Extension, Photoshop will automatically append the correct extension to your files.

11. Locate the newly created GIF file in Finder (Macintosh) or Explorer (Windows), and drag it to the Trash Can (Macintosh) or Recycle Bin (Windows).

12. From the File pull-down menu select Automate>Batch.

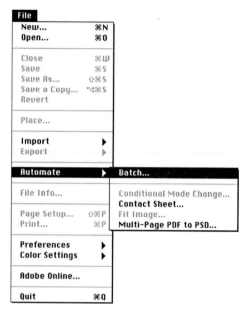

Make certain that Source is set to Folder. Click Choose and specify the **Buttons** folder. Change Destination to Folder; click Choose in the Destination box, and select the **Work in Progress** folder (not the **Buttons** folder). Leave all other settings at their defaults and click OK. Wait until Photoshop is no longer automatically opening files.

13. Examine the contents of your **Work in Progress** folder; note that there are now four GIF files in the folder, created by running the GIF Files Action.

The History Palette

One of the difficulties that Photoshop users have faced has been the inability to revert further than one step backward to correct an action or a task. The History palette corrects that difficulty by setting up a file, so to speak, of up to 100 actions taken on a Photoshop image. The default is 20. Be warned that the History palette is a RAM hog — add states only if you need them.

If you click the second box next to the Action name, Photoshop will display dialog boxes for the commands in the Actions.

The History palette maintains a record of non program-wide changes to the current working file as long as the file remains open. The Photoshop user can return to a previous change in the file through the History palette items, called "states," to review or change from that point. Once the file is closed and the work session is ended, these states are removed.

When the number of states exceeds the maximum states specified in History options, the older ones will "scroll off" the palette list. There is a way to maintain a state longer than the maximum levels specified — the Photoshop user can create a "snapshot" of the state, and keep it throughout the work session, or create a new file from a snapshot.

A program-wide change is a change to palettes, color settings, actions, and preference. Since these changes do not affect a particular file, they will not be stored in the History palette.

Using the History Palette

1. Open **CD Photo.TIF** from the **SF-Advance Photoshop** folder. Select Window>Show History and Window>Show Layers.

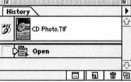

2. Notice that in the History palette, the image appears as a thumbnail with the History brush appearing to the left of the thumbnail, and Open appears as the first state.

3. Click the Type tool, and select a location in the center of the monitor screen. Select ATCRumRunnerScript Regular from the Font drop-down menu. Enter 30 points in the Size window. Click the Color window, and select 255 in the Red, Blue, and Green windows to produce white. Select the Center Type icon. Type the words "New CD Disc". Click OK. Notice that a new state, Type Tool, appears in the History palette.

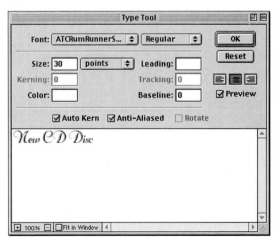

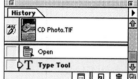

Make certain that your RAM allocation is sufficient to operate the History palette. Photoshop 5 works best with at least 64 MB of allocated RAM. Without the RAM allocation, the History palette, and Photoshop, will run slowly or possibly crash your computer.

4. Select the Magnetic Lasso tool. Double-click on it to show Options, or choose Window>Show Options. Set the Feather to 2, Lasso Width to 5, Frequency to 59, and Edge Contrast to 10%. Make certain that the Anti-Aliased box is selected. Select the edge of the CD in the image, closing the selection. A new state, Magnetic Lasso, appears in the History palette.

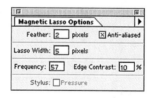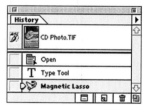

5. Use the Lasso tools to remove the center finger and complete the edge selection of the CD. Notice that every time a new task is finished, a new state appears in the History palette.

6. Select the Background layer in the Layers palette. Select Layer>New>Layer Via Copy. Deselect the CD. Double-click Layer 1 and rename it "CD Layer". Notice that all of these tasks appear as states in the History palette.

7. Deselect the Eye icons in the Background and New CD Disc layer, leaving only the CD Layer visible. Select the Magic Wand tool, select 2 in the Tolerance window of the Magic Wand Options palette, and make certain that Use All Layers is not selected. Select a point around the transparent area around the CD. Choose Select>Inverse, making the CD the selected area. Notice again that all of these actions appear as states in the History palette.

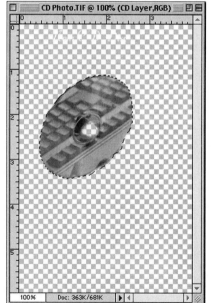 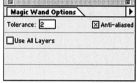

8. Turn on all the layers in the Layers palette. With the CD Layer selected as the active layer, select Edit>Transform>Flip Horizontal. Select the Move tool, and move the selection to the right, so that it looks like a mirror image of the original CD. Deselect the CD. Additional states appear in the History palette.

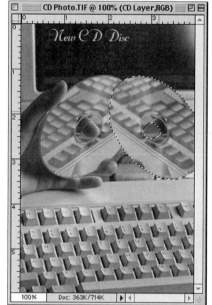 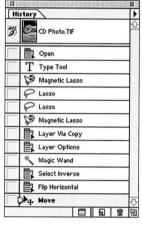

9. Select the box next to the Type state in the History palette and click on the Type Tool state. Notice that all of the states below the Type tool become gray and their names become italic. Select Delete from the History palette pull-down menu. Notice that all states disappear below the Type Tool state. Click Command/Control-Z to reinstate all of the deleted states.

10. With the Type Tool state still highlighted, click Create New Document from the Current state button at the bottom of the History palette.

A new document named **Type Tool**, having only the original image and the type appears on the screen with only Duplicate state appearing in the History palette. Close the Type Tool image without saving.

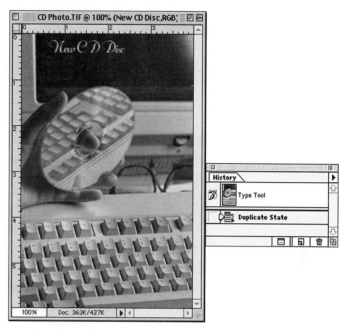

11. Select the Flip Horizontal state in the History palette, and the History Brush box next to the Flip Horizontal state. Notice that the image returns to the point prior to moving the CD Layer. Select the Delete button from the bottom of the History palette.

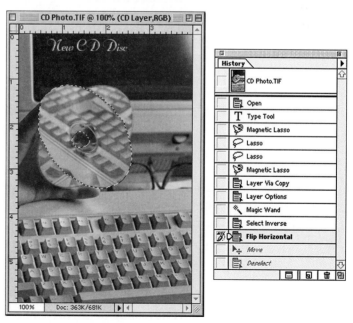

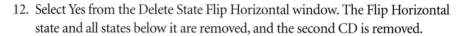

12. Select Yes from the Delete State Flip Horizontal window. The Flip Horizontal state and all states below it are removed, and the second CD is removed.

13. Close the file without saving.

Using the History palette saves time, headaches, and heartburn. As you use it on a variety of files, you will discover the power and value of this tool.

The Contact Sheet

Imagine working on a project with many Photoshop and Illustrator EPS files, supplied by a client with a tight deadline. The task is to color correct all these images with no knowledge of what the images look like. The problem is that there are no proofs of the images for organizing the files.

The Contact Sheet allows the Photoshop user to create one image of all the files in a particular folder. The images can be placed either in a horizontal row or vertical column order. The images can then be viewed like a contact sheet from a photographer.

Using the Contact Sheet

1. Choose File>Automate>Contact Sheet.

2. In the Contact Sheet dialog box, select the Choose button from the Source Folder area. Choose your **Work in Progress** folder from the **SF-Adv Photoshop** folder. Keep the defaults in the rest of the window. If you have only a black-and-white printer available, use Grayscale in the Mode pull-down window. Click OK.

Make certain that there are no folders with a folder, or Photoshop will stop making the Contact Sheet at the first folder.

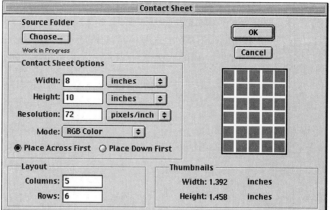

3. The Contact Sheet tool will adjust the thumbnail image size to fit onto the file by processing the files through a Preset Action set. Click OK.

4. After all the images are placed in one file, Select Flatten Image from the Layers palette pull-down menu to save storage space of the file.

5. Save the file as "WIP Contact.TIF" in your **Work in Progress** folder. Print the file, and see all the images on one sheet. Close the file.

Conditional Mode Change

Sometimes a job will contain several kinds of files, and each discrete file type may receive different treatment. For example, there may be RGB and grayscale images in a job that will be printed using traditional lithography. The Conditional Mode Change feature allows an "if/then"-type query: If a file is RGB, change it to CMYK; otherwise leave it alone.

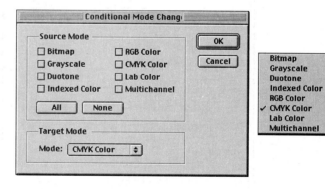

If the majority of your images are light, make certain that your background color in your Tool Bar is set for Black, for easier viewing.

Multi-Page PDF to PSD

Occasionally it may be desirable to convert a PDF document to another format, such as GIF or JPEG for inclusion on a web page. This automation feature opens each page of the PDF file (or the pages you select) into a separate Photoshop document.

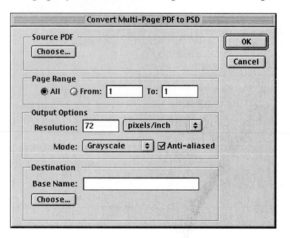

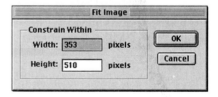

Fit Image

There may be a need to fit images to a specific height/width dimension (meaning to the greater of the two dimensions, with no distortion). Such projects could include catalogs or ads with standard "holes," such as automobiles or real estate. Simply applying this automation can save numerous steps.

This is generally equivalent to resizing the image with Image Sampling turned on. If the target size is larger than the original, unwanted interpolation may result.

Summary

Automation enables us to meet "impossible" client deadlines, deal with complex file issues, and free us from deadly boredom — at the same time it gives us the time to experiment and expand our skills. Tools alone are insufficient, however. They must be combined with appropriate planning of your workflow and continually expanding your knowledge base. Often, taking advantage of automation and shortcuts becomes the difference between productivity and frustration.

CHAPTER 16

SPECIAL EFFECTS

CHAPTER OBJECTIVE:

To learn how to create Photoshop's nearly infinite variety of special effects; to learn how to use special effects using type, line art, and images. By completing Chapter 16, you will:

- Learn how to import an EPS illustration.
- Learn how to create Jungle, Soft "Pillow" type, Type cutouts, and how to carve line art out of the Background.
- Learn about Photo edges, used for creating Vignette borders and Strokes, Rippled borders, Wood Weathered Decoupages, and Burnt Edges.
- Learn how to color images with Duotones, Tritones, and Quadtones.
- Learn how to create a "Pegboard" image.

PROJECTS TO BE COMPLETED:

- Pokey Creek Book Cover
- Retouching the Jones Family Portrait
- Head in the Clouds Ad
- Baby Shower Invitation
- Farm Fresh Logo
- **Photomat**
- **The Fix is in**

Special Effects

Photoshop is capable of creating a nearly infinite variety of special effects. Some can be achieved quickly, while others require several intertwined operations. This chapter demonstrates a few building block techniques that can be combined and varied to create hundreds of unique custom effects for all types of design projects.

Remember that all effects are developed through experimentation. With the skills learned so far, several have already been discovered. Because creativity is serendipitous and hard to duplicate, keep these items in mind:

While working through the exercises in this chapter, be certain to remember that we are only providing examples of what can be done artistically with Photoshop. We strongly encourage you to experiment with these techniques using your own artwork and image elements. These are fun techniques, and can provide hours of educational practice after the course is complete.

- Write down the steps used to create the effect as it's created. At least jot down the steps and values when trying something experimental. The History palette can be a reminder, but it has two drawbacks for this purpose. It doesn't display values in dialog boxes and it only goes back "so far" depending on memory and how many steps it is set to in History Options. Another possibility is to consider recording frequently used effects (such as borders) as Actions in the Actions palette.

- Try to recreate an effect at various resolutions. Some wonderful special effects only work as expected on low or high resolution files. Identify this and develop a work-around if resolution is a problem before wanting to use the effect again.

- Duplicate layers for experimentation. They can then be combined with the original layer using blend modes for additional effects. Also, duplicate original Selection channels before modifying them. The raw selection is often useful to combine with the Blurred, Offset, and Filtered channel to create the finished effect. The original selection remains available to try other possibilities. Consider duplicating the entire file for a worry-free creative environment.

- The History palette and History Brush add a different dimension to creating effects. They record and allow integration of various stages of the process, including Snapshots. Often, special effects work well on one area but destroy the work performed to perfection on another. These tools provide a great deal of freedom and documentation to repeat effects and get them just where they work best.

- Don't be afraid to try things that obviously won't work! Even stuff that "just isn't done," such as applying Sharpen More or Auto Levels. No one knows just what effect a filter or command will have on a particular image until it's tried!

Special Effects Using Type and Line Art

Although Photoshop is an image-editing program, type and line art are often important elements in the design. Line art from vector programs and Photoshop type can be included, edited, and integrated using special effects throughout the design process. The following exercises will demonstrate how type and line art can be manipulated into the image using filters and a combination of Photoshop effects.

About Raster and Vector Images

A fundamental difference between working in Photoshop and a vector-based drawing program such as Illustrator is the scalability of the results. Vector art is abbreviated — even to the extent that a rather elaborate design can be defined by only a few points (and the equations of the curve between them).

Visualize a Photoshop file as a logo printed on a balloon. By adding or subtracting air to the balloon, the logo will enlarge or reduce — usually looking crisper and denser when the balloon is at its proper or smaller size. As the balloon is inflated, the logo loses definition and density. A Photoshop file has the same problem: it won't enlarge or reduce forever without sacrificing quality.

The graphic below illustrates an aliased bitmap against a vector curve. Regardless of how much the image is enlarged, the vector curve will not change in quality, while the bitmap can only get worse. Anti-Aliasing — the softening of the bitmap edges — will help, but eventually it, too, will degrade.

It's not necessary to abandon Photoshop altogether in favor of Illustrator. The two applications coexist well, as shown when the Tropical Interiors logo was imported in the section on Channel Operations.

Importing an EPS Illustration

1. Open **Tropical Interiors.EPS** from the **SF-Adv Photoshop** folder. Set it to Rasterize into an RGB image at 100 ppi, 5″ wide.

2. Choose Image>Canvas Size to enlarge the canvas to 6″ × 2.5″. Anchor the current image in the center.

3. Choose Select>Load Selection, and load Layer 1 Transparency as a selection. Save the selection to a new channel and name it "Type". Deselect.

4. With the RGB composite active, Image>Adjust>Hue/Saturation to turn the logo black by dragging the Lightness slider to the far left.

5. Make certain that the Image Background color is white. Select Flatten Image from the Layers palette menu. Rename the Background layer "Type Layer".

"Distressed" type can be very effective. To invent your own, experiment with Text channels and the Noise and Pixelate filters.

Press Command/Control-F to repeatedly apply the exact same filter. Press Command-Option/Control Alt-F to repeat the same filter but change settings in the dialog box.

6. Save the image as "Tropical Type.PSD" to your **Work in Progress** folder.

Creating "Jungle" Type

1. With the Tropical Type file still open, duplicate the Type layer. On this layer use the following filters: Filter>Pixelate>Crystalize with an Amount of 3, Filter>Blur>Gaussian Blur 2.5 pixels, and Filter>Stylize>Find Edges. Finally, choose Filter>Sharpen>Sharpen More and repeat it nine more times.

2. For a cleaner look, load the Type channel, choose Select>Inverse, and Fill with white.

3. Save the selection as a mask for the background (name it "Background"). Create a New layer. Create an interesting texture on the new layer, such as one from Chapter 12. Start by Filling the layer with White before adding Noise, then use the Blend modes to combine the layers.

4. Save as "Jungle Type.PSD" in your **Work in Progress** folder.

Third-party plug-ins aren't all bad – learning the basics from doing the steps yourself can help you understand how the plug-in works more quickly and enable you to control it. Often, using a combination of manual techniques and plug-ins makes the image better and work time more efficient.

Many of the type effects shown in this book are best used with heavy typefaces. To use a light typeface, work in a higher resolution. Even then avoid fine serif lines that get lost in the pixels.

Creating Soft "Pillow" Type

1. Open **Tropical Type.PSD** if it is not already open.

2. Load the Type channel as a Selection. Feather the selection 4 pixels.

3. Save the new selection. Make the new Alpha 1 channel active.

4. Load the Type channel as a Selection. Choose Select>Inverse and Fill the area with White. Deselect.

5. Click on the RGB Composite channel. In the Layers palette, create a new layer and Fill it with White.

6. Load the Type channel selection and run the Lighting Effects filter. Enter the settings shown below. Use the Alpha 1 channel (feathered type selection) as the Texture channel. Drag the "spotlight" below the Preview window to the lower right corner. Click OK.

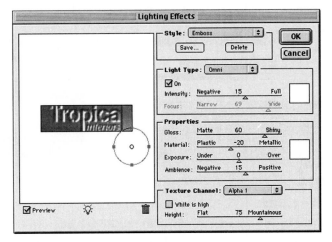

7. Return to the layer and choose Select>Inverse. Delete the background.

8. Colorize the type. Replace the original background, Type Layer, with a textured background and add a drop shadow (using Layer Effects) behind the type.

9. Close the file without saving.

Creating Type Cutouts

1. Open **Sandy Beach.TIF** from the **SF-Adv Photoshop** folder. Double-click the Background layer and rename it "Beach".

2. Place the **Tropical Interiors.EPS** logo into the document and position it on the horizon. Press the Return or Enter key to finish placing. Load the selection Tropical Interiors.EPS Transparency and drag the Tropical Interiors.EPS layer to the trash; we just needed the selection. The Beach layer should be active. Press the Delete key to cut the type out of the image and leave only transparency. Deselect.

3. Add a New layer and position it below the Beach layer. Name it "Shadow" and Fill the layer with Black.

4. Command/Control-click on the Beach layer to load the layer transparency as a selection. Choose Select>Inverse. With the Shadow layer active, Fill the selection with White. Deselect.

5. Choose Filter>Blur>Gaussian Blur 3 pixels. Choose the Move tool and use the Arrow keys to offset the Shadow layer down and right.

Notice that the smaller fine-lined type is engulfed by this effect.

6. In the History palette, return to the "Clear" step and create a new version using Layer Groups. This technique allows the cutout and shadow to be moved anywhere in the image.

7. Close the file without saving.

Carving a Line Art Image Out of the Background

1. Open **Slime.TIF** from the **SF-Adv Photoshop** folder.

2. Create a new Channel and Fill it with White. Choose File>Place **Fleur.EPS,** which is also located in the **SF-Adv Photoshop** folder.

3. Size and position the image, then press the Return key. Deselect. Choose Image>Adjust>Invert.

Cutouts can be used to great effect with two photos instead of using a photo and text. The top layer is cut out of the selection built from the bottom layer. For example, using the shape of a wine glass or house to mask an image of something else.

4. Return to the RGB composite and create a new layer above the Background layer. Name it "Image" and load the Alpha 1 channel as a Selection. Choose Select>Feather 1 pixel and Fill it with Black. Deselect.

5. Choose Filter>Stylize>Emboss. Set the Angle, Height, and Amount desired. This example uses a -45° angle, 3 pixels, and 250% for the Amount.

6. Click OK and set the Blend mode for this layer to Overlay.

7. Load the Alpha 1 channel as a Selection again and choose New Adjustment Layer from the Layer palette menu. Choose Levels for the type of Adjustment layer. In the Levels dialog, drag the shadow and/or midtone slider to the right to darken the inside of the carved area to enhance the effect.

8. Try replacing the background (since it's on an independent layer) to test the effect on different textures. Continue experimenting with this technique by adding a second texture on a new layer for the inside of the black-and-white image using the Alpha channel as a mask.

9. Close the file without saving.

Record each step taken to create a special effect. While it may seem that we stress this point too strongly, we know of a designer who created an engraved text effect which was approved by his client, then spent three weeks trying to recreate the effect for the actual job.

Photo Edges

Photo edges of various types have become quite popular. Though you can buy a selection of photo edges, many of these effects can be created easily in Photoshop.

The first edge that we will create is a mask for a vignette border, which is a soft, graduated edge that was originally created in the photographer's darkroom. You may have seen old photos that used this technique. With minor modifications, a basic vignette border can be used to create a variety of special photo edges.

Remember that all of the techniques used in this section can be applied to a border of any shape, not just a rectangular border. Simply create the initial selection using the Lasso tool instead of the Marquee Tool. They can also be created quickly using Quick Mask instead of channels if no need exists to save the selection effect.

Creating a Vignette Border

1. Open **Hammock.TIF** from the **SF-Adv Photoshop** folder.

2. Choose the Rectangular Marquee tool. Draw a rectangle in the middle of the image as shown below:

3. Choose Select>Feather, and enter a value of 5 pixels.

4. Save the selection, naming it "Edge", then Save the document as "Borders.PSD" to your **Work in Progress** folder.

5. With the RGB composite active, choose Select>Inverse. Fill the selection with White. This is a basic vignette border. Deselect and keep the file open for the next exercise.

Creating a Stroked, Rippled Border

1. Select Revert from the File menu.

2. Duplicate the Edge channel, saved in Step 4 above. On this new channel, choose Filter>Distort>Ocean Ripple. Drag the preview until an edge of the border is visible. Set Size to 5 and Magnitude to 10.

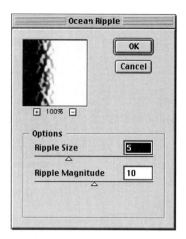

3. Select the RGB composite channel. Load the Alpha 1 channel. Choose Select>Inverse. Fill with White. Deselect.

4. For a variation of this, open the History palette. Click to select the step "Ocean Ripple" and thus return to the stage of this file just after the Ocean Ripple filter was used. Deselect. While active on the Alpha 1 channel, choose Image> Adjust>Levels and drag both Highlight and Shadow sliders toward the center. Click OK.

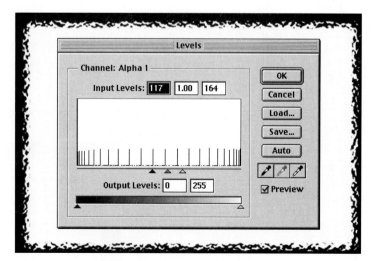

5. Choose the RGB composite and load the Alpha 1 channel as a Selection. Choose Select>Inverse and Fill the selection with White.

6. Choose Select>Inverse again. Choose a light blue for the Foreground color and Stroke this selection using a 5-pixel Width, Center Option.

7. Now we need to select all the border pixels. Choose Select>Modify>Border 5 pixels. With the Magic Wand tool, shift-click on areas of the blue border that were not included, then choose Select>Similar. Subtract from the selection any areas of the image that are included. Access Filter>Stylize>Emboss for just the border using a -45° Angle, 2-pixel Height, and 400% Amount.

8. Choose Image>Adjust>Hue/Saturation to uniformly colorize the embossed border as desired.

9. Make the Base layer transparent by double-clicking on it. Click OK to Save As Layer 0. Build a layer behind it and create the drop shadow. Use the Alpha 1 channel to trim the bordered image and generate the shadow.

Creating a Wood Weathered Decoupage

1. Select Revert from the File menu.

2. Activate the Edge channel. Drag a marque inside the area. Feather it 10 pixels. Choose Select>Inverse and Fill with Black to contract the transition area. Deselect.

3. Choose Filter>Pixelate>Mezzotint and select Long Strokes from the pop-up menu. Click OK.

4. Return to the RGB composite and add a new layer. Press D to return to default colors and select Filter>Render>Clouds.

5. Choose Filter>Blur>Motion Blur. Set the Angle to 0° with 150 for the Distance.

6. Add texture by choosing Filter>Texture>Craquelure and use the settings shown below:

7. Choose Image>Adjust>Hue/Saturation. Click "Colorize" and set Hue to 36, Saturation to 32, and Lightness to -25.

8. While still on the Texture layer, load the Edge channel as a Selection, choose Select>Inverse, and click on the Add Layer Mask icon in the Layers palette.

9. For a little extra ambiance, duplicate Layer 1 and delete its Layer mask. Choose Hard Light for the Blend mode and decrease the Opacity to about 25%.

10. Add a drop or carved shadow to enhance the depth of this effect.

11. Leave the file open for the next exercise.

Creating Burnt Edges

1. Select Revert from the File menu. Activate the Edge channel.

2. Choose Filter>Pixelate>Crystalize. Set Cell Size to 15.

3. With the Magic Wand tool, Tolerance set to 4, click on the white area inside, then shift-click on the solid black area of the channel. Choose Select>Inverse to get a selection of just the border edge. Choose Filter>Pixelate>Pointillize with a setting of 5.

4. Gaussian Blur the channel 0.5 pixels. Deselect.

5. With the RGB composite active, load the Edge channel and choose Select>Inverse. Press Command/Control-I to Invert the colors of the image outside the border.

6. Choose Select>Inverse again. Choose Select>Modify>Contrast, 16 pixels. Feather this selection 12 pixels and choose Select>Inverse. The outside edge should be selected with most of the border included in the feather.

7. To combine this with the Edge selection, choose Select>Load Selection. Choose the Edge channel and click to Intersect with the current selection. Select>Modify>Expand 1 pixel. Fill with Black.

8. Choose Image>Adjust>Hue/Saturation; click Colorize, then set Hue to 35, Saturation to 100, and Lightness to 10. Deselect.

9. Load the Edge channel. Expand 1 pixel. Save this as a New Selection.

To intersect a channel selection with the current selection, hold Command Option-Shift/Control-Alt - Shift and click on the other channel.

10. Load the Edge channel again and access Select>Inverse. Feather 6 pixels. Load the Alpha 1 channel to intersect with this selection. Fill with Black.

11. For a variation of this, choose the Crystallize step in the History palette. Apply Threshold to get a hard, jagged edge, then continue from Step 4.

12. Close the image without saving.

Special Effects and Images

Images often work great on their own. There are times, however, when your message can be made more effective by applying special effects to images.

Coloring an Image with Duotones, Tritones, and Quadtones

In the real world, the budget doesn't always allow for process color printing. But even when it does, using a Duotone, Tritone, or Quadtone can add richness, quality, and a dramatic mood to the image and the entire design piece.

Duotones are frequently used to reproduce an antique photographic method known as Sepia tone, but any combination that suits the mood of the piece is possible. If color tinting is the design objective, choose a color that most effectively communicates the feeling of the image and message being conveyed. For example, red conveys action, danger, or heat, while blue often represents calmness, security, or cold. Printing a black-on-black Duotone dramatically increases the tonal range of the image; Ansel Adams prints are often reproduced using this method. Since one grayscale emphasizes the highlight-to-midtone range and the second emphasizes the shadows, depth and intensity is added without obscuring detail.

Duotones can be tricky to output. Talk to the service provider before using them in a job to prevent problems before they occur.

Tritones and Quadtones can be used to add color tinting to an image as well but are most often used to create a full range grayscale look. This is accomplished by printing the image with process inks using separations that are generated in perfect gray balance throughout the image. The effect is manufactured by manipulating the curves of each grayscale version of the image in multichannel mode to capture a specific tonal range and balance for each ink. Using Photoshop's Duotone mode, it's possible to create most of these effects by manipulating the ink coverage curves.

The key to colorizing part of an image using Duotones is to isolate the part of the image that you want to be colored, and restrict the range of grays for that area. For example, if by restricting most of one image to grays in the 0–127 range, and the grays you want colored to the 128–255 range, you can add color to only the areas in the upper range of grays. The only catch to this procedure is that the lower range of grays must be inverted in order to create a smooth Duotone curve.

Colorizing with Duotones

1. Open **Berries.TIF** from the **SF-Adv Photoshop** folder. Choose Select>Color Range to select the red raspberries within the image.

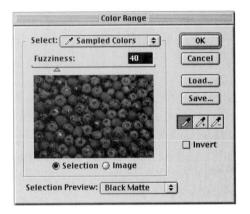

2. Save the newly created selection. Deselect. Activate the new channel Alpha #1. Choose Filter>Noise>Dust and Scratches to remove any unwanted areas from the channel. Slide the Radius until it looks clean.

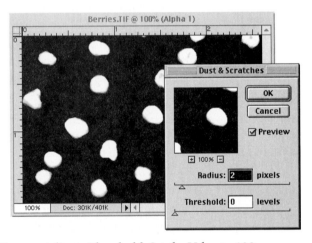

Be certain to completely select the raspberries, or you will end up with hard edges between the colors.

3. Choose Image>Adjust>Threshold. Set the Value to 128.

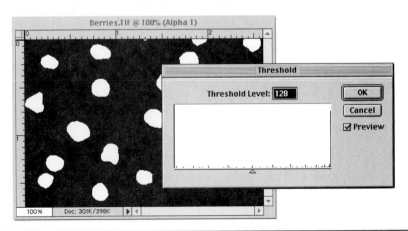

4. Activate the RGB composite channel. Choose Image>Mode>Grayscale. Images for Duotones mode must first be converted to Grayscale.

5. Choose Image>Adjust>Levels. Move the white Output slider (be certain to use the Output slider, not the Input slider) to 128.

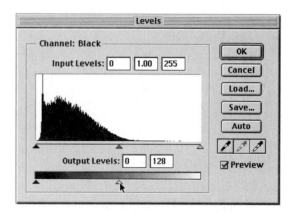

6. Load the Alpha 1 channel as a Selection. Press Command/Control-I. This will ensure that the raspberries encompass a different range of grays than the blueberries. In addition, inverting the map makes it easier to set a Duotone curve to cover the entire dynamic range of the raspberries.

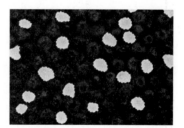

7. Choose Mode>Duotone. Make certain that Type is set to Duotone. Click on the color swatch for Ink 1 and change it to Pantone 2757. Click on the Ink 1 Curve icon and drag the Midpoint (50%) down to 0. The curve should look like the one shown below:

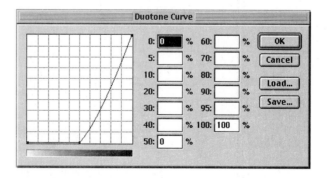

8. Click the Ink 2 color swatch and change its color to Pantone 202. Click the Ink 2 Curve icon. Drag the Midpoint (50%) and Shadow (100%) point to 0, and the Highlight (0%) to 100. Click OK.

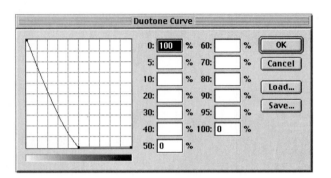

9. Choose Select>Inverse, then select Image>Adjust>Levels to adjust the Highlights and shadows of the blueberries. Drag the Highlight and Midtone sliders as shown below:

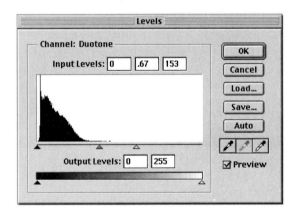

10. Choose Select>Inverse and Image>Adjust>Levels again. Drag the Highlight slider slightly in to adjust Highlights, increase the range of Shadows, and add detail to the image.

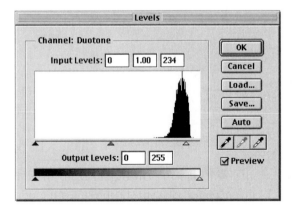

Note: Inverting the image requires that the White and Gamma slider move to the left to darken the image.

11. Close the file without saving.

The Writing on the Wall

1. Create a New document 300 pixels wide by 100 pixels high in RGB, with a Transparent background. Press D to set the colors to their defaults.

2. Select All. With Black as the Foreground color, choose Edit>Stroke. Set the Width to 6 pixels and use the Inside option. Deselect.

3. Change the Canvas Size to 150 pixels wide by 50 pixels high. Anchor the image in the upper left corner. After clicking OK, a warning will appear that doing this will crop the image. Click to proceed.

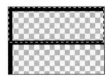

4. Select all of the image and choose Edit>Define Pattern. Close the file without saving.

5. Create a New RGB document, 150 pixels wide by 100 pixels high; set Contents to Transparent.

6. Fill the image with the defined pattern. Select the top half of the image, making certain that the Marquee goes through the middle horizontal line.

7. Choose Filter>Other>Offset. Set the Horizontal Offset to 75 pixels, and check Wrap Around.

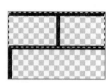

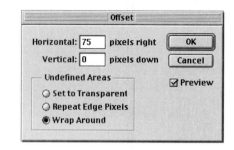

8. Deselect. Choose the Offset filter again. This time use 25 pixels for Vertical and Horizontal.

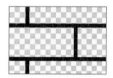

9. Duplicate Layer 1 and name it "Mortar". Choose Select>Load Selection. Choose "Mortar Transparency" as the Channel and check to Invert. Fill this selection with White.

10. Deselect. Choose Filter>Blur>Gaussian Blur 1 pixel.

11. Adjust Filter>Stylize>Emboss to a -40 degree Angle, 2 pixels Height, and Amount of 75. Change the Layer Blending mode to Hard Light.

12. Create a New layer below the embossed layer. Name it "Brick". Fill the layer with White. Select Filter>Noise>Add Noise. Choose Monochrome and Gaussian options and set Amount at 500. Adjust Filter>Stylize>Diffuse using Lighten Only.

13. Choose Filter>Blur>Gaussian Blur at 0.5 pixel Radius. Adjust Filter>Stylize>Emboss to a -40 degree Angle, 2 pixels Height, and Amount of 25.

14. Choose Image>Adjust>Hue/Saturation. Check "Colorize" and set Hue to 10, Saturation to 60, and Lightness to -30.

15. Activate Layer 1. Access Select>Load Selection. Choose Layer 1 transparency as the channel. Activate the Brick layer and choose Image>Adjust>Desaturate.

16. Choose Flatten from the Layers palette menu. Select All and Define it all as a Pattern.

17. Create a New RGB document, 5″ × 5″, 100 ppi with a White background.

18. Fill the new document with the pattern.

19. With the Type Mask tool, click on the lower left corner. In the dialog box, choose ATC Monsoon, 150 pt., and type "USA". Drag to center the type near the bottom.

20. Choose Select>Transform Selection and drag to stretch the type vertically almost to the top. Save this selection as "USA image" to your **Work in Progress** folder.

21. Open **Mt. Rush.TIF** from the **SF-Adv Photoshop** folder. Marquee just around Washington's head as shown and select Edit>Copy.

22. Close **Mt. Rush.TIF** without saving. Load the USA image channel. Choose Edit>Paste Into and position the image so that both eyes clear the mask.

23. While on this layer, choose Filters>Brush Strokes>Spatter (Radius 7, Smoothness 5) and Artistic>Cutout (# of Levels 4, Edge Simplicity 4, Edge Fidelity 2).

24. Use the Magic Wand tool on the Background layer with a Tolerance of 10. Click on the brick, then choose Select>Grow and Select>Similar. Save this selection.

25. Activate Layer 1. Choose Filter>Render>Lighting Effects. Apply these settings:

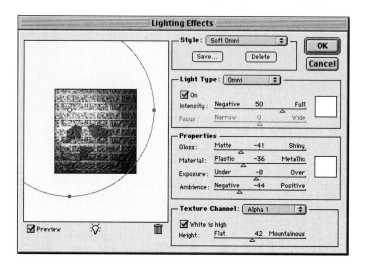

26. Choose Filter>Fade Lighting Effects. Use the Luminosity Mode at 40% Opacity.

27. Close the file without saving.

Creating a "Pegboard" Image

1. Create a New Grayscale document, 20 pixels wide and 20 pixels high with a White background and a resolution of 150 ppi.

2. Choose the Elliptical Marquee tool, then double-click on it to open the Options palette. Change the Style to Fixed Size. Enter Height and Width at 18 pixels.

3. Hold Option/Alt and click in the center of the image to position the circular selection. Fill with Black. Deselect. Press Command/Control-I to Invert the colors in the image.

4. Choose Select>All. Choose Edit>Define Pattern. Close the document without saving.

5. Open **Beach Boy.TIF** from the **SF-Adv Photoshop** folder.

6. Choose Image>Image Size. Change the pixel dimensions to 800 by 800 pixels.

7. Choose Filter>Pixelate>Mosaic. Set Cell Size to 20 pixels. Save the image as "Pegboard.TIF" in your **Work in Progress** folder.

8. Create a new channel for this image. Select Edit>Fill and Fill with Pattern at 100%. Rename the channel "Original".

9. Duplicate the Original channel. Name it "Shadow". Choose Filter>Blur> Gaussian Blur with a setting of 2 pixels.

10. Duplicate the Shadow channel and rename the copy "Highlight".

11. Press D to change the Background color to Black. Choose the Move tool and offset the Shadow channel down one pixel and to the right one pixel. Switch to the Highlight channel. Offset it up one pixel and to the left one pixel.

12. Choose Image>Calculations. Add the Original channel to the Shadow channel; make certain that the Invert checkbox is checked for the Shadow channel. Set Scale to 2.

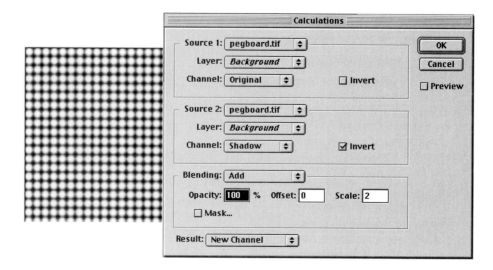

13. Choose Image>Calculations again. This time, choose Shadow for the Source 1 channel and Highlight for the Source 2 channel. Invert should be checked for the Shadow channel. Select Add Blending mode, 100% Opacity, and a Scale of 2. The Result should be a New Channel.

14. Activate the Alpha 2 channel created in Step 13. Choose Image>Adjust>Auto Levels to flatten the tones.

15. Choose Image>Calculations. Select the Alpha 1 and Alpha 2 channels respectively. Neither should be inverted. Set the Blending mode to Add, Scale of 2. The Result should be a New Channel. Click OK. Rename the channel "Bump Map".

16. Delete the channels Highlight, Shadow, Alpha 1, and Alpha 2. Original and Bump Map should be the only additional channels remaining.

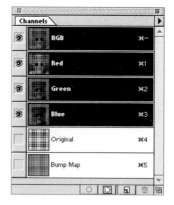

17. Activate the RGB Composite channel. Choose Filter>Render>Lighting Effects. Change the Light Type to Omni. Move the center of the light to the upper left corner of the window and drag the bottom handle down and to the right to make the light as big as possible. Click the color swatch in the Light Type section and change it to White. Select Bump Map as the Texture Channel and use the settings shown below:

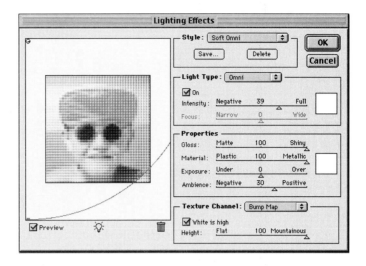

18. Load the Original channel as a Selection. Choose Select>Inverse. Fill the selection with Black. Deselect.

19. Open the original **Beach Boy.TIF** image from the **SF-Adv Photoshop** folder. Select Image>Image Size. Resize the image to 16 pixels by 16 pixels.

20. Double-click the Background layer of the **Beach Boy.TIF** image, then click OK to change its name to Layer 0 and thus allow transparency in the layer.

21. Select Image>Canvas Size. Change the size of the image to 20 pixels by 20 pixels. Select all of this image and choose Edit>Define Pattern. Close the Beach Boy image without saving.

22. Create a new layer in the **Pegboard.TIF** image. Fill the layer with the pattern. Change the Layer Blending mode to Darken and the Layer Opacity to 80%.

23. Choose Image>Adjust>Levels. Drag the White slider down to 175 to lighten the layer.

24. Select Flatten Image from the Layers palette menu. Choose Image>Adjust> Brightness & Contrast. Set both the Brightness and the Contrast to 20.

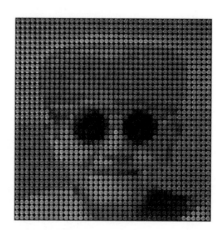

25. Close the file without saving.

3D Mt. Rushmore

1. Open **Mt. Rush.TIF** from the **SF-Adv Photoshop** folder.

2. Reset the Elliptical Marquee style to Normal. Using the Elliptical Marquee, select Washington's head. Select Edit>Copy.

3. Choose File>New. The dimensions are already preset. Click OK. Choose Edit>Paste.

4. Erase areas of the sky that were included, but leave pieces of surrounding rock.

5. Choose Filter>Render>3D Transform. Choose the Spherical tool and drag a circle around the entire head. Use the Selection and Direct Selection tools to position and mold the wire frame.

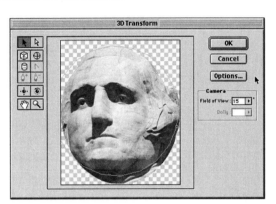

6. With the Track Ball tool, drag up and to the left to achieve this perspective.

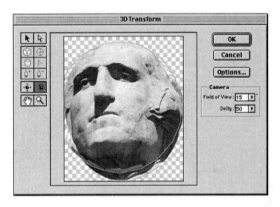

7. Click OK. In the Image window, perform a little retouching under Washington's chin to blend the rock.

8. Select All and choose Edit>Copy. Close this file without saving.

9. In the original **Mt. Rush.TIF**, Deselect and choose Edit>Paste. Perform a little retouching to blend the 3-D image into the rock. Check "Use all Layers" in the Rubber Stamp Options palette to source the background while painting on this new layer. Rename this layer "Washington".

10. With the Magnetic Lasso tool, select Jefferson's head, avoiding Washington. Choose Edit>Copy and Copy the selection to the clipboard. Open a new file and choose Edit>Paste.

Using the Track Ball tool requires only three things: practice, practice, and more practice. Work at it for long enough, and it will start to feel natural.

11. Choose Filter>Render>3D Transform. Select the Cube tool and drag to encompass Jefferson's head. Use the Direct Selection tool to move the lowest, front Corner point, aligning the front edge of the cube with his nose.

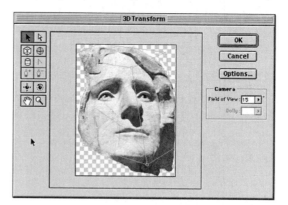

12. With the Track Ball tool, drag up and left to rotate the cube perspective.

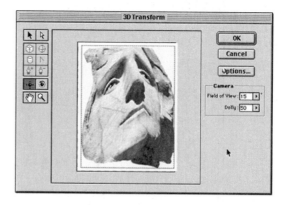

13. Click OK, and retouch the image a little to blend where necessary with the rock. Select All and choose Edit>Copy. Close this file without saving.

14. In the original **Mt. Rush.TIF**, choose Edit>Paste Into for the original selection left behind. Deselect and retouch around the edges with "Use all Layers" checked for the Rubber Stamp tool.

15. Select the Lincoln head with a combination of Lasso tools, including the blocks to the right of his chin. Choose Edit>Copy. Open a new file and select Edit>Paste.

16. Choose Filter>Render>3D Transform. Select the Cylindrical tool and drag to select most of Lincoln's head. The Cylindrical tool alone allows Anchor Points to be added and deleted. Adjust one new point slightly toward the shape of his chin.

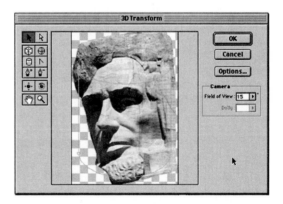

17. With the Track Ball tool, drag up and right to rotate the cylinder perspective to make it appear as if he's cocking his head. Shift the image with the Pan Camera tool to align it somewhat with the existing hair and beard. Click OK.

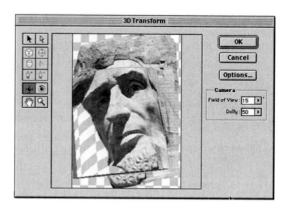

18. Retouch the image slightly. Most retouching will be performed back on the original image. Just erase solid gray areas along the bottom and left. Choose Select>All and Edit>Copy. Close this file without saving.

19. On the original **Mt. Rush.TIF**, choose Edit>Paste and position Lincoln to align him over himself. Use both the Rubber Stamp and History Brush to retouch the hair and beard into the Background layer. For the History Brush, use the Lasso state just before copying Lincoln from this file.

20. Now that the heads of several great presidents have been turned, the image is ready for additional special effects as desired. Close the file without saving.

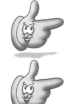

Complete Project F: Photomat

Complete Project G: The Fix Is In

REVIEW 2

CHAPTERS 9 THROUGH 16:

In Chapters 9 through 16, we learned how to use the Blur and Sharpen filters, the Remapping commands, how to apply Shadows and other Layer effects, create patterns and textures, how to use the Render filters, how to import and export files, how to work efficiently when performing color correction and file manipulation, and how to create a variety of Photoshop special effects. After completing the second half of Advanced Photoshop, you should:

- Know how to use the Blur and Sharpen filters to save bad scans or damaged photographs. You should know how to use Motion Blur and Radial Blur. You should realize the importance of Unsharp Mask (USM), and know how to use it properly. You should also understand Sharpening with Luminosity Only.

- Understand the Remapping commands, and know how to use them to map or recolor pixels. You should know how the Invert command creates the photographic negative of an image. You should understand the Equalize commands, and know the difference between the Threshold and Posterize commands.

- Know how to add special effects to layers. You should know how to create Multimedia buttons. You should know how to apply a drop shadow and inner glow to a Type layer.

- Understand how to create patterns and textures as backgrounds for almost any Photoshop job. You should understand basic tiling and alternating tiles. You should also know how to create Offset Graphic and Rubber Stamp tiles.

- Know how to use the Render filters to create specialized blending patterns and entire lighting schemes for images. You should have learned how the Clouds and Difference Clouds filters generate random color values based on the Foreground and Background colors.

- Understand how to import an Illustrator or Freehand file into a Photoshop document. You should know the two different file formats for use on the World Wide Web, and fully understand which is the appropriate format to use.

- Know how the Actions palette allows the recording of a series of commands for playback and application to files or file groups. You should know how to use the Contact Sheet. You should also understand the Conditional Mode Change.

Project A: Pokey Creek Book Cover

Book covers are comprised of a number of elements. While they normally would not be created entirely in Photoshop, it is a valid alternative to using the typical page layout application. This project will provide you with good experience in using a variety of features of the program.

Ultimately, the book cover will be displayed on a web page, displayed with other titles in the series on a large-format poster, and printed using traditional lithography.

Correcting Color Images

1. Open **Uncle Otie.TIF** from the **SF-Adv Photoshop** folder.

2. Notice the yellow cast in the image. Select Image>Adjust>Curves. With the White Point Eyedropper tool, select the snow at the top of the mountain.

3. Using the Black Point Eyedropper tool, select the darkest area in Otie's pants. Lock the quarter and three-quarter tone points. Slightly adjust the curve to lighten the midtone range.

Note that the yellow cast has been corrected, and no further correction is required.

4. Save the image as a TIFF file to your **Work in Progress** folder. Name it "Uncle Otie Corrected.TIF". Close the file.

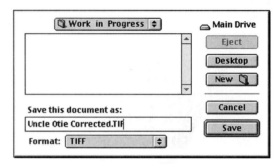

5. Open **Pokey.TIF** from the **SF-Adv Photoshop** folder. Notice that the image has a decided magenta cast.

6. Select Image>Adjust>Curves. Use the White Point Eyedropper tool to select the snow; use the Black Point Eyedropper tool to select the darkest shadows in the grass near the foreground of the image. Lock the midtone and raise the quarter tone to improve the contrast.

The water still has a decided magenta cast.

7. Select Image>Adjust>Curves. Adjust the Green channel to remove the cast from the water.

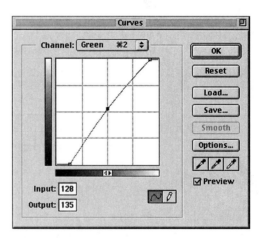

8. Save the image to your **Work in Progress** folder, and name it "Pokey Corrected.TIF". Close the file.

Even though we work in RGB due to the larger color gamut, we often "think better" in CMYK, and have tools available for specifying color in that mode. This is perfectly all right. The computer will perform the translation.

Creating a New Image

1. Create a New RGB document with a White background. Make it 11.5″ wide by 8″ high. Set the resolution to 100 ppi.

2. Click on the Foreground Color swatch. In the lower right corner of the Color Picker, change the Foreground color to 100 C; 0 M; 100 Y; and 40 K.

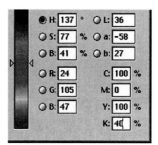

3. Activate the Swatches palette. Click the blank area at the end of the palette to add the Green channel to the palette so that you can select it as needed.

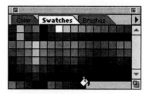

4. Fill the Background layer with your newly created Green channel.

5. Double-click the Rectangular Marquee tool. In the Options palette, change Style to Fixed Size. Change Width to 100 and Height to 800. (Note: at 100 ppi, this is equal to 1″ x 8″.)

6. Add a New layer to the image; it will become the book cover spine. With the Spine layer active, click anywhere on the image; Fill the selection with Black.

7. If the black bar is no longer selected, press Command/Control-A to Select All. Cut and Paste the black bar; this will center it perfectly within the layer. Make certain that the entire image is visible before you Paste.

8. Turn off the Background layer and click on the Spine layer. Click on the Green channel that you added earlier to the Swatches palette to change the Foreground color.

9. Activate the Vertical Type tool. Click in the image. Change the Font to ATCCoconuts ExtraBold. Change Size to 25 pixels. Make certain that Anti-Aliased is checked, and that Auto Kern is unchecked. Check the Rotate box. In all capital letters type "LIFE AT POKEY CREEK".

10. Double-click the T icon in the layer, and change the kerning between characters until you are satisfied with the results.

A single line of vertical type will automatically center in the layer.

11. Make certain that the Type layer is active. Activate the Move tool, and reposition the type to the top of the spine, centered horizontally.

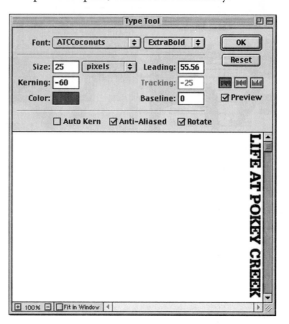

12. Activate the Vertical Type tool again and click on the image. Keep the settings the same. In all capital letters type "BAUER". To make this type slightly lighter, click on the Color swatch in the Type dialog box, and change the Luminance Value (the "L" in "L*a*b") to 46. This lightens the type color without changing the Hue or the current Foreground color.

13. With the BAUER layer selected, activate the Move tool and reposition the type at the bottom of the spine, centered below the book title.

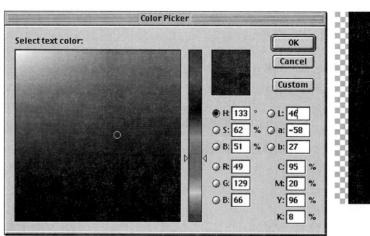

14. With the Spine layer selected, link the two Type layers by clicking in the second box.

15. Turn on the Background layer. Save the image as "Pokey Creek Book Cover.PSD" to your **Work in Progress** folder.

Adding Images

1. Open **Uncle Otie Corrected.TIF** from your **Work in Progress** folder and Select All. Copy the image to the clipboard, and Close the document. Make certain that the Info palette is open and visible on the desktop.

2. Select Edit>Paste. Name the layer "Back Cover Image".

3. With the Back Cover Image layer selected, choose Edit>Transform Numeric. Scale the image 75%.

4. Position the image with the Move tool so that it is centered in the left panel.

5. With the Back Cover Image layer selected, choose Layer>Effects>Inner Shadow. Change the Angle to 135° and the Distance and Blur to 9 pixels. Leave the Use Global Angle box checked.

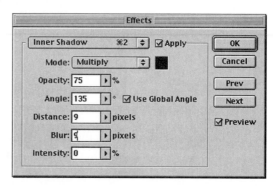

6. Turn on all layers. Save the image.

7. Open **Pokey Corrected.TIF** from your **Work in Progress** folder. Select All, then Copy the image to the clipboard. Close the image, then select Edit>Paste. Name the layer "Front Cover Image".

8. With the Move tool, move the image to the upper right corner of the cover, obscuring all of the Green in that corner.

9. With the Front Cover Image layer active, choose Edit>Transform>Scale. Press the Shift key while scaling, and scale the image to fill the layer vertically. Drag the layer so that it is below the Spine layer.

Never, never, never do this in real life! You're reducing the image data, which would deteriorate the quality of the printed image. Normally, you'd rescan the image with more resolution.

10. Double-click the Rectangular Marquee tool. In the Options palette change the Style to Normal. Select the left half of the image, intersecting the spine.

11. Press the Delete key to remove the left half of the image. Deselect and Save the file. Activate the Front Cover Image layer. Select Edit>Purge>Clipboard.

Adding Type

1. In the Swatches palette, select the Green channel that we created for this job.

2. Activate the Type tool and click near the top of the right panel in the image. Change the Font to ATCCoconuts ExtraBold, Size to 125 pixels, and Leading to 100. Make certain that Anti-Aliasing is on and Auto Kern is off. Click the Center Alignment button. In all capital letters type (including the returns):

LIFE
AT
POKEY
CREEK

3. Use the Move tool to center the type in the top of the right panel, as shown below:

4. Select Layer>Effects>Drop Shadow. Notice that the drop shadow Angle is set to the Global Angle that you changed earlier (135°). Set the Distance to 8 pixels, the Blur to 4 pixels, and the Intensity to 4 percent.

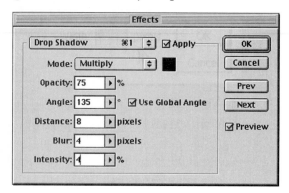

5. Click the Type tool in the bottom center of the right panel. Make certain that Font is still set to ATCCoconuts ExtraBold. Change Size to 45 pixels. In all caps, type "BY OTIE BAUER". Reposition the type if necessary.

6. Select Layer>Effects>Drop Shadow and apply the settings Distance 4 pixels, Blur 2 pixels, Intensity 4% (to take into effect the smaller size) to the BY OTIE BAUER layer.

7. With the Type tool, click in the middle of the left panel below the image. Set Font to ATCCoconuts ExtraBold, Color to Black, Size and Leading to 25 pixels, and click the Centered Alignment radio button. In the Type box, in upper and lower case, type (with returns):

Otie Bauer, the author
at home in Pokey Creek

8. Center the type below the image.

9. Save the image before closing or Save and proceed to the next section.

Prepare Files for Output

Now that you have a Photoshop file, you need to prepare a file for the printer and other distribution. Save all files to your **Work in Progress** folder.

Preparing Files for RGB-savvy Printers

1. Choose File>Save a Copy and select TIFF from the Format drop-down menu. Name the file "PCC_RGB.TIF".

2. Leave the file open for the next operation.

Preparing Files for the Web

1. From Image>Image Size, change the resolution to 72 ppi.

2. Choose File>Save a Copy and select JPEG from the Format drop-down menu. Name the file "PCC.JPG".

3. Choose an appropriate compression level. Greater compression (the lower the number) discards more data. Less compression results in a better-looking photo, but it loads much slower.

4. Leave the file open for the next operation.

Preparing Files for Traditional Lithographic Printing

1. Revert the file (File>Revert).

2. Choose Image>Mode>CMYK.

3. Choose File>Save a Copy and select TIFF from the Format drop-down menu. Name the file "PCC_CMY.TIF".

4. Close the file without saving.

Notes:

Project B: Retouching the Jones Family Portrait

This is a portrait of an extended family, taken on location. Although it is an excellent photograph, there are several areas that need attention. The first step in any successful project is to analyze the image and decide what needs to be done. In this case, three major changes will be made as well as general cleanup. The white sweater is very distracting, the foot at the left edge of the picture was distorted by the wide angle lens used to take the picture, and Gina, the woman holding the baby on the right, was unable to maintain a good pose due to the activity of a small child who was not really interested in having his portrait taken.

This photo could reasonably be included on the family's web page, or used for a short-run greeting card. In either case, it might be output to a RGB savvy printer.

Fixing the Sweater

1. Open **The Joneses.PSD** from the **SF-Adv Photoshop** folder. Rename the background layer "Jones".

2. Use the Lasso tool to draw a rough selection around the sweater. Don't worry about getting it close for now.

3. Add an Adjustment layer (Command/Control-click the layer) for Hue and Saturation. Set it to colorize and adjust the color by sliding first the Hue then the Saturation and Lightness sliders until the color of the sweater fits well with the overall color harmony of the group.

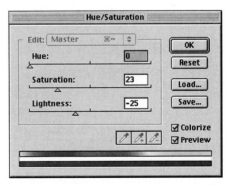

4. Select a soft edge brush. Type D to set the default colors and type X to toggle between Foreground and Background until Black is the Foreground color.

5. Making certain that the Hue/Saturation Adjustment layer is active. Use the soft-edge Black paintbrush to remove any color change that overlapped the boundaries of the sweater. As you can see by the icon in the Layer stack, the color change takes effect wherever white pixels appear on the Adjustment layer and not where the layer is filled with black. In this respect, Adjustment layers work just like Layer masks. If you make a mistake while editing the Adjustment layer,

type X to toggle to white, and paint over your error. In this way, the color of the sweater can be undetectably altered.

Podiatric Plastic Surgery

1. Make another loose selection with the Lasso tool — this time around the foot in the left Foreground. Be certain to include some of the carpet along with the foot since it will be needed to cover the original one. Copy the selected area. (Did you remember to make Jones the active layer?)

2. Paste the foot onto its own layer. Name this layer "Foot". Reduce the Opacity of the layer to 50% to allow a view of the underlying image.

3. Type Command/Control-T to activate Free Transform. Hold down the Shift key to maintain proportion and resize the foot to be just a little smaller. (A little goes a long way here.) Rotate the layer a small amount to the right. Move the resized and rotated foot until it is in a natural position and press the Enter key. Return the Opacity to 100%.

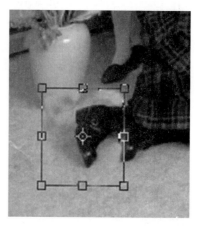

4. Add a Layer mask to the Foot layer. Use a soft edge paintbrush and black-and-white paint to blend the edges until a natural look is achieved. (Be certain that the Mask icon is active in the Layer stack when editing Layer masks.)

5. Merge the layer with the Background layer.

Picture Perfect Posture

1. Use the Lasso tool to draw a rough selection — this time around the legs of Mrs. Jones, the woman in the middle. Be certain not to get too close, because plenty of background will be needed for this step.

Even though both sets of legs now are identical, the overall look is enhanced. Identical sets of well posed legs are less distracting than the original awkward pose.

2. Copy and Paste her legs to a new layer. Name this new layer "Legs". Reduce the Opacity to 50%. Using the Move tool, cover Gina's legs with Mrs. Jones's legs. You can line them up by using the furniture as a guide.

3. Return the Opacity to 100% and add a Layer mask. You should be an old hand at this by now. Change back and forth between black-and-white and change brush sizes as needed to achieve a natural looking result.

Finishing

1. Using the Oval Marquee, select an oval around the group on the Jones layer. Feather the selection about 40 - 50 pixels and Invert the selection.

2. Add an Adjustment layer for levels.

3. Move the Midtone slider to the right. As you can see, this gives the effect of toning down the edges of the photograph in the same manner in which a custom printer tones down the edges in a darkroom.

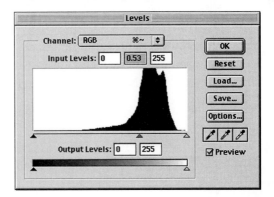

4. Move this layer above the Foot layer so that the changes affect that layer as well.

5. Add a New layer, name it "spotting", and move it to the top of the stack.

6. Set the Rubber Stamp tool to Use All Layers. Remove any dust spots, especially the one on the sweater. Since this file is sized to reproduce only at 3.5″ × 5″, there is not enough resolution to retouch faces, and because of the small size, facial lines won't show very much. If this file were reproduced at 10″ × 14″, the file size would be about 100 MB, and facial detail should be retouched.

7. Save the file to your Work in Progress folder as "The Jones.PSD". Close the file, or continue with the next section.

Prepare Files for Output

Now that you have a Photoshop file, you need to prepare a file for the printer and for other distribution. Save all files to your **Work in Progress** folder.

Preparing Files for RGB-savvy Printers

1. Choose File>Save a Copy and select TIFF from the Format drop-down menu. Name the file "Jones_RGB.TIF".

2. Leave the file open for the next operation.

Preparing Files for the Web

1. From Image>Image Size, change the Resolution to 72 ppi.

2. Choose File>Save a Copy and select JPEG from the Format drop-down menu. Name the file "Jones.JPG".

3. Choose an appropriate compression level. Greater compression (the lower the number) discards more data. Less compression results in a better-looking photo, but it loads much slower.

4. Close the file without saving.

Project C: Head in the Clouds Ad

This ad for Tropical Suites will be used in a variety of different formats. It's going to be used in the Tropical Suites web site, in addition to publication in national magazines, and will also be used as in-room promotion in each of the ten hotels in this small chain. Because there are few hotels in the chain, promotional posters will be printed in small quantities using RGB-savvy printers. The ads will be run in black and white in major metropolitan newspapers.

Creating a Density Mask

1. Open **Hammock.TIF** from the **SF-Adv Photoshop** folder.

2. Activate the Channels palette. Duplicate the Blue channel and rename it "Hammock Mask".

3. Select Image>Adjust Levels. Level the image to create a mask; eliminate the clouds in the upper right, and try to maintain as much detail in the hammock as possible. The Shadow Input level will be about 25. Click on the sky in the upper left to set the Highlight (about 103).

4. Gaussian Blur the channel 0.3 pixels to soften the edges.

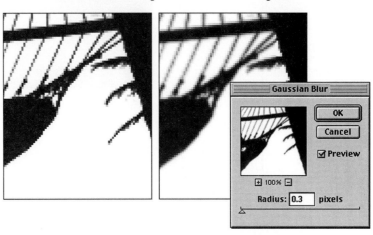

5. Press Command/Control-Tilde (~) to return to the Composite channel.

6. Save the image as "Head in the Clouds Ad.PSD" to your **Work in Progress** folder.

Creating a Composite Image

1. Open **Work.TIF** from the **SF-Adv Photoshop** folder.

2. Activate the Layers palette. Drag the Background layer onto the Hammock image. Close the **Work.TIF** image.

3. Scale the new layer, Layer 1, using Edit>Transform>Numeric. Scale to 55%.

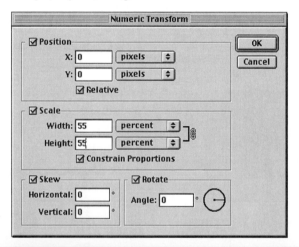

4. Activate the Channels palette and load the Hammock Mask channel as a Selection. Activate Layer 1 and choose Layer>Add Layer Mask>Reveal Selection.

5. Activate the Move tool. Click the Layer 1 Image icon.

When you click on the image thumbnail, the Selection icon, next to the Eye icon, will switch to the Paintbrush icon.

6. Notice the Link icon between the Image icon and the Image Mask icon of Layer 1. Click on the Link icon to unlink the Layer image from the Image mask.

7. Move the **Work.TIF** image so that it is centered above the hammock.

8. Turn off the Background layer. Choose Layer>Disable Layer Mask. A red "X" will appear through the Layer Mask icon, and the mask will no longer be applied to the layer.

9. Activate the Paths palette. Draw a closed path around the background surrounding the man's head and shoulders. We'll use this path to delete the background around his head. From the Paths palette menu, choose Make Selection.

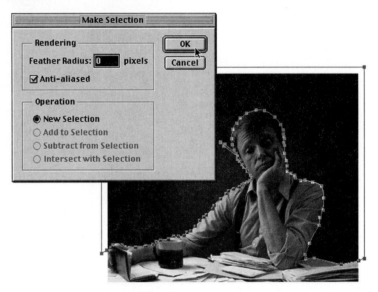

Turn off Paths from the Paths palette menu and press Delete. If any Background color remains outside the selection, use the Lasso tool (while holding the Shift key down) to modify the selection. Make certain that the Background color is White. Press Delete.

10. Deselect, then choose Layer>Enable Layer Mask with Layer 1 active to turn the Layer mask back on. Turn the Background back on.

11. Select the Move tool. Reposition the Work Image layer, but not the Layer mask, so that the composite resembles the image below:

12. Activate the Lasso tool. Select the area below the hammock; include part of the calculator. Feather the selection 6 pixels and Delete.

13. Rename the layer "Office" and Save the file to your **Work in Progress** folder.

Adding Type

1. Activate the Eyedropper tool. Select a golden color from the image in the lightest area of the sky just above the horizon. This will create the Foreground color to be used for the type.

2. Select the Type tool. Click in the middle of the image at the top. Change the Font to ATCTequila; change Size to 80 pixels, and select Center Alignment.

3. In the Text Box, type "Got your head in the clouds?", Track to -20, Kern to taste, Click OK, then reposition the type selection at the top center of the page. Change the Opacity of the new Type layer to 60%.

4. Click in the lower left corner of the new layer with the Type tool. Keep the Font set to ATCTequila and change the Size to 60 pixels. Change the Leading to 50 and keep the Tracking set to -20. Select the Align Left button to create the type flush left.

5. In the Type Box enter:

    Come Back
    To Earth At
    Tropical Suites

6. With the new Type layer selected, use the Layer>Effects>Drop Shadow command. Set the Angle to 135°, the Distance and Blur to 3 pixels, and the Intensity to 30%.

7. Move the modified Type layer flush with the headline. Leave the same amount of space on the bottom as there is on the left. Save the file.

Creating a Border

1. Create a New layer; name it "Border". Place the layer at the top of the Layers palette. With the Eyedropper tool, select the gold color in the headline.

2. Fill the layer with the gold Foreground color. Select Filter>Noise>Add Noise. Set Amount to 60, and make the Noise Gaussian and Monochromatic.

3. Select Filter>Blur>Radial Blur. Change the Blur Method to Zoom. Set Amount to 100 and make certain that Quality is set to Good. Click OK. Be patient; this may take a while. Leave the Blur in the center of the Dialog Box Placement window.

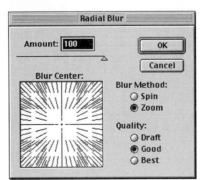

4. Choose Select>All and Select>Modify>Border. Create a 32-pixel border.

5. Choose Select>Inverse and press the Delete key.

6. Save the file before closing, or Save and proceed to the next section.

Prepare Files for Output

Now that you have a Photoshop file, you need to prepare a file for the printer and other distribution. Save all files to your **Work in Progress** folder.

Preparing Files for RGB-savvy Printers

1. Choose File>Save a Copy and select TIFF from the Format drop-down menu. Name the file "HIC_RGB.TIF".

2. Leave the file open for the next operation.

Preparing Files for the Web

1. From Image>Image Size, change the Resolution to 72 ppi.

2. Choose File>Save a Copy and select JPEG from the Format drop-down menu. Name the file "HIC.JPG".

3. Choose an appropriate compression level. Greater compression (the lower the number) discards more data. Less compression results in a better-looking photo, but it loads much slower.

4. Leave the file open for the next operation.

Preparing Files for Traditional Lithographic Printing

1. Revert the file (File>Revert).

2. Choose Image>Mode>CMYK.

3. Choose File>Save a Copy and select TIFF from the Format drop-down menu. Name the file "HIC_CMY.TIF".

4. Leave the file open for the next operation.

Preparing Files for the Newspaper

1. Select Image>Mode>Grayscale.

2. Choose File>Save a Copy and select TIFF from the Format drop-down menu. Name the file "HIC_GS.TIF".

3. Close the file without saving.

Notes:

Project D: Baby Shower Invitation

In this project we will create an invitation for a baby shower. This exercise takes advantage of Photoshop's Erase to Layer function.

Needless to say, we're not going to print thousands of these invitations, but we will take advantage of technology that allows us to print from a few dozen to a few hundred — it all depends on how many friends we have.

Isolating from the Background

1. Open **Baby Background.TIF** from the **SF-Adv Photoshop** folder. This picture will act as the background for the babies.

2. Open **Baby01.TIF** from the **SF-Adv Photoshop** folder. This cute baby is going to be the first picture that you place onto the "stage." There's only one problem: Our little baby has to be isolated from the background. We will do this using the Magnetic Lasso tool. This tool snaps to the edges of your image, allowing you to easily select the edges of your picture. The Magnetic Lasso tool is located on the toolbar on the left side, under the standard Lasso tool. Click and hold the button and the tool will "pop out."

3. Click somewhere along the edge of the baby. A Starting "Node" point will appear. Slowly move your mouse around the edge of the baby. A series of nodes will appear and will snap to the outside of the Baby image. When you reach the beginning, click on the original node. The nodes will disappear and "marching ants" will appear.

4. You will notice that the marching ants do not completely enclose the baby. We will have to add and subtract some areas with the Lasso tool. This will give us a good clean selection area of the baby.

5. Find an area of the picture where the image is not completely surrounded by the marching ants. (This will probably be down near the baby's hands.) Zoom in to the section. Select the regular Lasso tool and hold down the Shift key. Surround the area that is not included. This will allow you to add to the Selection area.

6. Slowly move around the image and add in all of the areas that the Magnetic Lasso tool missed. If you over-select an area, you can delete that area by holding down the Option/Alt key and drawing around the over-selected spot.

7. The baby should now be completely enclosed by the marching ants. It is not critical that the selection is perfect. We will solve that problem later.

Creating a Path

8. Selecting those edges was a lot of work! Wouldn't it be nice if you could keep that selection information so that you wouldn't have to repeat this procedure every time you need that baby? With Photoshop's Path tool, you can archive your selection so that you can use it any time you need that image. If it is not already open, pull down the window and select Show Paths.

9. Hold down the mouse on the little black triangle located at the top right side of the menu. Select Make Work Path. A dialog box will appear. Select a Tolerance of 2.0 pixels and click OK. A line will appear around your picture. This line holds all the information you so carefully isolated a moment ago.

10. Let's give this line a name. Double-click on the Work Path box that has now appeared on the Side menu. A dialog box will appear. Name your path "Path 1". Click OK. This new Path will now be part of your image when you save it. Save this image with its new information.

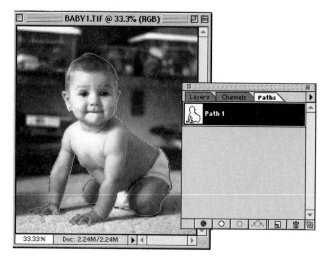

11. Once the picture has a path, that path can easily be changed into a selection. Click on the top right black triangle and select Make Selection. Set the Feather Radius to zero and check the Anti-Aliased box. Click OK. A set of marching ants will now appear around the image.

12. Now we'll turn the path off so that we can transfer the image to the background. Click on the top right black triangle and select Turn Off Path.

13. Position **Baby Background.TIF** and **Baby01.TIF** so that you can see both pictures. Be careful not to deselect the marching ants in the **Baby01.TIF** picture.

14. Select the Move Tool (V) and slowly drag the baby over to the Background picture. As you move the picture, a Gray box will appear around the Background picture. This tells you that you are correctly moving the picture. Release the mouse. The baby will now appear as Layer 1 on the Background.

15. That Baby sure is large! Let's size him down a little so we have room for all the other babies. If you cannot see the Layer menu, pull down the Window menu and select Show Layer Menu. Layer 1 should be the active layer.

16. In the Edit menu, select Transform, then select Scale. A set of white handles will appear around your baby. Hold down the Shift key (this constrains the selection) and grab a corner handle. Slowly drag the handle toward the center of the picture. The baby will begin to get smaller. When you are satisfied with the size change, press the Return key. If you change your mind, Undo (Command/Control-Z) the Scale and try again.

17. If you zoom in, you will notice that the edges around the baby are too sharp. The baby needs to be blended into the background. We'll use the Eraser tool to accomplish this. Select the Eraser tool. In the Brush menu, select the soft Brush in the second row, two over from the left. Zoom in to 150%, to the area of the baby's hands.

18. The Background color on the Side palette should be White. Hold down the mouse button and slowly erase around the edges where the hands meet the water. A soft edge should appear. Be careful not to erase too many of the pixels. You are trying to create a natural feel.

Creating a Layer Mask

19. You want the baby to appear to be in the water. We will accomplish this with a Layer mask. Make certain that Layer 1 is still active. In the Layer menu, select Add Layer Mask, Reveal All. A White square will appear in the Layer window. Now double-click the Linear Gradient tool. For the effect to work, Black must be the Foreground color and White the Background color on the palette. The Linear Gradient Options box will be displayed. Under the box entitled Gradient, select Foreground to Transparent.

20. Click somewhere below the baby's hands and slowly drag the line up to about the baby's elbow. The baby will appear to blend into the water.

21. Let's blend the baby into the background just a little more. Click back on the picture of the baby in the Layer menu box. Change the Opacity to 98%. This causes the baby to sit a little more into the background and makes the picture more realistic.

Creating a Composite

22. Now let's bring the rest of those babies into the picture. Click the Close box to **Baby01.TIF** and Save any changes. Open **Baby02.TIF** from the **SF-Adv Photoshop** folder. This picture will be added to the first picture.

A Path has been created for you in each of the Baby pictures. You may use that Path or create a new one for practice.

23. Repeat Steps 11 through 21. This will use the paths that were already created for the images. You will be dragging the **Baby02.TIF** image to the **Baby Background.TIF** picture. Remember that there will now be two Layers plus the Background. Be certain that Layer 2 is active when you are making a Layer mask.

24. When you have completed the above steps and are satisfied, click the Close box for **Baby02.TIF**. Open **Baby03.TIF** from the **SF-Adv Photoshop** folder. Now we have a new problem. This baby is facing in the wrong direction. Let's fix that.

25. Make certain that **Baby03.TIF**'s path is not active. Pull down the Image menu and select Rotate Canvas. Select Flip Horizontal. Notice that the Path changes as well.

26. Our picture is a little dark compared to the others. Let's lighten him up using the Curves Dialog box. Pull down the Image Menu>Adjust>Curves. The Curves Dialog box will appear.

27. Select a point along the curve line, close to the center. Pull that line up slightly. The entire image will lighten up. When you are satisfied with the results, click OK.

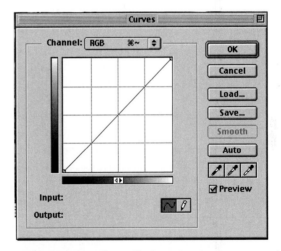

28. Repeat Steps 11 through 21. This will place **Baby03.TIF** onto the page with the other babies. Let's take a look at the file size. If you look at the button to the left of the Picture window, you will notice that the file has grown from its original size of 4.29 MB to about 9 MB. Each of those layers holds all of the pixel information plus the mask information for your picture. If you have lots of RAM, this is not a problem, but if you need to make the file smaller, Photoshop provides the means. It is called Merge, and it is a very powerful function.

29. You will see an Eye icon in the Layer menu. Click and turn off the Eye icon on the Background layer. The babies will look as if they are sitting on a checkerboard pattern.

Although merging layers makes the file smaller, it also makes it more difficult to move and edit individual components. Only merge when it is necessary.

30. Click on Layer 1. It should be the active layer. Hold down the button on the sideways black triangle and select Merge Visible. This will make your three babies one layer, but still keep the Background separate. Click on the Eye icon to turn the Background layer back on.

31. Save the image to your **Work in Progress** folder as "Invitation.PSD".

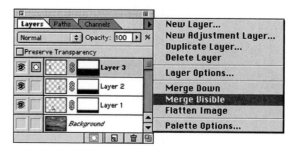

32. Open each of the remaining Baby pictures and repeat Steps 11 through 21. There are 14 different babies for you to place on the page. After every three or four pictures, Merge the layers (Steps 29 and 30). Don't forget to periodically Save your image (Command/Control-S).

Creating the Type

Now that we have all of our cute little babies in place, let's create some type for our invitation.

33. Choose the Type tool and click on the bottom left side of the image. Click on the Fit in Window box at the bottom of this dialog box. This lets the type fit in so that you can see what you are typing. Make certain that Anti-Aliased is checked. Select ATCIsland Bold 60 points and type "Come to a Baby Shower". Let's make that type Blue. With the Eyedropper tool, select a shade of Blue from the sky.

34. Photoshop 5.0 has some great effects features. Lets use one of them. In the Layer menu, Select Effects>Bevel and Emboss. Make the selections as shown below. When you are satisfied with the results, click OK.

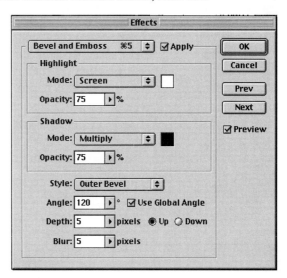

35. Use the Move tool to center the type on the invitation. Save the image before closing, or proceed to the next steps.

Prepare Files for Output

Now that you have a Photoshop file, you need to prepare a file for the printer and other distribution. Save all files to your **Work in Progress** folder.

Preparing Files for RGB-savvy Printers

1. Choose File>Save a Copy and select TIFF from the Format drop-down menu. Name the file "PCC_RGB.TIF".

2. Close the file without saving.

Notes:

Project E: Farm Fresh Logo

Logos will be used across the board in every medium into which a company enters. Chances are that Farm Fresh will have some short run point-of-purchase signage, in addition to the labels that will be affixed to all their products. They'll also want their logo in black-and-white ads for newspaper, and, of course, it will be prominent on their web page.

Creating Type

1. Create a New RGB document. Make it 4.5″ wide x 3″ high at 100 pixels per inch.

2. Activate the Channels palette. Create a new channel; name it "Original".

3. From the **SF-Adv Photoshop** folder, choose File>Place to Place the file **Farm Fresh.EPS**. Use Edit>Transform>Numeric to scale the placed file to about 85% of its original size. Center within the channel and Fill with White. Deselect.

4. Duplicate the Original channel; name the copy "Edge".

5. Select Filter>Other>Maximum. Enter a value of 5 pixels.

6. Load the Original channel as a Selection; Fill the selection with Black. Deselect.

7. Duplicate the Original channel. Rename the new channel "Highlights". Use Filter>Blur>Gaussian Blur to Blur the channel 4 pixels.

8. Select Filter>Stylize>Emboss. Enter an Angle of 140, Height of 7, and Amount of 150.

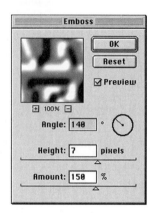

9. Duplicate the Highlights channel using the Channel drop-down menu and rename the copy "Shadows". Select the Invert box to create a negative of the channel.

10. Activate the Highlights channel. Select Image>Adjust>Levels. Select the Black Point Eyedropper tool and click on the Gray background. Click OK.

11. Activate the Shadows channel. Choose Image>Adjust>Levels. Select the Black Point Eyedropper tool and click on the Gray background. Click OK.

12. Load the Edge channel as a selection. Select the Invert box and Fill the selection with Black. Do not deselect.

13. Activate the Highlights channel; Fill the selection with Black. Deselect.

14. Duplicate the Original channel; name the new channel "Inside Shadow".

15. Gaussian Blur the channel 5 pixels. Press D to make certain that your Background color is set to Black. Activate the Move tool and use the Arrow keys to move the channel 3 pixels down and 3 pixels right.

16. Load the Original channel as a Selection, Inverted. Fill the selection with White. Deselect, then press Command/Control-I to Invert the colors in the image.

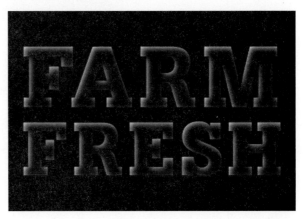

17. Select the RGB Composite. Activate the Layers palette. Create a New layer and click on it to activate it. Fill it with 50% Gray (from the Edit>Fill menu) at 100% Opacity.

18. Load the Highlights channel as a Selection. Press Command/Control-L to activate the Levels command. Use Levels to lighten the selection. Click OK.

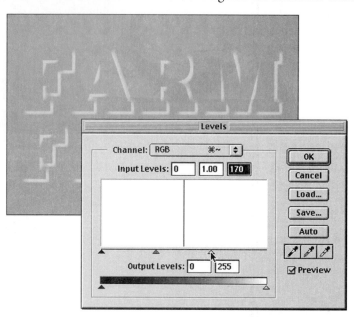

19. Load the Shadows channel. Press Command/Control-L to activate the Levels dialog box. This time, use Levels to darken the selection. Click OK.

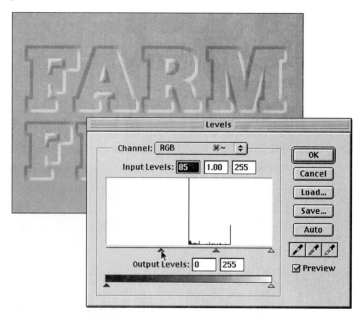

20. Load the Inside Shadow channel. Press Command/Control-L and darken the selection a lot — we're looking for a nice, hard line where the shadow meets the edge of the type. Click OK.

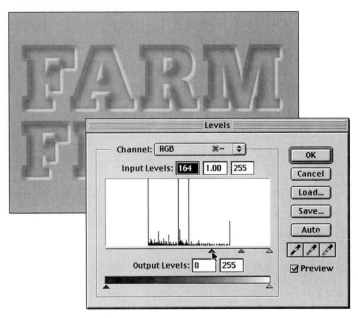

21. Press Command/Control-D to Deselect. Rename Layer 1 as "Type". Delete the Edge, Shadows, Highlights, and Inside Shadow Alpha channels.

22. Save the image as "Farm Fresh.PSD" to your **Work in Progress** folder.

Adding Background Texture

1. Activate the Background layer. Turn off the Type layer. Fill the Background layer with a medium-dark Green.

2. Select Filter>Noise>Add Noise. Add Gaussian Monochromatic Noise with Amount set to 50.

3. Filter>Blur>Motion Blur the selection 45° and 20 pixels.

4. Use the Levels, Curves, or Brightness/Contrast commands to increase the contrast and bring out texture in the image.

5. Double-click the Background layer and name it "Texture".

6. Activate the Type layer, and set the Layer Blending mode to Hard Light.

7. Activate the Texture layer. Load the Original channel as a selection, and press Delete. Deselect.

8. Save the image.

Filling the Text with an Image

1. Open **Market Oranges.TIF** from the **SF-Adv Photoshop** folder.

2. Press Command/Control-A to Select the image, Command/Control-C to Copy it to the clipboard, then Close the file.

3. Select Edit>Paste. Place the new layer below the Texture layer.

4. Use Edit>Transform>Numeric to scale the image to 40%.

5. Press Command/Control-A to Select All, then Command/Control-X to Cut the oranges from the layer and place them on the clipboard.

6. Select the F in the word FARM with the Lasso tool. Choose Edit>Paste Into to Paste the oranges inside the selection. Adjust the position of the oranges if necessary to completely fill the letter.

7. Select the A in the word FARM with the Lasso tool. Use Paste Into to Paste a copy inside the letter. Reposition to fill the letter, if necessary.

8. Repeat the Lasso, Paste Into, and Repositioning on each letter in the image. Turn off the Type and Texture layers and press Command/Control-Shift-E to Merge the visible layers. Turn all the layers on.

9. Duplicate the Type layer. Change Layer Opacity of the Type Copy layer to 50%. Save the document.

Creating Water Droplets

1. Activate the Channels palette. Add a new channel to the image.

2. Select Filter>Noise>Add Noise. Make the Noise Monochromatic, Gaussian and set Amount to 999.

3. Gaussian Blur the channel 4 pixels.

4. Choose Image>Adjust>Threshold. Adjust the slider so that the channel is filled with white water droplet shapes. The shapes will be rough.

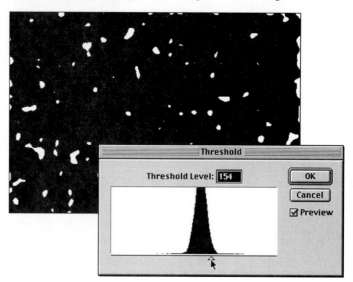

5. Rename the channel "Droplets". Gaussian Blur the channel 2 pixels. Select Image>Adjust>Levels and Level the channel until the edges of the drops are hard again, but some Anti-Aliasing still exists.

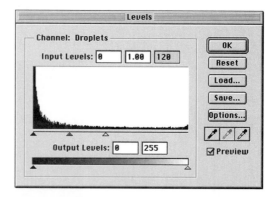

6. Load the Original channel as a Selection. Use Edit>Fill to Fill the selection with Black. Choose Select>Inverse, then use the Painting tools with a hard brush to remove any droplets that intersected with the type, and therefore have a hard edge. Clicking the Eye icon next to the Original channel to make it visible makes it easier to spot the drops that intersect the type. Just make certain that the Droplets channel is the Active channel, not the Original channel.

7. Click the Eye icon next to the Original channel to turn it off. Deselect.

8. Duplicate the Droplets channel. Name the copy "Drop Shadows". Gaussian Blur the new channel 3 pixels.

9. Duplicate the Drop Shadows channel. Name the duplicate "Drop Highlights".

10. Activate the Move tool. Make certain that your Background color is set to Black (press D). With the Arrow keys, nudge the channel up 2 pixels and left 2 pixels.

11. Activate the Drop Shadows channel. Nudge the channel down 2 pixels and right 2 pixels.

12. Select Image>Calculations. Set the Blending mode to Add the Drop Shadows channel, with Layer Merged and the Invert box checked, to the Drop Highlights channel, also set with Layer Merged. Set Scale to 2.

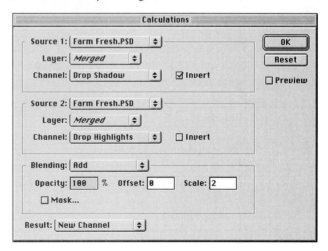

13. Load the Droplets channel as a selection. Click the Invert box and choose Edit>Fill to Fill the image with 50% Gray at 50% Opacity. Deselect.

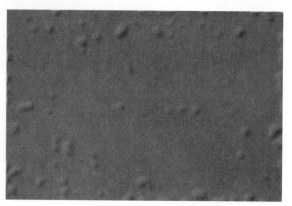

14. Rename the new channel "Drops 1 Channel".

15. Select Image>Calculations again. Set the Blending mode to Add the Droplets channel with Layer Merged to the Drop Shadows channel. Make certain that Drop Shadows is set to Layer Merged and that the Invert checkbox is checked. Set Scale to 2.

16. Rename the new channel "Drops 2 Channel".

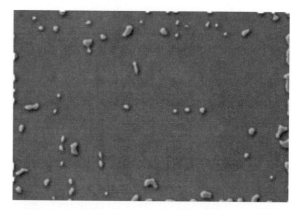

17. Make certain that the RGB composite is selected. Activate the Layers palette. Create a New layer and Fill it with Black. Rename the layer "Drops 1 Layer".

18. Duplicate Drops 1 layer. Name the duplicate "Drops 2 Layer". Position these as the top two layers.

19. Load Drops 2 channel as a selection. Choose Edit>Fill to Fill with White. Change the layer to Hard Light mode; set Opacity at 50%.

20. Activate Drops 1 layer. Load the Drops 1 Channel as a Selection and Fill with White. Change the layer to Hard Light. Deselect.

21. Save the image.

22. Activate the Channels palette. Activate Drops 1 channel. Choose Select>All and Copy to the clipboard.

23. Create a New grayscale document. Let the sizes default.

24. Paste the contents of the clipboard into the new document and Save As "Displacement Map" to your **Work in Progress** folder. Close the **Displacement Map** image.

25. In the **Farm Fresh.PSD** image, activate the Channels palette, and Delete all of the Alpha channels.

26. Activate the Layers palette and select the Texture layer.

27. Select Filter>Distort>Displace. The Displacement filter offsets the pixels in one image according to the gray values in a second image. White will move pixels down and left; black moves pixels up and right. By using the Drops channel we created as a Displacement map, we'll distort the green texture underneath the drops, similar to distortion caused by real water droplets.

28. Set both Horizontal and Vertical to 5, the click OK.

29. Select the **Displacement Map** image and click Open.

30. Crop the image to remove artifacts around the edges.

31. Save the file before closing, or Save and proceed to the next section without closing.

Prepare Files for Output

Now that you have a Photoshop file, you need to prepare a file for the printer and other distribution. Save all files to your **Work in Progress** folder.

Preparing Files for RGB-savvy Printers

1. Choose File>Save a Copy and select TIFF from the Format drop-down menu. Name the file "FF_RGB.TIF".

2. Leave the file open for the next operation.

Preparing Files for the Web

1. From Image>Image Size, change the Resolution to 72 ppi.

2. Choose File>Save a Copy and select JPEG from the Format drop-down menu. Name the file "FF.JPG".

3. Choose an appropriate compression level. Greater compression (the lower the number) discards more data. Less compression results in a better-looking photo, but it loads much slower.

4. Leave the file open for the next operation.

Preparing Files for Traditional Lithographic Printing

1. Revert the file (File>Revert).

2. Choose Image>Mode>CMYK.

3. Choose File>Save a Copy and select TIFF from the Format drop-down menu. Name the file "FF_CMY.TIF".

4. Leave the file open for the next operation.

Preparing Files for the Newspaper

1. Select Image>Mode>Grayscale.

2. Choose File>Save a Copy and select TIFF from the Format drop-down menu. Name the file "FF_GS.TIF".

3. Close the file without saving.

Project F: Photomat

This project is designed specifically to allow you to experiment with a variety of Photoshop effects, and as such, is more personal than "publishing" related. It would reasonably be printed on an RGB-savvy printer.

The Shapes of the Frames

1. Because it is much easier and more precise to create geometric shapes in Adobe Illustrator, you will find those shapes prefabricated for you. Open the document **Frames.AI** from within Photoshop.

2. In the Layers palette, double-click on Layer 1. When the dialog box appears, rename it "Frames" and click OK.

3. Click the arrow at the top right of the Layers palette, and select New Layer from the menu. Name this layer "Background".

4. Create another new layer, and name it "Photos". Then create one more, and name this one "Shadows".

5. Drag the original Frames layer to the top of the list so that the layers, from top to bottom, read Frames – Shadow – Photos – Background.

6. Save your work as "PhotoFrames.PSD" to your **Work in Progress** folder. Continue to Save frequently as you work.

To open an Illustrator document as a Photoshop document, either open it from Photoshop's File menu, or drag its icon onto the Photoshop icon. This opens a new Photoshop file, leaving the original Illustrator file untouched.

Painting and Textures

1. A well-designed commercial framing device would probably have a more unified look than this piece. The treatments of each frame would be more similar, integrated. But since this is a learning exercise, you will be creating a variety of effects — a different look for each frame, and for the photos within. The objective of this exercise is to acquaint you with the range of tools in Photoshop, not necessarily to create something which is tastefully understated.

2. To help make these frames more visible, you will now Fill the background with color. Activate the Background layer by clicking on it.

3. Press Command/Control-A to Select the entire background. Choose the Swatches palette, and click on the lightest Grey swatch. Press Option-Delete (Macintosh) or Alt-Backspace (Windows), and the background will Fill with this Grey.

4. With the background still selected, go to the Filter menu, and choose Noise: Add Noise. In the dialog box, set these parameters: Amount = 50, Distribution = Uniform, and check the box next to Monochromatic. This will result in a nice Gray texture that will aid in unifying the eclectic colors of the frames. Deselect the background using Command/Control-D.

To set these frames off from the background, you will add a drop shadow. This is one of Photoshop's most frequently used effects, but it is useful in augmenting contrast and readability.

5. Click on the Frames layer, and choose Load Selection from the Select menu. The default "Frames Transparency" selects all occupied pixels in the chosen layer, so just click OK.

Depending on your working routine, you might find it more convenient to deselect by clicking the Selection tool anywhere in the image, or with the keyboard shortcut, Command-D. In general, keyboard shortcuts save time, but depending on which tool is active at any moment, it may be more convenient to click the mouse. As you grow more familiar with Photoshop, you will devise your own methods of using time efficiently.

6. Without deselecting, click on the Shadows layer. Fill the selected area with Black. Deselect. You won't see any black until, using the Move tool, you reveal the Black selection. Using the cursor keys, move the selection 6 pixels down and to the right.

7. Select the Filter menu, and choose Blur: Gaussian Blur. Set the Radius to 20 pixels and click OK.

   If you should happen to Blur the layer while the shapes are still selected, the results will be far less pleasing. Make certain that you deselect first.

8. In the Layers palette, set the Opacity to 25%. This will make the shadow much more subtle, while still adding a sense of depth to the image.

Modeling the Outer Frame

1. Click on the Frames layer, then select the Magic Wand tool and click on the large, outer frame.

2. In the Swatches palette, choose a light Brown (Color Value R = 169, G = 131, B = 79). Fill the frame with the color. Deselect.

3. To imitate the way most natural frames are constructed, one segment per side, you must isolate the four segments before airbrushing highlights and shadows on them. The light would strike each segment in a different way because of its alignment. This is called "modeling."

4. Since the opposite sides of the frame are so far from each other (left is far from right, top is far from bottom), they can be easily isolated.

5. Select the Polygon Lasso tool (pull out the submenu next to the regular Lasso tool). The icon for the Polygon Lasso tool is made up of straight lines, as opposed to the round, regular Lasso tool.

6. For precision, use the Magnifying Glass tool, or click Command/Control-(+) to enlarge the upper left section of the image. Make your first click in that upper left corner where you see the arrow in the graphic above. Make your next click outside the image, but still within Photoshop's border, so that the line cuts the two edges right at the corner.

7. Release, and drag the mouse to the right, and when you reach the right border of Photoshop's border, click again at a point very near the upper right. Click once again down inside the image, so that once again, you have divided the segments.

8. Continue down and repeat this at the bottom. When you are about to click on your starting point again to complete a sort of "spool" shape, your cursor will momentarily change to signal you that you are about to finish the shape.

9. In the Select menu, choose Save Selection. Don't change the defaults. Name it "Spool".

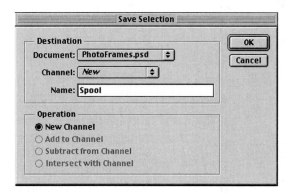

10. You have created a shape that will isolate the top and bottom segments from the left and right segments. First, you will deal with the left and right.

11. Deselect. Choose Load Selection from the Select menu. The default channel will be Frames Transparency. Click OK.

12. Immediately return to the Select menu>Load Selection. This time, choose Spool for the channel, and specify Subtract from Selection. The Spool shape will be subtracted from the outer frame, and what remains is the left and right segments. Now you can airbrush them.

Airbrushing

1. Since the shadows you created make it appear that light is being cast from the upper left, we must be consistent with the modeling of the frame. Segments will be lighter on the left and top, darker on the right and bottom.

2. Without deselecting, hide the marching ants by pressing Command/Control-H.

3. Choose the Airbrush tool, and in the Brushes palette, choose a brush 45 pixels wide. In the Options palette, set the Pressure to 15%. Choose Black from the Swatches palette.

4. Begin with the left segment. Go to its top right corner, click and drag the mouse down to the bottom while pressing the Shift key to constrain your movement to a straight line. Then do the same thing on the right side of the right segment.

    The Undo function is useful for making strokes with any Painting tool. If you don't like the way it came out the first time, press Command/Control-Z and try again. If you want to Undo the Undo, press Command/Control-Z again to restore to a pre-Undo state.

5. For the Bright highlight, you'll need to increase the Pressure in the Options palette to 30%, and choose White from the Swatches palette.

6. Start on the left side of the left segment, and airbrush the highlight, remembering to constrain your movement with the Shift key. Then do the same with the right segment. Deselect.

7. To continue with airbrushing the top and bottom segments, you need to select them in the same manner in which you earlier selected the left and right segments.

8. Choose Load Selection from the Select menu. The default channel will be Frames Transparency. Click OK.

9. Return to the Select menu and choose Load Selection again. Choose Spool for the channel. But this time, click the check mark next to Invert, then specify Subtract from Selection.

10. This will result in the top and bottom segments being selected, but it will also select the frames in the interior, which you don't want to deal with yet. Choose the Rectangular Marquee; press and hold the Option/Alt key while you make a rectangle that encompasses the interior frames. This way, you deselect them while retaining the selection of the top and bottom segments. Press Command/Control-H to hide the marching ants.

11. With the Airbrush tool, Paint the segments, remembering to change the Pressure option between 30% for White and 15% for Black. Paint White on the top edge of each segment, and Black on the bottom edge.

12. The end result will be a rounded-looking frame. Select the Channels palette, and drag the Spool channel to the trash.

Pasting an Image Into a Frame

1. Click the Magic Wand tool to select the largest interior frame, the rectangular frame in the upper left corner. Open **Clouds.TIF** from the **SF-Adv Photoshop** folder.

2. Select All. Copy. Close the **Clouds.TIF** file.

3. In the **PhotoFrames.PSD** file, press Command-Shift-V (Macintosh) or Control-Shift-V (Windows) to Paste Into the selected shape.

4. You now have a frame painted with clouds. The clouds that you pasted in now exist on a new layer named Layer 1, so go to the submenu in the Layers palette and select Merge Down. Layer 1 will merge with the Frames layer, one layer below it.

Painting Tiger Stripes

1. Use the Magic Wand tool to select the next frame — the round one at the top right. Fill it with Yellow (R = 250, G = 230, B = 0). Hide the marching ants (Command/Control-H).

2. Change the Foreground color to Black. Choose the Brush tool. In the Options palette, set Opacity to 100%. In the Brushes palette, start with the largest visible hard-edged brush, which has a diameter of 19 pixels.

3. Draw a couple of squiggly lines across the O-shaped frame. If you aren't 100% thrilled with a line, Undo it.

4. Choose a smaller brush, perhaps 9 pixels, and draw a couple of lines. Make the thick and thin lines work with each other to add variety.

5. Return to the first thicker brush, and draw some more lines. Maybe you'd like an even thicker brush, perhaps 30 pixels. You'll have to create it. Click and hold the arrow on the Brushes palette to reveal the submenu, and choose New Brush. Enter a value of 30 for the Diameter, and click OK.

6. Continue alternating between these three brushes in a visually interesting way until the frame is filled up.

If the diameter of a brush is not labeled, you can double-click on the brush to display its dialog box.

Here comes the tricky part — applying the same type of airbrush shading to this Tiger Skin frame as you applied to the Outer frame, except that this frame doesn't have sections. The same principles apply — the highlights are on the top left, the shadows are on the bottom right.

7. Reveal the hidden marching ants. With the Selection tool, drag the marching ants slightly up and to the left, maybe one-third of the width of the frame.

8. You want to use this selection as an airbrush artist would use a frisket, except that you can soften the edge of your frisket. Since you don't want to airbrush in the Selection area, but use it to selectively block the airbrush, press Command/Control-Shift-I to Invert the selection. Now, although the marching ants look the same, everything is selected except the inside of the O shape.

9. To achieve a soft-edged frisket, press Command-Option-D (Macintosh) or Control-Alt-D (Windows) to display the Feather dialog box. Enter a value of 10 pixels. Hide the marching ants again.

10. One further aid for your frisketing: by checking the Preserve Transparency box in the Layers palette, you will only be allowed to paint on pixels which are already occupied in the layer on which you're working. That prevents your paint from going onto the background.

11. Using the same values for your airbrush as you did before (Pressure = 15%, Brush = 45 pixels, Color = Black), paint around the lower right edge of the O shape. Remember to also paint the corresponding area on the inside. Take your time, go slowly, and remember that you can always Undo.

12. Make the marching ants visible again for a moment, and using the Selection tool, drag the selection down and to the right to about one-third the width of the frame. Hide the marching ants again.

13. Set the foreground color to White, and set the Pressure Value to 60% in the Options palette. Airbrush the highlights on the top left surfaces.

14. Deselect, and uncheck the Preserve Transparency box.

Swirling Colors

1. For the next frame, the other oval in the second row, you will place another photograph. But first you'll transform it into an abstract. Open the file **Forest.TIF** from the **SF-Adv Photoshop** folder.

2. Nice, tasteful, vibrant colors. You're going to make them even more vibrant by using the Adjust: Brightness/Contrast command in the Image menu. Increase the Brightness by 10%, and the Contrast by 25%.

3. Here comes the "Timothy Leary" effect, better known in the Filter>Distort menu as "Twirl". It will look as though this image were printed on taffy, which is swirling down a drain. You'll note that we're not going for realism here.

4. Since subtlety has very little to do with this effect, let's set a value of 999 in the dialog box. Click OK.

5. Now you'll see how such a bizarre look can actually be used in a subtle manner. Select All, Copy, and Close the **Forest.TIF** file without saving.

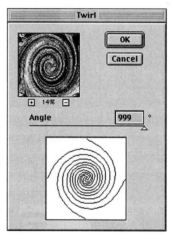

6. Return to the **PhotoFrames.PSD** file and click to select the oval in the bottom row with the Magic Wand tool. Then Paste Into the oval shape. With the Move tool, drag the swirled image around within the oval, trying out some possible placements. You can achieve an impression of antique woodcarving, or marbling, if you have an active imagination.

7. Once you are pleased with the effect, pull down the submenu on the Layers palette and choose Merge Down. Then the visible portion of the image is all that remains, and it is part of the Frames layer.

When artwork has been Pasted Into a selection, as opposed to just Pasted, it gets a layer of its own, and parts of it still exist which cannot be seen. You can resize, rotate, and perform various edits until it is just the way you want it.

Wood Grain

1. The frame in the center of the bottom row will have a more traditional look — wood grain. Start by selecting the frame with the Magic Wand tool.

2. So this frame doesn't resemble too closely the colors in the large outer frame, let's start with a warmer light brown tone: R = 200, G = 165, B = 110. Press Option-Delete or Alt/Backspace to Fill the rectangle.

3. Choose a darker brown: R = 140, G = 100, B = 50. Select the Paintbrush tool, as you did with the tiger stripes. This time, select a 5-pixel brush. Hide the marching ants.

4. Look at some real wood grain, and try to imitate the lines you see. Loose and wavy, burls and swirls. Not too straight or regular.

5. When you have filled the shape with wavy, wood-like lines, keep the marching ants invisible and choose Filter>Blur>Gaussian Blur. Enter a value of three pixels. Click OK. Deselect.

6. This type of natural treatment cries out for some modeling. But this time, you're not going to go to any great lengths to mask the frame. Simply check the Preserve Transparency box in the Layers palette. That will mask off the background, but won't protect the other frames, so be careful not to extend your painting too far.

7. Start with Black, 45 pixel airbrush, Pressure 15%. White should have a Pressure Value of 30%. Remember that the shadow goes on the bottom and right edges, highlights on the top and left. Constrain your paths with the Shift key, and remember you can always Undo.

If your monitor resolution is less than 1024 × 768, you might need to choose a smaller brush.

8. To add to the homespun effect of this frame, let's carve the word MOM into the frame. Choose the Type tool, and click it on the bottom segment of the frame. Make certain that Black is selected as the Foreground color.

9. Choose ATCBahama, and set the type size at 20 points. Type MOM, Select and Track 300, then click OK. The layer will be named MOM.

10. To be able to work with the type as a series of pixels, you have to Render the Type layer that was created. This cannot be done from the Layers palette submenu; you must select Layers>Type>Render Layer.

11. Choose the Select menu>Load Selection, using the MOM Transparency channel. Copy and Paste it. That will create a new layer called Layer 1. Drag Layer 1 below the MOM layer. Select it by choosing Select>Load Selection, and paint it White. Deselect. With the Move tool, position it so that it is just slightly down and to the right of the original.

12. Deselect and choose Filter>Blur>Gaussian Blur. Enter a value of 1 pixel. Click OK.

13. If it is positioned correctly, it should suggest that the lettering has been carved into the wood. Activate the MOM layer and select Merge Down. Do the same with Layer 1. Now the carved MOM is on the Frames layer.

Chrome

1. The final frame will be a simulation of chrome. This is purely an airbrush effect. Select the frame with the Magic Wand tool. Choose Black as the Foreground color. Look at some examples of rendered chrome to see how the light hits. It's fairly easy to fake. Start with a larger soft-edged brush, 150 pixels, and a Pressure Value of 30%.

2. Paint about four diagonal stripes across the frame. Don't space them too perfectly. Allow some irregularity.

3. Just those four stripes are enough to give an illusion of chrome, but it will look more metallic if it has a slight bluish tint. Select the Image menu: Adjust: Variations. Move the cursor one step toward Fine, and select More Blue. Click OK.

4. Deselect, and if you haven't been saving your work all along, make certain to Save it now.

If your monitor resolution is less than 1024 × 768, you might need to choose a smaller brush.

Content for the Frames

Now that the frames are created, it's time to start placing your pictures in them. You can use the photos provided with the exercise, or some of your own scanned photos or images that you have created.

Watercolors

1. First you will Fill the large Cloud frame. Open **Scuba.TIF** from the **SF-Adv Photoshop** folder. This is a good natural image to go with the sky in the frame.

2. Turn it into a watercolor effect. Select the entire image, then select Filter> Artistic>Watercolor. Set Brush Detail to 12, Shadow Intensity to 0, and Texture to 1. Or play around with these values until you find something you like better.

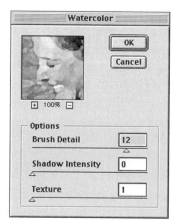

3. Copy the image, then Close the **Scuba.TIF** image without saving the changes.

4. In the **PhotoFrames.PSD** file, in the Frames layer, click the interior of the Cloud frame with the Magic Wand tool to select the rectangle inside. Then click on the Photos layer. Paste Into the selected space.

5. The image will appear in a new layer of its own called Layer 1. Position and resize to taste. Merge Down to the Photos layer.

6. Click on the Frames layer, use the Magic Wand tool to select the interior of the Tiger Skin frame, then return to the Photos layer.

7. Open **Watermelon.TIF** from the **SF-Adv Photoshop** folder. From the Filter menu, choose Artistic>Paint Daubs. Enter Brush Size = 8, Sharpness = 7, Brush Type = Sparkle. Click OK. This yields a different painting effect.

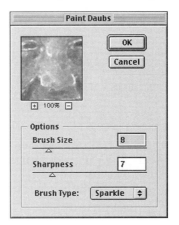

8. Select the entire image, Copy, and then Close the **Watermelon.TIF** image without saving.

9. Back in the **PhotoFrames.PSD** file, press Paste Into the selected oval space. Adjust to taste and Merge Down into the Photos layer.

Posterization and Noise

1. In the Frames layer, select the interior of the bottom left Oval frame with the Magic Wand tool. Then click on the Photos layer. Open **Teen Picnic.TIF** from the **SF-Adv Photoshop** folder.

2. In the Image menu, choose Adjust>Posterize, and enter a value of 4 levels. Click OK.

It is important to keep track of which layer you are working in, especially during times when you must be frequently jumping back and forth between layers.

3. It looks more interesting, but somewhat harsh. Select the Filter menu: Noise: Add Noise. Set the Amount at 50, the Distribution at Gaussian, and choose Monochromatic. Click OK.

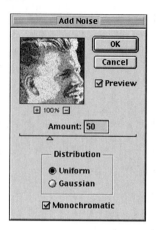

4. Select All, Copy, then Close **Picnic.TIF** without saving. Return to **PhotoFrames.PSD**.

5. Paste Into the bottom oval. Adjust and Merge Down.

Sepia Tone

1. Open **Mom.TIF** from the **SF Adv Photoshop** folder. Convert the image to grayscale, then to a Duotone.

2. We're going to make this image a Process Tritone. Set the Duotone curves for the inks as follows:

Black:	50% = 40%, 80% = 90%
Process Yellow:	10% = 05%, 30% = 30%, 100% = 80%
Process Magenta:	50% = 25%, 100% = 70%

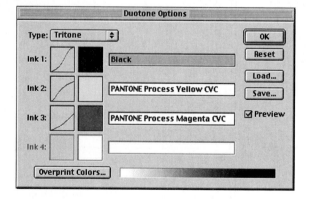

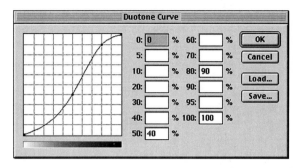

3. Now make this look old and weathered. Select the Filter menu: Texture: Craquelure. Set Values of Crack Spacing = 20, Crack Depth = 5, Crack Brightness = 10. Click OK.

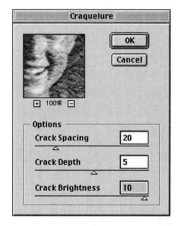

4. Select All, and Copy. Close the **Mom.TIF** image without saving. Return to **PhotoFrames.PSD**.

5. In the Frames layer, select the interior of the wooden MOM frame. Then move to the Photos layer. Paste Into, Adjust and Merge Down to the Photos layer.

Pastels

1. Finally, it's time to fill the Chrome frame. Open **TrueLove.TIF** from the **SF-Adv Photoshop** folder. Choose the Filter menu: Artistic: Rough Pastels. Set these Values: Stroke Length = 2, Stroke Detail = 15, Texture = Canvas, Scaling = 100%, Relief = 20, Light Direction = Top Left. Click OK.

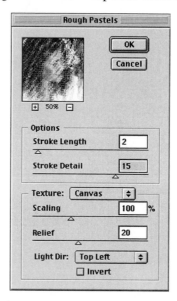

2. Select All and Copy. Close **TrueLove.TIF** without saving. Return to **PhotoFrames.PSD**. Select and Copy the interior of the Chrome frame, and return to the Photos layer. Paste Into the selected area. Adjust and Merge down to the Photos layer.

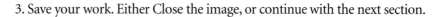

3. Save your work. Either Close the image, or continue with the next section.

Prepare Files for Output

Now that you have a Photoshop file, you need to prepare a file for the printer and other distribution. Save all files to your **Work in Progress** folder.

Preparing Files for RGB-savvy Printers

1. Choose File>Save a Copy and select TIFF from the Format drop-down menu. Name the file "Frames.TIF".

2. Close the file without saving.

Notes:

Project G: The Fix Is In

This image comes to us from the Veronica Cass School of Photographic Arts in Hudson, Florida, where it is used to teach both conventional and digital retouching. This project is quite typical of the type of work found in the world of retouching. The assignment is in two parts: first, the image needs to be repaired (arms added, scratches removed, and a new background created), then the image will be colorized to recreate the hand-colored effect that was in vogue when the original was taken.

The image could be reproduced on disk or a web page to show off your work, or it could be printed using an RGB-savvy printer.

Retouching the Image

1. Open the file **Cop.TIF** from the **SF-Adv Photoshop** folder. (Cop is not a derogatory term but an acronym for constable on patrol.)

   Always begin by analyzing the image. It is apparent that the scan was made from a copy of the original image. This was done to allow for extra room for the arms and a larger background. It is a necessary step when doing conventional retouching since there is no way to add canvas as can be accomplished in Photoshop.

2. Choose the Pen tool. Although there are magnetic features to the Pen and the Lasso tools, the standard version of the Pen tool works best here due to the similarity of tone in areas of the background and foreground.

3. Start at his shoulder and draw a path all the way around the cop. His slicked-down style haircut makes this job easier. Continue to draw the path where his arm should be. Don't panic if you can't draw well; just make several curves to suggest folds in the cloth.

4. When your path is finished, double-click the Work path and name it "Cop", then go to the bottom of the Path palette and click on the dotted circle. This will turn your path into a selection. Click in the palette away from the path to turn off the path. (If you forget to turn off the path you will find a fine line where the path was.)

5. With the selection active on the Background layer, you are ready to paint in his arms. Feather the selection by about 1.5 pixels.

6. Select the Rubber Stamp tool ("S" key) and begin adding cloth to the area where his arms should be. Use as many different areas to clone from as possible using the existing folds and seams to add detail and realism to your work. The Selection Marquee keeps you from having to worry about drawing the edge of the coat since you can only paint inside the lines. It's like having a magic coloring book.

7. At the same time, fix the damaged areas that fall inside the Selection Marquee. Don't worry about the area outside the selection; you will soon replace that with a new background. Take as much time as necessary to do a good job.

8. Rename the Background layer "Cop". Add a Layer mask to the Cop layer. When this is done with a selection active, only the selected layer remains visible. Add a new layer and position it below the Cop layer. This will be part of your new background.

9. Type D to set the default colors to Black and White. With the new layer active, select the Filter menu and choose Render Clouds. Your new layer should be filled with Photoshop clouds. Add another layer and Fill it with a linear gradient from dark at the top to white at the bottom. Blend the layers by adjusting the Opacity of whichever one is on top. Different effects can be achieved with different Opacity settings and by changing which one is on top. Experiment until you are satisfied.

10. One last trick before you begin to colorize. The badge is without detail because it has been copied too many times. Use the Rubber Stamp tool set at a low Opacity (20%) to add just a suggestion of detail from one of the uniform buttons. Don't add too much, just enough to make the viewer think he can see detail.

11. Save the image as "Cop.PSD" to your **Work in Progress** folder.

You'll want to save after every major step below, both as a matter of safe computing, and to avoid running out of RAM.

Colorizing the Image

1. Select Image>Mode>RGB. Do not flatten the image. Be certain that the Cop layer is active.

2. Add an Adjustment layer for Hue and Saturation. Check the box to Group with Previous Layer. When the dialog box appears, check the Colorize box. Move the sliders until a sepia tone is achieved.

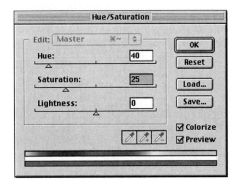

3. Using the Lasso tool, loosely select the area around his hair. Add another Hue and Saturation layer, grouped with the previous layer. Adjust the sliders until you are happy with the hair color; don't worry about the sloppy edges. If you make the color too bright you can always reduce the effect by lowering the Opacity slider for the Adjustment layer. This is especially useful when adding color to the lips; you don't want him to look like a cross-dresser.

4. Reset the colors to default (B&W).

5. Select a soft-edge brush. Be certain that Black is the Foreground color. Paint on the Hue and Saturation layer to remove the sloppy edges. If you paint into the hair area, type X to switch Foreground and Background and paint over your mistake. When you paint with White on this layer you will change the underlying pixels to the color specified in the Adjustment layer.

6. Use the same technique to colorize his lips and jacket. Each will have its own Hue and Saturation Adjustment layer. When you have finished the jacket, use the Black brush to remove the blue from his buttons and badge. (Don't forget his collar numbers.)

7. When doing the eyes, follow the same technique, but colorize only the iris and pupil. Go to the very first (sepia tone) Adjustment layer and remove the sepia color in the whites of his eyes using the Black soft-edged brush. If you want to be thorough, you can go back to the eyes and remove the color from the pupil and highlights by using the soft-edge Black brush on the Adjustment layer that gives the eyes their color.

8. Duplicate the Jacket Adjustment layer. (Drag it to the New Layer icon at the bottom of the stack.)

9. Select Image>Adjust>Invert. At this point, the buttons and his face will all turn blue. Don't panic! Simply use the Marquee tool to select the area around his head and Fill with Black. (Be certain that you are still in the New Adjustment layer.) That will remove the change from his face. Double-click this new layer to display the dialog box and adjust the sliders to make the buttons and badge a nice brassy yellow.

10. Finally, choose the Background layers. (Activate the one just below the Cop layer.) Add an Adjustment layer for Hue and Saturation (do not click Link to the Previous Layer). Click Colorize and decide on a color for your background.

You now have a completely editable version of the Cop in color. By double-clicking on the various Adjustment layers, you can change him to your heart's content, giving him any color hair, eyes, lips, jacket, and/or buttons. You can even alter his skin tone and the background. Good luck and happy pixel pushing.

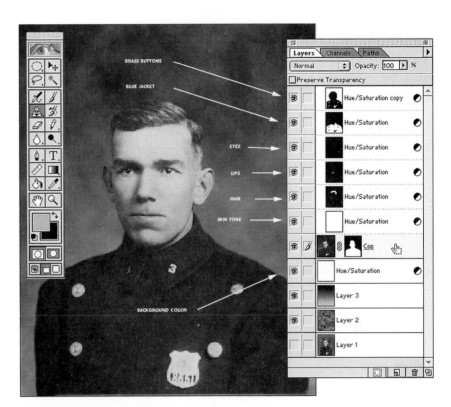

11. Save the image. Either Close the image or go on to the next section.

Prepare Files for Output

Now that you have a Photoshop file, you need to prepare a file for the printer and other distribution. Save all files to your **Work in Progress** folder.

Preparing Files for RGB-savvy Printers

1. Choose File>Save a Copy and select TIFF from the Format drop-down menu. Name the file "Cop_RGB.TIF".

2. Leave the file open for the next operation.

Preparing Files for the Web

1. From Image>Image Size, change the Resolution to 72 ppi.

2. Choose File>Save a Copy and select JPEG from the Format drop-down menu. Name the file "Cop.JPG".

3. Choose an appropriate compression level. Greater compression (the lower the number) discards more data. Less compression results in a better-looking photo, but it loads much slower.

4. Close the file without saving.

Notes:

Achromatic

By definition, having no color; therefore, completely black or white or some shade of gray.

Acrobat

This program by Adobe Systems, Inc. allows the conversion (using Acrobat Distiller) of any document from any Macintosh or Windows application to PDF format, which retains the page layout, graphics, color, and typography of the original document. It is widely used for distributing documents online because it is independent of computer hardware. The only software needed is a copy of Acrobat Reader, which can be downloaded free.

Adaptive Palette

A sampling of colors taken from an image, and used in a special compression process usually used to prepare images for the world wide web.

Additive Color Process

The additive color process is the process of mixing red, green, and blue light to achieve a wide range of colors, as on a color television screen. See Subtractive Color.

Adjacent Color

The eye will respond to a strong adjacent color in such a way as to affect the perception of the particular color in question. That is, a color having different adjacent colors may look different than it does in isolation. Also referred to as metamerism.

Adobe Systems Incorporated

A major software developer responsible for the creation of the PostScript page description language (see PostScript), used in almost all graphic arts environments. PostScript resides in a printer or Raster Image Processor (see Raster Image Processor) and is used to convert graphics from the screen to high-resolution output. Adobe also develops the highly popular Photoshop, Illustrator, PageMaker, and Premiere graphics and video applications, in addition to a range of others.

Algorithm

A specific sequence of mathematical steps to process data. A portion of a computer program that calculates a specific result.

All signature folding dummy

A folding dummy in which all of the signatures that make up the job are used to determine the page arrangement for each signature. Also known as a Job Worksheet.

Alpha Channel

An 8-bit channel of data that provides additional graphic information, such as colors or masking. Alpha channels are found in some illustration or graphics programs, and are used in video production.

Anti-Aliasing

A graphics software feature that eliminates or softens the jaggedness of low-resolution curved edges.

Archival storage

The process of storing data in a totally secure and safe manner. Archiving differs from backup in that it's meant to be used to restore entire systems or networks, rather than providing quick and easy access to specific files or folders.

Art

Illustrations and photographs in general; that is, all matter other than text that appears in a mechanical.

Artifact

By definition, something that is artificial, or not meant to be there. An artifact can be a blemish or dust spot on a piece of film, or unsightly pixels in a digital image.

Ascender

Parts of a lower-case letter that exceed the height of the letter "x". The letters b, d, f, h, k, l, and t have ascenders.

ASCII

The American Standard Code for Information Interchange, which defines each character, symbol, or special code as a number from 0 to 255 (8 bits in binary). An ASCII text file can be read by any computer, and is the basic mode of data transmission on the Internet.

ATM (Adobe Type Manager)

A utility program which causes fonts to appear smooth on screen at any point size. It's also used to manage font libraries.

Backing Up

The process of making copies of current work or work-in-progress as a safety measure against file corruption, drive or system failure, or accidental deletion. Backing up work-in-progress differs from creating an archive (see Archiving) for long-term storage or system restoration.

Banding

A visible stair-stepping of shades in a gradient.

Banner

A large headline or title extending across the full page width, or across a double-page spread.

Baseline

The implied reference line on which the bases of capital letters sit.

Bézier Curves

Curves that are defined mathematically (vectors), in contrast to those drawn as a collection of dots or pixels (raster). The advantage of these curves is that they can be scaled without the "jaggies" inherent in enlarging bitmapped fonts or graphics.

Bindery marks

Marks that appear on a press sheet to indicate how the sheet should be cropped, folded, collated, or bound.

Binding

In general, the various methods used to secure signatures or leaves in a book. Examples include saddle-stitching (the use of staples in a folded spine), and perfect-bound (multiple sets of folded pages sewn or glued into a flat spine).

Bit (Binary Digit)

A computer's smallest unit of information. Bits can have only two values: 0 or 1. This can represent the black and white (1-bit) pixel values in a line art image. Or in combination with other bits, it can represent 16 tones or colors (4-bit), 256 tones or colors (8-bit), 16.8 million colors (24-bit), or a billion colors (30-bit). These numbers derive from counting all the possible combinations (permutations) of 0 or 1 settings of each bit: $2 \times 2 \times 2 = 16$ colors; $2 \times 2 \times 2 \times 2 \times 2 \times 2 \times 2 \times 2 = 256$ colors; $2 \times 2 = 16.8$ million colors.

Bitmap image

An image constructed from individual dots or pixels set to a grid-like mosaic. Each pixel can be represented by more than one bit. A 1-bit image is black and white because each bit can have only two values (for example, 0 for white and 1 for black). For 256 colors, each pixel needs eight bits (2 8). A 24-bit image refers to an image with 24 bits per pixel (2 24), so it may contain as many as 16,777,216 colors. Because the file must contain information about the color and position of each pixel, the disk space needed for bitmap images is usually quite significant. Most digital photographs and screen captures are bitmap images.

Bitmapped

Forming an image by a grid of pixels whose curved edges have discrete steps because of the approximation of the curve by a finite number of pixels.

Black

The absence of color; an ink that absorbs all wavelengths of light.

Blanket

The blanket, a fabric coated with natural or synthetic rubber wrapped around the cylinder of an offset press, transfers the inked image from the plate to the paper.

Bleed

Page data that extends beyond the trim marks on a page. Illustrations that spread to the edge of the paper without margins are referred to as "bled off."

Blend

See Graduated fill.

Blind Emboss

A raised impression in paper made by a die, but without being inked. It is visible only by its relief characteristic.

Blow up

An enlargement, usually of a graphic element such as a photograph.

Body Copy

The text portion of the copy on a page, as distinguished from headlines.

Border

A continuous line that extends around text; or a rectangular, oval, or irregularly-shaped visual in an ad.

Bounding Box

The imaginary rectangle that encloses all sides of a graphic, necessary for a page layout specification.

Brightness

1. A measure of the amount of light reflected from a surface. 2. A paper property, defined as the percentage reflection of 457-nanometer (nm) radiation. 3. The intensity of a light source. 4. The overall percentage of lightness in an image.

Bullet

A marker preceding text, usually a solid dot, used to add emphasis; generally indicates that the text is part of a list.

Burn

1. To expose an image onto a plate. 2. To make copies of ROM chips or CD-ROMs. 3. To darken a specific portion of an image through photographic exposure.

Byte

A unit of measure equal to eight bits (decimal 256) of digital information, sufficient to represent one text character. It is the standard unit measure of file size. (See also Megabyte, Kilobyte, and Gigabyte).

Cab

See Flat.

Calibration

Making adjustments to a color monitor and other hardware and software to make the monitor represent as closely as possible the colors of the final printed piece.

Calibration Bars

A strip of reference blocks of color or tonal values on film, proofs, and press sheets, used to check the accuracy of color registration, quality, density, and ink coverage during a print run.

Callout

A descriptive label referenced to a visual element, such as several words connected to the element by an arrow.

Camera Ready

A completely finished mechanical, ready to be photographed to produce a negative from which a printing plate will be made.

Cap Line

The theoretical line to which the tops of capital letters are aligned.

Caps

An abbreviation for capital letters.

Caps and Small Caps

A style of typesetting in which capital letters are used in the normal way, while the type that would normally be in lower case has been changed to capital letters of a smaller point size. A true small-caps typeface does not contain any lower-case letters.

Caption

The line or lines of text that identify a picture or illustration, usually placed beneath it or otherwise in close proximity.

CD-ROM

A device used to store approximately 600MB of data. Files are permanently stored on the device and can be copied to a disk but not altered directly. ROM stands for Read-Only Memory. Equipment is now available on the consumer market for copying computer files to blank CD-ROMs.

Center marks

Press marks that appear on the center of all sides of a press sheet to aid in positioning the print area on the paper.

Character Count

The number of characters (letters, figures, signs or spaces) in a selected block of copy. Once used to calculate the amount of text that would fit on a given line or region when physically setting type.

Choke

See Trapping.

Chooser

A part of the Macintosh operating system that permits selection of a printer or other peripheral device. Chooser is also used to access resources on a network.

Chroma

The degree of saturation of a surface color in the Munsell color space model.

Cromalin

A single-sheet color proofing system introduced by DuPont in 1971 and still quite popular in the industry. It uses a series of overlaid colorants and varnish to simulate the results of a press run.

Chromaticity Diagram

A graphical representation of two of the three dimensions of color. Intended for plotting light sources rather than surface colors. Often called the CIE diagram.

Cicero/Didot Point

The cicero is a unit of horizontal distance slightly larger than the pica, used widely in continental Europe. A cicero equals 0.178 inches, or 12 Didot points.

Clipboard

The portion of computer memory that holds data that has been cut or copied. The next item cut or copied replaces the data already in the clipboard.

Cloning

Duplication of pixels from one part of an image to another.

CMS

See Color Management System

CMYK

Acronym for cyan, magenta, yellow, and black, the four process color inks which, when properly overprinted, can simulate a subset of the visible spectrum. See also color separation. Also refers to digital artwork that contains information necessary for creating color separations.

CMYK (Cyan, Magenta, Yellow, Black)

Acronym for the process colors cyan, magenta, yellow, and black (subtractive primaries) used in color printing. The letter K stands for "Key," although it is commonly used to refer to the Black ink that is added to the three colors when necessary. When printing black text as part of a four-color process, only the black ink is used. A normal four-color separation will have a plate for each of the four colors. When combined on the printed piece, the half-tone dots of each color give the impression of the desired color to the eye.

Coated

Printing papers having a surface coating (of clay or other material) to provide a smoother, more even finish with greater opacity.

Cold type

Type produced by photographic or digital methods, as opposed to the use of molten metal as in the old Linotype machine.

Collate

To gather separate sections or leaves of a publication together in the correct order for binding.

Collate and cut

Multiple signatures that are stacked then cut to be later placed in sequential order, drilled, and placed in three-ring binders.

Color Balance

The combination of yellow, magenta, and cyan needed to produce a neutral gray. Determined through a gray balance analysis.

Color Cast

The modification of a hue by the addition of a trace of another hue, such as yellowish green, pinkish blue, etc. Normally, an unwanted effect that can be corrected.

Color Chart

A printed chart of various combinations of CMYK colors used as an aid for the selection of "legal" colors during the design phase of a project.

Color Control Strip

A printed strip of various reference colors used to control printing quality. This strip is normally placed outside the "trim" area of a project, as a guide and visual aid for the pressman.

Color Conversion

Changing the color "mode" of an image. Converting an image from RGB to CMYK for purposes of preparing the image for conventional printing.

Color Correction

The process of removing casts or unwanted tints in a scanned image, in an effort to improve the appearance of the scan or to correct obvious deficiencies, such as green skies or yellowish skin tones.

Color Gamut

The range of colors that can be formed by all possible combinations of the colorants of a given reproduction system (printing press) on a given type of paper.

Color Key

An overlay color proof of acetate sheets, one for each of the four primary printing inks. The method was developed by 3M Corporation and remains a copyrighted term.

Color Management System

A process or utility that attempts to manage color of input and output devices in such a way that the monitor will match the output of any CMS-managed printer.

Color Model

A system for describing color, such as RGB, HLS, CIELAB, or CMYK.

Color overlay

A sheet of film or paper whose text and art correspond to one spot color or process color. Each color overlay becomes the basis for a single printing plate that will apply that color to paper.

Color Picker

A function within a graphics application that assists in selecting a color.

Color Proof

A printed or simulated printed image of the color separations intended to produce a close visual representation of the final reproduction for approval purposes and as a guide to the press operator.

Color Separation

The process of transforming color artwork into four components corresponding to the four process colors. If spot colors are used, additional components may be created containing only those items that will appear in the corresponding spot color layer. Each component is imaged to film or paper in preparation for making printing plates that correspond to each ink.

Color Sequence

The color order of printing the cyan, magenta, yellow, and black inks on a printing press. Sometimes called rotation or color rotation.

Color Space

Because a color must be represented by three basic characteristics depending on the color model, the color space is a three-dimensional coordinate system in which any color can be represented as a point.

Color Temperature

The temperature, in degrees Kelvin, to which a blackbody would have to be heated to produce a certain color radiation. (A "blackbody" is an ideal body or surface that completely absorbs or radiates energy.) The graphic arts viewing standard is 5,000 K. The degree symbol is not used in the Kelvin scale. The higher the color temperature, the bluer the light.

Color Transparency

A positive color photographic image on a clear film base that must be viewed by transmitted light. It is preferred for original photographic art because it has higher resolution than a color print. Transparency sizes range from 35mm color slides up to 8x10in. (203x254mm).

Colorimeter

An optical measuring instrument designed to measure and quantify color. They are often used to match digital image values to those of cloth and other physical samples.

Column rule

A thin vertical rule used to separate columns of type.

Combination signatures

Signatures of different sizes inserted at any position in a layout.

Comp

Comprehensive artwork used to present the general color and layout of a page.

Compose

To set copy into type, or lay out a page.

Composite proof

A version of an illustration or page in which the process colors appear together to represent full color. When produced on a monochrome output device, colors are represented as shades of gray.

Compression

A digital technique used to reduce the size of a file by analyzing occurrences of similar data. Compressed files occupy less physical space, and their use improves digital transmission speeds. Compression can sometimes result in a loss of image quality and/or resolution.

Condensed Type

A typeface in which the width of the letters has been reduced. Condensed type can be a specific font, or the result of applying a percentage of normal width by a formatting command.

Continuous Tone

An image such as an original photograph in which the subject has continuous shades of color or gray tones through the use of an emulsion process. Continuous tone images must be screened to create halftone images in order to be printed.

Contrast

The relationship between the dark and light areas of an image.

Copyright

Ownership of a work by the originator, such as an author, publisher, artist, or photographer. The right of copyright permits the originator of material to prevent its use without express permission or acknowledgment of the originator. Copyright may be sold, transferred, or given up contractually.

CorelDRAW

A popular drawing program originally designed for the Windows environment, but now available as a Macintosh program. CorelDRAW is known to create files that can cause printing and/or output problems in many prepress environments.

Creep

The progressive extension of interior pages of the folded signature beyond the image area of the outside pages. Shingling is applied to correct for creep.

Crop Marks

Printed short, fine lines used as guides for final trimming of the pages within a press sheet.

Cropping

The elimination of parts of a photograph or other original that are not required to be printed.

Crossover

An element in a book (text, line art, or other graphic) that appears on both pages of a reader spread crossing over the gutter.

Custom printer description file

A file containing information specific to a type of output device; used in conjunction with a standard PPD file to customize the printing process.

DCS (Desktop Color Separation)

Acronym for Desktop Color Separation, a version of the EPS file format. DCS 1.0 files are composed of five PostScript files for each color image: cyan, magenta, yellow, and black file, plus a separate low-resolution FPO image to place in a digital file. In contrast, DCS 2.0 files have one file that stores process color and spot color information.

Default

A specification for a mode of computer operation that operates if no other is selected. The default font size might be 12 point, or a default color for an object might be white with a black border.

Densitometer

An electronic instrument used to measure optical density. Reflective (for paper) and transmissive (for film).

Descender

The part of a lower-case letter that extends below the baseline (lower edge of the x-height) of the letter. The letters y, p, g, and j contain descenders.

Desktop

1. The area on a monitor screen on which the icons appear, before an application is launched. 2. A reference to the size of computer equipment (system unit, monitor, printer) that can fit on a normal desk; thus, desktop publishing.

Desktop Publishing (DTP)

Use of a personal computer, software applications, and a high-quality printer to produce fully composed printed documents. DTP is, in reality, an incorrect term these days. In the early days of Macintosh and PostScript technology, the term Desktop Publishing inferred that the materials produced from these systems was somehow inferior (as opposed to professional publishing). Now, the overwhelming majority of all printed materials - regardless of the quality - are produced on these systems, up to and including nationally famous magazines, catalogs, posters, and newspapers

Die line

In a digital file, the outline used to mark where cutting, stamping, or embossing the finished printed piece will occur. Uses to create a particular shape, such as a rolodex card.

Digital

The use of a series of discrete electronic pulses to represent data. In digital imaging systems, 256 steps (8 bits, or 1 byte) are normally used to characterize the gray scale or the properties of one color. For text, see ASCII.

Digital Camera

A camera which produces images directly into an electronic file format for transfer to a computer.

Digital Proofs

Digital proofs are representations of what a specific mechanical will look like when output and reproduced on a specific type of printing press. The difference with a digital proof is that it is created without the use of conventional film processes and output directly from computer files.

Dingbat

A font character that displays a picture instead of a letter, number or punctuation mark. There are entire font families of pictographic dingbats; the most commonly used dingbat font is Zapf Dingbats. There are dingbats for everything from the little airplanes used to represent airports on a map, to telephones, swashes, fish, stars, balloons - just about anything.

Direct-to-plate

Producing printing plates directly from computer output without going through the film process.

Disk Operating System (DOS)

Software for computer systems that supervises and controls the running of programs. The operating system is loaded into memory from disk by a small program which permanently resides in the firmware within the computer. The major operating systems in use today are Windows95 and WindowsNT from Microsoft, the Macintosh OS from Apple Computer, and a wide range of UNIX systems, such as those from Silicon Graphics, SUN Microsystems, and other vendors.

Dithering

A technique used in images wherein a color is represented using dots of two different colors displayed or printed very close together. Dithering is often used to compress digital images, in special screening algorithms (see Stochastic Screening) and to produce higher quality output on low-end color printers.

Document

The general term for a computer file containing text and/or graphics.

Dongle

A security device that usually plugs into your keyboard or printer port, that allows copy-protected software to run on your system. Such protected software will only run on systems with the dongle present. This prevents a single copy of software from running on any but one machine at a time.

Dot Gain

The growth of a halftone dot that occurs whenever ink soaks into paper. This growth can vary from being very small (on a high-speed press with fast-drying ink and very non-porous paper) to quite dramatic, as is the case in newspaper printing, where a dot can expand 30% from its size on the film to the size at which it dries. Failure to compensate for this gain in the generation of digital images can result in very poor results on press. Generally speaking, the finer the screen (and therefore, the smaller the dot) the more noticeable dot gain will be.

Double-page Spread

A design that spans the two pages visible to the reader at any open spot in a magazine, periodical, or book.

Downloadable Fonts

Typefaces that can be stored on disk and then downloaded to the printer when required for printing.

DPI (Dots Per Inch)

The measurement of resolution for page printers, phototypesetting machines and graphics screens. Currently graphics screens use resolutions of 60 to 100 dpi, standard desktop laser printers work at 600 dpi, and imagesetters operate at more than 1,500 dpi.

Drop Shadow

A duplicate of a graphic element or type placed behind and slightly offset from it, giving the effect of a shadow.

Drum Scanner

A color scanner on which the original is wrapped around a rotary scanning drum. See Scanner.

DSC

Acronym for the Adobe Document Structure Conventions, designed to provide a standard order and format for information so applications that process PostScript, such as PressWise, can easily find information about a document's structure and imaging requirements. These conventions allow specially formatted PostScript comments to be added to the page description; applications can search for these comments, but PostScript interpreters usually ignore them. TrapWise requires that the PostScript in incoming files is formatted using conventional DSC comments, so certain functions may not work properly if the file is not DSC-conforming.

Duotone

The separation of a black-and-white photograph into black and a second color having different tonal values and screen angles. Duotones are used to enhance photographic reproduction in two-three-or sometimes four-color work. Often the second, third, and fourth colors are not standard CMYK inks.

Dye

A soluble coloring material, normally used as the colorant in color photographs.

Dye Transfer

A photographic color print using special coated papers to produce a full color image. Can serve as an inexpensive proof.

Electrostatic

The method by which dry toner is transferred to paper in a copier or laser printer, and liquid toners are bonded to paper on some large-format color plotters.

Element

The smallest unit of a graphic, or a component of a page layout or design. Any object, text block, or graphic might be referred to as an element of the design.

Elliptical Dot Screen

A halftone screen having an elliptical dot structure.

Embedding

1. Placing control codes in the body of a document. 2. Including a complete copy of a text file or image within a desktop publishing document, with or without a link (see Linking).

Emulsion

The coating of light-sensitive material (silver halide) on a piece of film or photographic paper.

En Dash

A dash - often used in hyphenated word pairs - that is usually half the width of an em dash.

En Space

A space that is usually equal to half the width of an em space.

EPS

Acronym for encapsulated PostScript, a single-page PostScript file that contains grayscale or color information and can be imported into many electronic layout and design applications.

EPS (Encapsulated PostScript)

Acronym for file format used to transfer PostScript data within compatible applications. An EPS file normally contains a small preview image that displays in position within a mechanical or used by another program. EPS files can contain text, vector artwork, and images.

Expanded Type

Also called extended, a widened version of a typeface design. Type may be extended artificially within a DTP application, or designed as such by the typeface designer. See also Condensed Type.

Export

To save a file generated in one application in a format that is readable in another application.

Extension

A modular software program that extends or expands the functions of a larger program. A folder of Extensions is found in the Macintosh System Folder.

Fill

To add a tone or color to the area inside a closed object in a graphic illustration program.

Film

Non-paper output of an imagesetter or phototypesetter.

Film assembly

See Stripping.

Filter

In image editing applications, a small program that creates a special effect or performs some other function within an image.

First signature folding dummy

A folding dummy that determines the page arrangement for a single signature layout template. This template can then be applied to a job that requires multiple signatures, and PressWise will correctly impose all the pages based on the numbering sequence and binding method specified by the first signature.

Flat

Individual film assembled onto a carrier readied for contacting or platemaking. Referred to as a cab in gravure printing.

Flat Color

Color that lacks contrast or tonal variation. Also, flat tint.

Flatbed Scanner

A scanner on which the original is mounted on a flat scanning glass. See Scanner.

Flexographic printing

A rotary letterpress process printing on a press using a rubber plate that stretches around a cylinder making it necessary to compensate by distorting the plate image. Flexography is used most often in label printing, often on metal or other non-paper material.

Floating Accent

A separate accent mark that can be placed under or over another character. Complex accented characters such as in foreign languages are usually available in a font as a single character.

Flood

A user-defined screened or solid box that prints on and completely covers a PressWise blank page. Can be used to print a flat tint on the page, or to produce a mask for manual stripping in existing film-based pages.

Flop

To make a mirror image of visuals such as photographs or clip art.

Folder

1. The digital equivalent of a paper file folder, used to organize files in the Macintosh and Windows operating systems. The icon of a folder looks like a paper file folder. Double-clicking it opens it to reveal the files stored inside. 2. A mechanical device which folds preprinted pages into various formats, such as a tri-fold brochure.

Folding dummy

A template used for determining the page arrangement on a form to meet folding and binding requirements. See also All signature folding dummy and First signature folding dummy.

Font

A font is the complete collection of all the characters (numbers, uppercase and lowercase letters and, in some cases, small caps and symbols) of a given typeface in a specific style; for example, Helvetica Bold.

Force Justify

A type alignment command which causes the space between letters and words in a line of type to expand to fit within a line. Often used in headlines, and sometimes used to force the last line of a justified paragraph, which is normally set flush left, to justify.

Form

In PressWise, the front or back of a signature.

Four-color Process

See Process Colors

FPO

Acronym for For Position Only, a term applied to low-quality art reproductions or simple shapes used to indicate placement and scaling of an art element on mechanicals or camera-ready artwork. In digital publishing, an FPO can be low-resolution TIFF files that are later replaced with high-resolution versions. An FPO is not intended for reproduction but only as a guide and placeholder for the prepress service provider.

Frame

An area or block into which text or graphics can be placed.

FreeHand

A popular vector-based illustration program available from Macromedia.

Full Measure

A line set to the entire line length.

G (Gigabyte)

One billion (1,073,741,824) bytes (230) or 1,048,576 kilobytes.

Galley Proof

Proofs, usually of type, taken before the type is made up into pages. Before desktop publishing, galley proofs were hand-assembled into pages.

Gamma

A measure of the contrast, or range of tonal variation, of the midtones in a photographic image

Gamma Correction

1. Adjusting the contrast of the midtones in an image. 2. Calibrating a monitor so that midtones are correctly displayed on screen.

Gamut

See Color Gamut

GASP

Acronym for Graphic Arts Service Provider, a firm that provides a range of services somewhere on the continuum from design to fulfillment.

GCR (Gray component replacement)

A technique for adding detail by reducing the amount of cyan, magenta, and yellow in chromatic or colored areas, replacing them with black.

GIF - Graphics Interface File

A CompuServe graphics file format that is used widely for graphic elements in Web pages.

Global Preferences

Preference settings which affect all newly created files within an application.

Gradient fill

See Graduated fill.

Graduated fill

An area in which two colors (or shades of gray or the same color) are blended to create a gradual change from one to the other. Graduated fills are also known as blends, gradations, gradient fills, and vignettes.

Grain

Silver salts clumped together in differing amounts in different types of photographic emulsions. Generally speaking, faster emulsions have larger grain sizes.

Graininess

Visual impression of the irregularly distributed silver grain clumps in a photographic image, or the ink film in a printed image.

Gray Balance

The values for the yellow, magenta, and cyan inks that are needed to produce a neutral gray when printed at a normal density.

Gray Component Replacement

See GCR

Grayscale

1. An image composed in grays ranging from black to white, usually using 256 different tones of gray. 2. A tint ramp used to measure and control the accuracy of screen percentages on press. 3. An accessory used to define neutral density in a photographic image.

Greeking

1. A software technique by which areas of gray are used to simulate lines of text below a certain point size. 2. Nonsense text use to define a layout before copy is available.

Grid

A division of a page by horizontal and vertical guides into areas into which text or graphics may be placed accurately.

Grind-off

The roughing up at the back (or spine) of a folded signature, or of two or more gathered signatures, in preparation for perfect binding.

Gripper edge

The leading edge of a sheet of paper, which the grippers on the press grab to carry the paper through a press.

Group

To collect graphic elements together so that an operation may be applied to all of them simultaneously.

GUI

Acronym for Graphical User Interface, the basis of the Macintosh and Windows operating systems.

Gutter

Extra space between pages in a layout. Sometimes used interchangeably with Alley to describe the space between columns on a page. Gutters can appear either between the top and bottom of two adjacent pages or between two sides of adjacent pages. Gutters are often used because of the binding or layout requirements of a job — for example, to add space at the top or bottom of each page or to allow for the grind-off taken when a book is perfect bound.

Hairline Rule

The thinnest rule that can be printed on a given device. A hairline rule on a 1200 dpi imagesetter is 1/1200 of an inch; on a 300 dpi laser printer, the same rule would print at 1/300 of an inch.

Halftone

An image generated for use in printing in which a range of continuous tones is simulated by an array of dots that create the illusion of continuous tone when seen at a distance.

Halftone Tint

An area covered with a uniform halftone dot size to produce an even tone or color. Also called flat tint or screen tint.

Hard Drive

A rigid disk sealed inside an airtight transport mechanism that is the basic storage mechanism in a computer. Information stored may be accessed more rapidly than on floppy disks and far greater amounts of data may be stored.

High Key

A photographic or printed image in which the main interest area lies in the highlight end of the scale.

High Resolution File

An image file that typically contains four pixels for every dot in the printed reproduction. High-resolution files are often linked to a page layout file, but not actually embedded in it, due to their large size.

Highlights

The lightest areas in a photograph or illustration.

HLS

Color model based on three coordinates: hue, lightness (or luminance), and saturation.

HSV

A color model based on three coordinates: hue, saturation and value (or luminance).

HTML (HyperText Markup Language)

The language, written in plain (ASCII) text using simple tags, that is used to create Web pages, and which Web browsers are designed to read and display. HTML focuses more on the logical structure of a page than its appearance.

Hue

The wavelength of light of a color in its purest state (without adding white or black).

Hyperlink

An HTML tag directs the computer to a different Anchor or URL (Uniform Resource Locator). The linked data may be on the same page, or on a computer anywhere in the world.

Hyphenation Zone

The space at the end of a line of text in which the hyphenation function will examine the word to determine whether or not it should be hyphenated and wrapped to the next line.

Icon

A small graphic symbol used on the screen to indicate files or folders, activated by clicking with the mouse or pointing device.

Illustrator

A vector editing application owned by Adobe Systems, Inc.

Imaging

The process of producing a film or paper copy of a digital file from an output device.

Imagesetter

A raster-based device used to output a computer page-layout file or composition at high resolution (usually 1000 - 3000 dpi) onto photographic paper or film, from which to make printing plates.

Import

To bring a file generated within one application into another application.

Imposition

The arrangement of pages on a printed sheet, which, when the sheet is finally printed, folded and trimmed, will place the pages in their correct order.

Indexed Color Image

An image which uses a limited, predetermined number of colors; often used in Web images. See also GIF.

Indexing

In DTP, marking certain words within a document with hidden codes so that an index may be automatically generated.

Initial Caps

Text in which the first letter of each word (except articles, etc.) is capitalized.

Inline Graphic

A graphic that is inserted within a body of text, and may be formatted using normal text commands for justification and leading; inline graphics will move with the body of text in which they are placed.

Intensity

Synonym for degree of color saturation.

International Paper Sizes

The International Standards Organization (ISO) system of paper sizes is based on a series of three sizes A, B and C. Series A is used for general printing and stationery, Series B for posters, and Series C for envelopes. Each size has the same proportion of length to width as the others. The nearest ISO paper size to conventional 8-1/2 x 11 paper is A4.

ISO

The International Standards Organization.

Jaggies

Visible steps in the curved edge of a graphic or text character that results from enlarging a bitmapped image.

Job state

The state of working in PressWise while one or more jobs are open. Opposite of no-job state.

JPG or JPEG

A compression algorithm that reduces the file size of bitmapped images, named for the Joint Photographic Experts Group, an industry organization that created the standard; JPEG is a "lossy" compression method, and image quality will be reduced in direct proportion to the amount of compression.

Justification

The alignment of text along a margin or both margins..

Kelvin (K)

Unit of temperature measurement based on Celsius degrees, starting from absolute zero, which is equivalent to -273 Celsius (centigrade); used to indicate the color temperature of a light source.

Kerning

Moving a pair of letters closer together or farther apart, to achieve a better fit or appearance.

Key (Black Plate)

In early four-color printing, the black plate was printed first and the other three colors were aligned (or registered) to it. Thus, the black plate was the "key" to the result.

Keyline

A thin, often black border around a picture or a box indicating where to place pictures. In digital files, the keylines are often vector objects while photographs are usually bitmap images.

Kilobyte (K, KB)

1,024 (210) bytes, the nearest binary equivalent to decimal 1,000 bytes. Abbreviated and referred to as K.

Knockout

A printing technique that represents overlapping objects without mixing inks. The ink for the underlying element does not print (knocks out) in the area where the objects overlap. Opposite of overprinting.

L*a*b

The lightness, red-green attribute, and yellow-blue attribute in the CIE Color Space, a three-dimensional color mapping system.

Landscape

Printing from the left to right across the wider side of the page. A landscape orientation treats a page as 11 inches wide and 8.5 inches long.

Laser printer

A high quality image printing system using a laser beam to produce an image on a photosensitive drum. The image is transferred to paper by a conventional xerographic printing process. Current laser printers used for desktop publishing have a resolution of 600 dpi. Imagesetters are also laser printers, but with higher resolution and tight mechanical controls to produce final film separations for commercial printing.

Layer

A function of graphics applications in which elements may be isolated from each other, so that a group of elements may be hidden from view, locked, reordered or otherwise manipulated as a unit, without affecting other elements on the page.

Layout

The arrangement of text and graphics on a page, usually produced in the preliminary design stage.

Leaders

A line of periods or other symbols connecting the end of a group of words with another element separated by some space. For example, a table of contents may consist of a series of phrases on separate lines, each associated with a page number. Promotes readability in long lists of tabular text.

Leading ("ledding")

Space added between lines of type. Usually measured in points or fractions of points. Named after the strips of lead which used to be inserted between lines of metal type. In specifying type, lines of 12-pt. type separated by a 14-pt. space is abbreviated "12/14," or "twelve over fourteen."

Letterspacing

The insertion or addition of white space between the letters of words.

Library

In the computer world, a collection of files having a similar purpose or function.

Ligature

Letters that are joined together as a single unit of type such as oe and fi.

Lightness

The property that distinguishes white from gray or black, and light from dark color tones on a surface.

Line Art

A drawing or piece of black and white artwork, with no screens. Line art can be represented by a graphic file having only one-bit resolution.

Line Screen

The number of lines per inch used when converting a photograph to a halftone. Typical values range from 85 for newspaper work to 150 or higher for high-quality reproduction on smooth or coated paper.

Linking

An association through software of a graphic or text file on disk with its location in a document. That location may be represented by a "placeholder" rectangle, or a low-resolution copy of the graphic.

Linotype-Hell

The manufacturer of imagesetters such as the Linotronic that process PostScript data through an external Raster Image Processor (RIP) to produce high resolution film for printing.

Lithography

A mechanical printing process used for centuries based on the principle of the natural aversion of water (in this case, ink) to grease. In modern offset lithography, the image on a photosensitive plate is first transferred to the blanket of a rotating drum, and then to the paper.

Lossy

A data compression method characterized by the loss of some data.

Loupe

A small free-standing magnifier used to see fine detail on a page. See Linen Tester.

LPI

Lines per inch. See Line Screen.

Luminosity

The amount of light, or brightness, in an image. Part of the HLS color model.

LZW

The acronym for the Lempel-Ziv-Welch lossless data- and image-compression algorithm.

M, MB (Megabyte)

One million (1,048,576) bytes (220) or 1,024 Kilobytes.

Macro

A set of keystrokes that is saved as a named computer file. When accessed, the keystrokes will be performed. Macros are used to perform repetitive tasks.

Margins

The non-printing areas of page, or the line at which text starts or stops.

Mask

To conform the shape of a photograph or illustration to another shape such as a circle or polygon.

Masking

A technique that blocks an area of an image from reproduction by superimposing an opaque object of any shape.

Match Print

A color proofing system used for the final quality check.

Mechanical

A pasted-up page of camera-ready art that is to be photographed to produce a plate for the press.

Mechanical Dot Gain

See Dot Gain

Medium

A physical carrier of data such as a CD-ROM, video cassette, or floppy disk, or a carrier of electronic data such as fiber optic cable or electric wires.

Megabyte (MB)

A unit of measure of stored data equaling 1,024 kilobytes, or 1,048,576 bytes (1020).

Megahertz

An analog signal frequency of one million cycles per second, or a data rate of one million bits per second. Used in specifying computer CPU speed.

Menu

A list of choices of functions, or of items such as fonts. In contemporary software design, there is often a fixed menu of basic functions at the top of the page that have pull-down menus associated with each of the fixed choices.

Metafile

A class of graphics that combines the characteristics of raster and vector graphics formats; not recommended for high-quality output.

Metallic Ink

Printing inks which produce an effect of gold, silver, bronze, or metallic colors.

Midtones or Middletones

The tonal range between highlights and shadows.

Misregistration

The unwanted result of incorrectly aligned process inks and spot colors on a finished printed piece. Misregistration can be caused by many factors, including paper stretch and improper plate alignment. Trapping can compensate for misregistration.

Modem

An electronic device for converting digital data into analog audio signals and back again (Modulator-DEModulator.) Primarily used for transmitting data between computers over analog (audio frequency) telephone lines.

Moiré

An interference pattern caused by the out-of-register overlap of two or more regular patterns such as dots or lines. In process-color printing, screen angles are selected to minimize this pattern.

Monochrome

An image or computer monitor in which all information is represented in black and white, or with a range of grays.

Monospace

A font in which all characters occupy the same amount of horizontal width regardless of the character. See also Proportional Spacing.

Montage

A single image formed by assembling or compositing several images.

Mottle

Uneven color or tone.

Multimedia

The combination of sound, video images, and text to create a "moving" presentation.

Nested signatures

Multiple signatures that are folded, gathered, and placed one inside another, and then saddle-stitched at the spine.

Network

Two or more computers that are linked to exchange data or share resources. The Internet is a network of networks.

Neutral

Any color that has no hue, such as white, gray, or black.

Neutral density

A measurement of the lightness or darkness of a color. A neutral density of zero (0.00) is the lightest value possible and is equivalent to pure white; 3.294 is roughly equivalent to 100% of each of the CMYK components.

Noise

Unwanted signals or data that may reduce the quality of the output.

Non-breaking Space

A typographic command that connects two words with a space, but prevents the words from being broken apart if the space occurs within the hyphenation zone. See Hyphenation Zone.

Non-reproducible Colors

Colors in an original scene or photograph that are impossible to reproduce using process inks. Also called out-of-gamut colors.

Normal Key

A description of an image in which the main interest area is in the middle range of the tone scale or distributed throughout the entire tonal range.

Nudge

To move a graphic or text element in small, preset increments, usually with the arrow keys.

Object-oriented art

Vector-based artwork composed of separate elements or shapes described mathematically rather than by specifying the color and position of every point. This contrasts to bitmap images, which are composed of individual pixels.

Oblique

A slanted character (sometimes backwards, or to the left), often used when referring to italic versions of sans-serif typefaces.

Offset

In graphics manipulation, to move a copy or clone of an image slightly to the side and/or back; used for a drop-shadow effect.

Offset Lithography

A printing method whereby the image is transferred from a plate onto a rubber covered cylinder from which the printing takes place (see Lithography).

Opacity

1. The degree to which paper will show print through it. 2. Settings in certain graphics applications that allow images or text below the object whose opacity has been adjusted, to show through.

OPI

1. Acronym for Open Prepress Interface. 1. A set of PostScript language comments originally developed by Aldus Corporation for defining and specifying the placement of high-resolution images in PostScript files on an electronic page layout. 2. Incorporation of a low resolution preview image within a graphic file format (TIF, EPS, DCS) that is intended for display only. 3. Software device that is an extension to PostScript that replaces low-resolution placeholder images in a document with their high-resolution sources for printing.

Optical Disks

Video disks that store large amounts of data used primarily for reference works such as dictionaries and encyclopedias.

Output device

Any hardware equipment, such as a monitor, laser printer, or imagesetter, that depicts text or graphics created on a computer.

Overlay

A transparent sheet used in the preparation of multicolor mechanical artwork showing the color breakdown.

Overprint

A printing technique that lays down one ink on top of another ink. The overprinted inks can combine to make a new color. The opposite of knock-out.

Overprint Color

A color made by overprinting any two or more of the primary yellow, magenta, and cyan process colors.

Overprinting

Allowing an element to print over the top of underlying elements, rather than knocking them out (see Knockout). Often used with black type.

Page Description Language (PDL)

A special form of programming language that describes both text and graphics (object or bit-image) in mathematical form. The main benefit of a PDL is that makes the application software independent of the physical printing device. PostScript is a PDL, for example.

Page Layout Software

Desktop publishing software such as PageMaker or QuarkXPress used to combine various source documents and images into a high quality publication.

Page Proofs

Proofs of the actual pages of a document, usually produced just before printing, for a final quality check.

PageMaker

A popular page-layout application produced by Adobe Systems.

Palette

1. As derived from the term in the traditional art world, a collection of selectable colors. 2. Another name for a dialog box or menu of choices.

Panose

A typeface matching system for font substitution based on a numeric classification of fonts according to visual characteristics.

Pantone Matching System

A system for specifying colors by number for both coated and uncoated paper; used by print services and in color desktop publishing to assure uniform color matching.

Parallel fold

A folding method in which folds of a signature are parallel.

Pasteboard

In a page layout program, the desktop area outside of the printing page area, on which elements can be placed for later positioning on any page.

PCX

Bitmap image format produced by paint programs.

PDF (Portable Document Format)

Developed by Adobe Systems, Inc. (and read by Adobe Acrobat Reader), this format has become a de facto standard for document transfer across platforms.

Perfect binding

A binding method in which signatures are "ground off" at the spine of the book and then bound with adhesive, so each page is glued individually to the spine.

Perspective

The effect of distance in an image achieved by aligning the edges of elements with imaginary lines directed toward one to three "vanishing points" on the horizon.

Photoshop

The Adobe Systems image editing program commonly used for color correction and special effects on both the Macintosh and PC platforms.

Pi Fonts

A collection of special characters such as timetable symbols and mathematical signs. Examples are Zapf Dingbats and Symbol. See also Dingbats.

Pica

A traditional typographic measurement of 12 points, or approximately 1/6 of an inch. Most DTP applications specify a pica as exactly 1/6 of an inch.

PICT/PICT2

A common format for defining bitmapped images on the Macintosh. The more recent PICT2 format supports 24-bit color.

Pixel

Abbreviation for picture element, one of the tiny rectangular areas or dots generated by a computer or output device to constitute images.

PMS

See Pantone Matching System

PMT

Photo Mechanical Transfer - positive prints of text or images used for paste-up to mechanicals.

Point

A unit of measurement used to specify type size and rule weight, equal to (approximately, in traditional typesetting) 1/72 inch.

Polygon

A geometric figure consisting of three or more straight lines enclosing an area. The triangle, square, rectangle, and star are all polygons.

Portrait

Printing from left to right across the narrow side of the page. Portrait orientation on a letter-size page uses a standard 8.5-inch width and 11-inch length.

Positive

A true photographic image of the original made on paper or film.

Posterize, Posterization

The deliberate constraint of a gradient or image into visible steps as a special effect; or the unintentional creation of steps in an image due to a high LPI value used with a low printer DPI.

Postprocessing Applications

Applications, such as trapping programs or imposition software, that perform their functions after the image has been printed to a file, rather than in the originating application.

PostScript

1. A page description language developed by Adobe Systems, Inc. that describes type and/or images and their positional relationships upon the page. 2. An interpreter or RIP (see Raster Image Processor) that can process the PostScript page description into a format for laser printer or imagesetter output. 3. A computer programming language.

PostScript Printer Description file

See PPD.

PPD

Acronym for PostScript Printer Description, a file format developed by Adobe Systems, Inc., that contains device-specific information enabling software to produce the best results possible for each type of designated printer.

PPI

Pixels per inch; used to denote the resolution of an image.

Preferences

A set of defaults for an application program that may be modified.

Prepress

All work done between writing and printing, such as typesetting, scanning, layout, and imposition.

Prepress Proof

A color proof made directly from electronic data or film images.

Press sheet

In sheet-fed printing, the paper stock of common sizes that is used in commercial printing.

Primary Colors

Colors that can be used to generate secondary colors. For the additive system (i.e., a computer monitor), these colors are red, green, and blue. For the subtractive system (i.e., the printing process), these colors are yellow, magenta, and cyan.

Printer Command Language

PCL — a language, that has graphics capability, developed by Hewlett Packard for use with its own range of printers.

Printer fonts

The image outlines for type in PostScript that are sent to the printer.

Process colors

The four transparent inks (cyan, magenta, yellow, and black) used in four-color process printing. See also Color separation; CMYK.

Profile

A file containing data representing the color reproduction characteristics of a device determined by a calibration of some sort.

Proof

A representation of the printed job that is made from plates (press proof), film, or electronic data (prepress proofs). It is generally used for customer inspection and approval before mass production begins.

Proportional Spacing

A method of spacing whereby each character is spaced to accommodate the varying widths of letters or figures, thus increasing readability. Books and magazines are set proportionally spaced, and most fonts in desktop publishing are proportional. With proportionally spaced fonts, each character is given a horizontal space proportional to its size. For example, a proportionally spaced "m" is wider than an "i."

Pt.

Abbreviation for point.

QuarkXPress

A popular page-layout application.

Queue

A set of files input to the printer, printed in the order received unless otherwise instructed.

QuickDraw

Graphic routines in the Macintosh used for outputting text and images to printers not compatible with PostScript.

RAM

Random Access Memory, the "working" memory of a computer that holds files in process. Files in RAM are lost when the computer is turned off, whereas files stored on the hard drive or floppy disks remain available.

Raster

A bitmapped representation of graphic data.

Raster Graphics

A class of graphics created and organized in a rectangular array of bitmaps. Often created by paint software, fax machines, or scanners for display and printing.

Raster Image Processor (RIP)

That part of a PostScript printer or imagesetting device that converts the page information from the PostScript Page Description Language into the bitmap pattern that is applied to the film or paper output.

Rasterize

The process of converting digital information into pixels at the resolution of the output device. For example, the process used by an imagesetter to translate PostScript files before they are imaged to film or paper. See also RIP.

Reflective Art

Artwork that is opaque, as opposed to transparent, that can be scanned for input to a computer.

Registration

Aligning plates on a multicolor printing press so that the images will superimpose properly to produce the required composite output.

Registration Color

A default color selection that can be applied to design elements so that they will print on every separation from a PostScript printer. "Registration" is often used to print identification text that will appear outside the page area on a set of separations.

Registration marks

Figures (often crossed lines and a circle) placed outside the trim page boundaries on all color separation overlays to provide a common element for proper alignment.

Resolution

The density of graphic information expressed in dots per inch (dpi) or pixels per inch (ppi).

Retouching

Making selective manual or electronic corrections to images.

Reverse Out

To reproduce an object as white, or paper, within a solid background, such as white letters in a black rectangle.

RGB

Acronym for red, green, blue, the colors of projected light from a computer monitor that, when combined, simulate a subset of the visual spectrum. When a color image is scanned, RGB data is collected by the scanner and then converted to CMYK data at some later step in the process. Also refers to the color model of most digital artwork. See also CMYK.

Rich Black

A process color consisting of sold black with one or more layers of cyan, magenta, or yellow.

Right Reading

A positive or negative image that is readable from top to bottom and from left to right.

Right-angle fold

A folding method in which any successive fold of a signature is at right angles to the previous fold.

RIP

See Raster Image Processor

ROM

Read Only Memory, a semiconductor chip in the computer that retains startup information for use the next time the computer is turned on.

Rosette

The pattern created when color halftone screens are printed at traditional screen angles.

Rotation

Turning an object at some angle to its original axis.

RTF

Rich Text Format, a text format that retains formatting information lost in pure ASCII text.

Rubylith

A two-layer acetate film having a red or amber emulsion on a clear base used in non-computer stripping and separation operations.

Saddle-stitching

A binding method in which each signature is folded and stapled at the spine.

Sans Serif

Sans Serif fonts are fonts that do not have the tiny lines that appear at the top of and bottom of letters.

Saturation

The intensity or purity of a particular color; a color with no saturation is gray.

Scaling

The means within a program to reduce or enlarge the amount of space an image will occupy by multiplying the data by a scale factor. Scaling can be proportional, or in one dimension only.

Scanner

A device that electronically digitizes images point by point through circuits that can correct color, manipulate tones, and enhance detail. Color scanners will usually produce a minimum of 24 bits for each pixel, with 8 bits each for red, green, and blue.

Screen

To create a halftone of a continuous tone image (See Halftone).

Screen Angle

The angle at which the rulings of a halftone screen are set when making screened images for halftone process-color printing. The equivalent effect can be obtained electronically through selection of the desired angle from a menu.

Screen Frequency

The number of lines per inch in a halftone screen, which may vary from 85 to 300.

Screen Printing

A technique for printing on practically any surface using a fine mesh (originally of silk) on which the image has been placed photographically. Preparation of art for screen printing requires consideration of the resolution of the screen printing process.

Screen Shot

A printed output or saved file that represents data from a computer monitor.

Screen Tint

A halftone screen pattern of all the same dot size that creates an even tone at some percentage of solid color.

SCSI

Small Computer Systems Interface, a standard software protocol for connecting peripheral devices to a computer for fast data transfer.

Selection

The act of placing the cursor on an object and clicking the mouse button to make the object active.

Self-Cover

A cover for a document in which the cover is of the same paper stock as the rest of the piece.

SEP

A PostScript file format created from PageMaker that can contain multiple pages as well as links in the form of OPI comments to high-resolution images, in color or in black and white.

Separation

See Color separation.

Serif

A line or curve projecting from the end of a letter form. Typefaces designed with such projections are called serif faces.

Service Bureau

A business that specializes in producing film for printing on a high-resolution imagesetter.

SGML

Standard Generalized Markup Language, a set of semantics and syntax that describes the structure of a document (the nature, content, or function of the data) as opposed to visual appearance. HTML is a subset of SGML (see HTML).

Sharpness

The subjective impression of the density difference between two tones at their boundary, interpreted as fineness of detail.

Shortcut

1. A quick method for accessing a menu item or command, usually through a series of keystrokes. 2. The icon that can be created in Windows95 to open an application without having to penetrate layers of various folders. The equivalent in the Macintosh is the "alias."

Silhouette

To remove part of the background of a photograph or illustration, leaving only the desired portion.

Skew

A transformation command that slants an object at an angle to the side from its initial fixed base.

Small caps

A type style in which lowercase letters are replaced by uppercase letters set in a smaller point size.

Smart Quotes

The curly quotation marks used by typographers, as opposed to the straight marks on the typewriter. Use of smart quotes is usually a setup option in a word processing program or page layout application

Snap-to (guides or rulers)

An optional feature in page layout programs that drives objects to line up with guides or margins if they are within a pixel range that can be set. This eliminates the need for very precise, manual placement of an object with the mouse.

Soft or Discretionary Hyphen

A hyphen coded for display and printing only when formatting of the text puts the hyphenated word at the end of a line.

Soft Return

A return command that ends a line but does not apply a paragraph mark that would end the continuity of the style for that paragraph.

Spectrophotometer

An instrument for measuring the relative intensity of radiation reflected or transmitted by a sample over the spectrum.

Specular Highlight

The lightest highlight area that does not carry any detail, such as reflections from glass or polished metal. Normally, these areas are reproduced as unprinted white paper.

Spine

The binding edge at the back of a book that contains title information and joins the front and back covers.

Spot Color

Any pre-mixed ink that is not one of or a combination of the four process color inks, often specified by a Pantone swatch number.

Spread

Two facing pages that can be worked on as a unit, and will be viewed side by side in the final publication.

Stacking Order

The order of the elements on a PostScript page, wherein the topmost item may obscure the items beneath it if they overlap.

Standard Viewing Conditions

A prescribed set of conditions under which the viewing of originals and reproductions are to take place, defining both the geometry of the illumination and the spectral power distribution of the light source.

Step-and-repeat

A layout in which two or more copies of the same piece are placed on a single plate. This is useful for printing several copies of a small layout, such as a business card, on a single sheet. Also called a multiple-up layout.

Stet

Used in proof correction work to cancel a previous correction. From the Latin; "let it stand."

Stochastic Screening

A method of creating halftones in which the size of the dots remains constant but their density is varied; also known as frequency-modulated (or FM) screening.

Stripping

The act of manually assembling individual film negatives into flats for printing. Also referred to as film assembly.

Stroke, Stroking

Manipulating the width or color of a line.

Stuffit

A file compression utility used in the Macintosh environment.

Style

A set of formatting instructions for font, paragraphing, tabs, and other properties of text.

Style Sheet

A file containing all of the tags and instructions for formatting all parts of a document; style sheets create consistency between similar documents.

Subhead

A second-level heading used to organize body text by topic.

Subscript

Small-size characters set below the normal letters or figures, usually to convey technical information.

Substitution

Using an existing font to simulate one that is not available to the printer.

Subtractive Color

Color which is observed when light strikes pigments or dyes, which absorb certain wavelengths of light; the light that is reflected back is perceived as a color. See CMYK and Process Color.

Superscript

Small characters set above the normal letters or figures, such as numbers referring to footnotes.

System Folder

The location of the operating system files on a Macintosh.

Tabloid

Paper 11 inches wide x 17 inches long.

Tagged Image File Format (TIFF)

A common format for used for scanned or computer-generated bitmapped images.

Tags

The various formats in a style sheet that indicate paragraph settings, margins and columns, page layouts, hyphenation and justification, widow and orphan control and other parameters.

Template

A document file containing layout and styles by which a series of documents can maintain the same look and feel.

Text

The characters and words that form the main body of a publication.

Text Attribute

A characteristic applied directly to a letter or letters in text, such as bold, italic, or underline.

Text wrap

See Wrap

Texture

1. A property of the surface of the substrate, such as the smoothness of paper. 2. Graphically, variation in tonal values to form image detail. 3. A class of fills in a graphics application that give various appearances, such as bricks, grass, etc.

Thin Space

A fixed space, equal to half an en space or the width of a period in most fonts.

Thumbnails

1. The preliminary sketches of a design. 2. Small images used to indicate the content of a computer file.

TIFF

See Tagged Image File Format

Tile

1. A type of repeating fill pattern. 2. Reproduce a number of pages of a document on one sheet. 3. Printing a large document overlapping on several smaller sheets of paper.

Tint

1. A halftone area that contains dots of uniform size; that is, no modeling or texture. 2. The mixture of a color with white.

Tip In

The separate insertion of a single page into a book either during or after binding by pasting one edge.

Toggle

A command that switches between either of two states at each application. Switching between Hide and Show is a toggle.

Tracking

Adjusting the spacing of letters in a line of text to achieve proper justification or general appearance.

Transfer Curve

A curve depicting the adjustment to be made to a particular printing plate when an image is printed.

Transparency

A full color photographically produced image on transparent film.

Transparent Ink

An ink that allows light to be transmitted through it.

Trapping

The process of creating an overlap between abutting inks to compensate for imprecise registration in the printing process.

Trim

After printing, mechanically cutting the publication to the correct final dimensions. The trim size is normally indicated by marks on the printing plate outside the page area.

Trim page size

Area of the finished page after the job is printed, folded, bound, and cut.

TrueType

An outline font format used in both Macintosh and Windows systems that can be used both on the screen and on a printer.

Type 1 Fonts

PostScript fonts based on Bézier curves encrypted for compactness that are compatible with Adobe Type Manager.

Type Family

A set of typefaces created from the same basic design but in different weights, such as bold, light, italic, book, and heavy.

Typesetting

The arrangement of individual characters of text into words, sentences, and paragraphs.

Typo

An abbreviation for typographical error. A keystroke error in the typeset copy.

UCR (undercolor removal)

A technique for reducing the amount of magenta, cyan, and yellow inks in neutral or shadow areas and replacing them with black.

Undertone

Color of ink printed in a thin film.

Unsharp Masking

A digital technique (based on a traditional photographic technique) performed after scanning that locates the edge between sections of differing lightness and alters the values of the adjoining pixels to exaggerate the difference across the edge, thereby increasing edge contrast.

Uppercase

The capital letters of a typeface as opposed to the lowercase, or small, letters. When type was hand composited, the capital letters resided in the upper part of the type case.

Utility

Software that performs ancillary tasks such as counting words, defragmenting a hard drive, or restoring a deleted file.

Varnish Plate

The plate on a printing press that applies varnish after the other colors have been applied.

Varnishing

A finishing process whereby a transparent varnish is applied over the printed sheet to produce a glossy or protective coating, either on the entire sheet or on selected areas.

Vector Graphics

Graphics defined using coordinate points, and mathematically drawn lines and curves, which may be freely scaled and rotated without image degradation in the final output. Fonts (such as PostScript and TrueType), and illustrations from drawing applications are common examples of vector objects. Two commonly used vector drawing programs are Illustrator and FreeHand. A class of graphics that overcomes the resolution limitation of bitmapped graphics.

Velox

Strictly, a Kodak chloride printing paper, but used to describe a high-quality black & white print of a halftone or line drawing.

Vertical Justification

The ability to automatically adjust the interline spacing (leading) to make columns and pages end at the same point on a page.

Vignette

An illustration in which the background gradually fades into the paper; that is, without a definite edge or border.

Visible Spectrum

The wavelengths of light between about 380 nm (violet) and 700 nm (red) that are visible to the human eye.

Watermark

An impression incorporated in paper during manufacturing showing the name of the paper and/or the company logo. A "watermark" can be applied digitally to printed output as a very light screened image.

Web Press

An offset printing press that prints from a roll of paper rather than single sheets.

White Light

Light containing all wavelengths of the visible spectrum.

White Space

Areas on the page which contain no images or type. Proper use of white space is critical to a well-balanced design.

Window Shade

A type of text block used in certain applications, such as PageMaker. Windowshades have handles at the top and bottom which, when dragged with the mouse, will reveal or conceal text.

Wizard

A utility attached to an application or operating system that aids you in setting up a piece of hardware, software, or document.

WYSIWYG

An acronym for "What You See Is What You Get," (pronounced "wizzywig") meaning that what you see on your computer screen bears a strong resemblance to what the job will look like when it is printed.

X-height

The height of the letter "x" in a given typeface, which represents the basic size of the bodies of all of the lowercase letters (excluding ascenders and descenders).

Xerography

A photocopying/printing process in which the image is formed using the electrostatic charge principle. The toner replaces ink and can be dry or liquid. Once formed, the image is sealed by heat. Most page printers currently use this method of printing.

Zero Point

The mathematical "origin" of the coordinates of the two-dimensional page. The zero point may be moved to any location on the page, and the ruler dimensions change accordingly.

Zip

1. To compress a file on a Windows-based system using a popular compression utility (PKZIP). 2. A removable disk made by Iomega (a Zip disk) or the device that reads and writes such disks (a Zip drive).

Zooming

The process of electronically enlarging or reducing an image on a monitor to facilitate detailed design or editing and navigation.